World Disasters Report

2007

Focus on discrimination

 International Federation
of Red Cross and Red Crescent Societies

Editorial team: Yvonne Klynman, Nicholas Kouppari, Mohammed Mukhier

Design and Production Team: Jean-Charles Chamois, Avishan Chanani, Jorge Perez, Patrick Piper

Reviewers: Madhavi Ariyabandu, Sally Baker, Iñigo Barrena, Kate Burns, Thomaz Carlzon, Maitreyi Das, Esther Dingemans, Jan Gelfand, Barbara E. Harrell-Bond, George Kent, Isabel Mota Borges, Valérie Scherrer, Michaela Told, Eva von Oelreich, Ben Wisner, Anthony Zwi

We would also like to thank all those who assisted contributors during travel and research for this issue.

Typesetting by Strategic Communications SA, Geneva, Switzerland

Printed by ATAR Roto Presse, Satigny/Vernier, Switzerland

Contact details:
International Federation of Red Cross and Red Crescent Societies
17, chemin des Crêts, P.O. Box 372
CH-1211 Geneva 19, Switzerland
Tel.: + 41 (0) 22 730 4222. Fax: + 41 (0) 22 733 0395
E-mail: secretariat@ifrc.org; wdr@ifrc.org
Web: http://www.ifrc.org

To order the *World Disasters Report*, contact:

Kumarian Press Inc
1294 Blue Hills Ave
Bloomfield CT 06002, USA
Tel.: +1 860 243 2098
Fax: +1 860 243 2867
E-mail: kpbooks@kpbooks.com
Web: http://www.kpbooks.com

Eurospan
3 Henrietta Street, Covent Garden
London WC2E 8LU, UK
Tel.: +44 (0)17 6760 4972
Fax: +44 (0)17 6760 1640
E-mail: eurospan@turpin-distribution.com
Web: http://www.eurospangroup.com

International Federation
of Red Cross and Red Crescent Societies

Contents

Focus on discrimination

International Federation
of Red Cross and Red Crescent Societies

International Federation
of Red Cross and Red Crescent Societies

World Disasters Report 2007

Focus on discrimination

 International Federation
of Red Cross and Red Crescent Societies

Reaching everyone in need

In any emergency, the response by governments and aid organisations can only be said to be successful when it has reached everyone in need. But in disaster zones worldwide, despite the best efforts of many, a great need remains.

Those already marginalized by society – the elderly, women and girls, minority groups and people with disabilities – can become the most vulnerable in a time of crisis.

The level of discrimination they face in everyday life is heightened when disaster strikes. Then, too often, these people are invisible both within their own societies and to the national, regional and global communities that mobilize emergency aid.

Exclusion, prejudice, cultural norms and isolation can increase the vulnerability of these groups across the world.

Ethnicity, gender, language, religion, political opinions, national or social origin, economic condition are just some of the entrenched causes of discrimination that can compromise efforts to assist them.

The answer to this discrimination must be dialogue, openness and understanding. Aid agencies need to work to change attitudes, ensure inclusion and advocate. Discrimination thrives in the shadows; we need to chase those shadows away.

This year's *World Disasters Report* aims to address this issue by examining how and why different groups are marginalized during humanitarian emergencies. How does discrimination manifest itself? How does it increase vulnerability? In what ways are organizations reinforcing it? What can we do about it?

This report is not an exhaustive examination of discrimination but rather an attempt to stimulate debate, and to encourage humanitarian organizations and governments to reassess their emergency planning and response to limit the effects of discrimination and its consequences.

Markku Niskala
Secretary General

International Federation
of Red Cross and Red Crescent Societies

Disasters do not discriminate: people do

The scene was the Kibumba refugee camp in 1994. Sprawling in the shadow of Mount Nyiragongo, in what was then eastern Zaire, Kibumba was home to a quarter of a million refugees. Almost all of them were Hutus who had crossed the border from Rwanda. Many had been implicated in the slaughter of minority Tutsis and moderate Hutus, and feared reprisals from the victorious, Tutsi-led army that had halted the genocide. Having walked for weeks with their families, the refugees were exhausted and hungry. Kibumba camp sprang up when thousands were simply unable to carry on.

Among the Hutu refugees were a small number of Twa, a Pygmy people who were the original settlers of the Great Lakes region. Kibumba was unplanned, chaotic and, for the Twa, a nightmare of discrimination.

The camp was made up of 'communes' charged with distributing hundreds of tonnes of food aid from the International Federation of Red Cross and Red Crescent Societies each week. Since there were few Twa – before the war, they made up less than 1 per cent of the Rwandan population – they did not have their own commune. Dispersed throughout the camp, they had to struggle among crowds of Hutus and were often beaten and robbed of the aid they collected.

One day, three of them turned up at an International Federation camp management meeting. A glum spokesman, who stood maybe one and a half metres high, rose from the chair he shared with his friends and said: "No one sees us in the crowd. We are pushed around and sometimes we don't get anything."

Hutu leaders laughed, pointing at the man as if he were a clown. Kibumba was bad. Being small made it totally miserable.

A relatively basic solution was found. The International Federation would introduce separate Twa lines at communal distribution points. The simple move worked and Zaire Red Cross volunteers monitored their journeys home for good measure.

Disasters do not discriminate. They affect minorities and majorities, the able-bodied and persons with disabilities, young and old, men and women. But discrimination can multiply the effects of a crisis on vulnerable people.

In the case of the Twa, the problem was solved – once it had been made visible to those running the camp. But often discrimination remains invisible, and unless

Photo opposite page: A survivor of the 2005 South Asia earthquake sits in despair amid the rubble. The response to the disaster revealed discriminatory attitudes and practices towards marginalized groups.

© Arzu Ozsoy/ International Federation

governments and aid agencies know in advance what they are likely to encounter, they may not be able to address it.

Discrimination was and is inherent in many societies, with disasters often magnifying the problem. However, we now have the research and the means to try to eliminate it, as this report will illustrate.

Every emergency involves people who cannot access food and shelter simply because of their age, ethnicity, gender or disability. People already on the margins of society as a result of discrimination are made even more vulnerable through a crisis. Persons with disabilities who are hidden from view by their families may be excluded from emergency shelters. Older people, who are routinely denied food by their families, may be unable to walk to food distribution sites. Women often become targets of sexual violence in crisis situations.

When this happens, unacceptable pockets of human suffering can develop, unseen and unaddressed by governments and aid agencies alike.

The *World Disasters Report 2007* looks at discrimination based on gender, ethnicity, age and disability, and asks key questions such as: How does discrimination affect the vulnerable in an emergency? How can we spot it? What can we do about it?

Not only does already-embedded discrimination put vulnerable individuals at greater risk in a crisis, but sometimes governments and aid agencies themselves are guilty of discrimination, albeit unintentional.

This report looks at what legislation exists to protect the rights of vulnerable people and whether it is enough. Is there a need for legally binding treaties that ensure states protect against discrimination specifically within the context of an emergency? Are current guidelines on vulnerable groups for aid agencies sufficient?

There is no universal definition of discrimination in international law. Some conventions address it within the context of a particular group, but neither the Universal Declaration of Human Rights nor the United Nations International Covenant defines it.

The UN Convention on the Elimination of All Forms of Discrimination against Women and the International Convention on the Elimination of All Forms of Racial Discrimination define gender and racial discrimination as any distinction, exclusion, restriction or preference based on gender, race, colour etc., which has the purpose or effect of nullifying or impairing the recognition, enjoyment or exercise, on an equal footing, of human rights and fundamental freedoms in the political, economic, social, cultural or any other field of public life.

In disaster responses, discrimination is a broader concept and also includes social exclusion and restrictions resulting from marginalization and vulnerability.

This lead chapter offers an overview of subsequent chapters and provides a summary of cases to be discussed in detail.

Chapter 5, which focuses on women, argues that the misuse of power lies at the heart of discrimination, with devastating effects.

The misuse of power occurs within families, communities and the state as a whole (see Box 1.1). In an emergency, abuse of power within these relationships may increase. Humanitarian workers also have power because of their resources, information, contacts and authority. They decide who is vulnerable, who needs protection and who receives aid, and they define their working relationship with communities and individuals.

"The risk of discrimination is high. The success of disaster operations and the prevention of discrimination may depend on the way in which power is exercised," writes Judi Fairholm (see Chapter 5, Box 5.3).

An overview of vulnerable groups in disasters reveals common experiences across the world:

- Discrimination exists before disaster strikes but is exacerbated during an emergency.
- Existing discrimination is often invisible largely because of a lack of official data on the numbers of older people, ethnic minorities and persons with disabilities – some of whom are so hidden by their families that they are not included in national censuses or other formal registration processes.
- This invisibility is made worse when aid agencies carry out emergency assessments that do not include an analysis of vulnerable people and their needs.
- Vulnerable groups are often excluded from the disaster planning process before, during and after an emergency.

Discrimination in an emergency setting is life-threatening. And it affects not only people's ability to survive the crisis, but also to recover and to regain their livelihoods afterwards. The chapters that follow explain more about what this means in practice for the elderly, persons with disabilities, children, minorities and women.

It is clear that greater awareness is required by governments and by those who run relief and recovery operations – and that they need more tools to help reduce discrimination. Guidelines on *what* should be done are not hard to find, but the focus on *how* is inadequate (see Box 1.2).

Box 1.1 Nowhere to go but out: gender and sexuality-based persecution on a small island

He was certainly taking a big risk in Jamaica. Wearing heavy make-up, high-heeled shoes, long, shiny earrings, a fitted blouse and with a handbag slung over his shoulder, walking in Falmouth's Water Square could have easily spelt a death sentence that morning for the cross-dresser.

Once spotted, the question of whether he was going to live or die would either be left to the angry crowds, the health services, the policemen or the judges. Yet no one, it seems, can be counted on to take the side of lesbians, gays, bisexuals and transgendered people in Jamaica.

"Where the police station?" the frightened man screamed as crowds armed with whatever weapons they could find attacked him with the all-too-familiar cries of "battyman fi dead" (gay men must die).

This man was lucky. He made it to hospital thanks to a police escort, but only after crowds had beaten him to a pulp.

Countless others have not been so fortunate. According to Amnesty International, gay men and lesbians in Jamaica are subject to unprecedented levels of discrimination, which often manifests itself in extreme, spontaneous brutality towards them in public places.

Earlier this year, on Valentine's Day, a 200-strong, homophobic lynch mob besieged three gay men in a shopping centre in the capital, Kingston. The men were threatened by the crowds and then roughed up by the policemen who had rescued them from the mob. Two months later, the funeral congregation of a gay man was attacked by a mob at the church where the service was being held.

Jamaica's prevailing sodomy laws provide a pretext for many people to rationalize violence against those whose gender identity fails to conform to society's expectations. Under Jamaican law, being caught engaging in a homosexual act can result in a lengthy prison sentence. To be seen to be upholding the law appears to provide an excuse for policemen, politicians and other figures in society who play an active part in condoning violence against gay men and lesbians. Notoriously, in 2002, both main political parties used homophobic slogans in their campaign manifestos.

According to Robert Carr, currently coordinator of the Caribbean Centre of Communication for Development at the University of the West Indies, the highly gendered role of children's identity formation in poor communities in Jamaica plays a part, not only in reinforcing discrimination and violence against gays and lesbians, but also in reinforcing dangerous stereotypes about the roles of men and women in society.

Phoebe, living alone in Jamaica, has been raped three times. She does not know whether she has been continuously targeted for sexual violence because she is a woman living alone or because she is a lesbian. Deep-rooted Christian beliefs combined with socio-economic pressures result in a historical condemnation of any form of sexual or gender role variance. It is, therefore, hard to get a sense of how many victims there truly are because many homosexual men and women in Jamaica live as invisibly as possible, often coexisting in heterosexual relationships for fear of being identified and persecuted together with their children.

Not only does this situation lead to extreme misery and marginalization for the individuals and for their families, but it also

International Federation
of Red Cross and Red Crescent Societies

contributes towards driving underground a growing HIV prevalence rate. In Jamaica, high-risk populations such as men who have sex with men are understandably reluctant to seek treatment in the health services. Such is the climate of fear and intolerance that there have been numerous examples of health providers deliberately 'outing' people with HIV and knowingly exposing them to further danger and persecution within their communities. The practice of homosexuals engaging in heterosexual sex and invariably – out of a fear of discrimination – identifying themselves as heterosexuals, means that the pandemic has virtually no traceable boundaries. In any case, the Jamaican Ministry of Health only reports on the heterosexual transmission of HIV, so the true extent of the epidemic is all but invisible.

For the cross-dresser, leaving the hospital was not going to be the end of the story. A group was waiting outside to continue its job on him once he was well enough to be discharged. His only real chance of survival and respect for his inalienable human rights and dignity would be to leave Jamaica and seek asylum in another country. For most Jamaican men and women who dare to express any form of sexual or gender variance this is simply not an option, and they will remain living on this beautiful island mindful of a constant, irrational and unpredictable threat to their lives and the reality of very little, or no, recourse to protection. ■

What can aid agencies do?

One-size-fits-all relief planning is unhelpful in overcoming discrimination. If agencies go into a situation with 100,000 people to help, they need to know who those 100,000 are and how to reach the marginalized among them. This form of analysis is difficult to do in the first five to seven days after an emergency, but it is essential to carry out as soon as possible to avoid needless suffering.

Mass distribution through air drops, for example, excludes the young, old and persons with disabilities. Emergency shelters often exclude persons with disabilities. And poorly designed camps make women vulnerable to sexual violence or can inadvertently prevent minorities from accessing aid.

Dialogue is fundamental to good programme design, monitoring and evaluation. Systematic efforts to listen to people affected by disaster can help pre-empt and remedy discrimination.

Many agencies have policies and guidelines to address these issues. The Inter-Agency Standing Committee (IASC), which exists to help key UN and non-UN players coordinate humanitarian assistance, has published guidelines on how to prevent gender-based violence in an emergency. The *IASC Operational Guidelines* mentions persons with disabilities in terms of camp security, non-discriminatory access to aid, inclusion in the long-term planning of resettlement, reconstruction and livelihoods and so on. Special guidelines have also been produced that focus on minorities and children.

Box 1.2 Media matters

Where the media decides to shine, or not shine, a spotlight can spell inclusion or exclusion for people in great need.

News agendas, of course, are not always fashioned by need. Politics, national interest and conventional wisdom can colour the coverage, particularly when news is determined by news desks and not by journalists in the field. Reluctant correspondents can be posted to crises away from their usual beats and from issues they consider to be more important.

"Look, I need a good story and I need it fast. I need an excuse not to go to Kosovo," a senior television correspondent appealed to an International Federation of Red Cross and Red Crescent Societies contact in Nairobi when the Kosovo crisis erupted. A story was breaking in Tanzania, where refugees continued to flee from the conflict in the Democratic Republic of the Congo. But by the time the contact called to confirm he could help her, the correspondent had already received her marching orders.

Along with many other Africa hands, she was on her way to the biggest story of the moment. There was no denying the importance of Kosovo, but the Congolese hardships were far greater. Aid agencies, however, were on the self-same road as the journalists and resources for Africa were diverted to Europe. Soon, food stocks in Tanzania were so low that the World Food Programme and the International Federation had sufficient for half rations only and hungry Congolese in refugee camps began stoning Red Cross vehicles.

Most journalists would agree that this was also an important story, but no one was around to record it.

The direct effect that coverage has on support for humanitarian action makes the development of relationships with the media, the provision of access, information and honest evaluation before, during and after crises, all the more important for aid organizations. Proactive dialogue and partnership pay dividends for all.

The media can also entrench or exacerbate discrimination. Following what it described as the demonizing of a Tunisian linked to a gruesome murder case, the United Nations refugee agency, UNHCR, has been working with the Italian media to draw up a code of conduct for refugee and immigration coverage.

What prompted the action was the case, in December 2006, of three women found stabbed to death in the northern Italian town of Erba, along with the two-year-old son of one of the women who had had his throat cut.

Some sections of the Italian media quickly blamed the Tunisian husband of one of the women who had been to prison for drug offences. As it turned out, he had been in Tunisia at the time and the police eventually arrested some neighbours with whom there had been trouble over noise.

UNHCR argued the case showed media attitudes needed to change and told editors-in-chief in a letter: "Strong and rather unexpected evidence of xenophobic sentiments emerged, as did a media system ready to act as the sounding board for the worst manifestations of hate."

Proposing the opening of serious dialogue on the coverage of refugee and immigration issues, it said alarmist and warlike language had influenced public opinion.

The media responded positively and a technical committee was soon set up to draft a code of conduct. It included representatives from UNHCR, the Italian national press federation, the national journalists' association and the anti-discrimination departments of the ministries of the interior, equal opportunity and social solidarity, as well as a professor of international law and selected Italian and foreign journalists. ■

Older people have perhaps received the least attention. Although some agreements, such as the Madrid International Plan of Action on Ageing, say older people need equal access to food, shelter and medical care in a disaster, many of these policies are not widely known. This, combined with the fact that many of their needs are not comprehensively articulated, is a key reason for discrimination against older people in disasters.

A crucial question is why, despite existing guidelines and policies, aid agencies rarely mainstream vulnerable groups into their disaster and emergency programmes. One important reason is a lack of official data, compounded by a lack of information gathered during the emergency planning stage.

But what can begin as neglect – the product of inadequate assessment – can become discrimination. Neglect can be remedied through greater awareness, advocacy and the generation of greater or targeted resources. Discrimination, however, requires the changing of attitudes, supported by legislation.

State responsibilities and international legislation

The need to ensure that discrimination is addressed when an emergency strikes is clearly not just the role of aid agencies but government agencies as well.

Some countries have developed national disaster response plans, but there is no existing international law on the extent of their statutory role in an emergency situation.

A certain amount of international legislation addresses discrimination and human rights, much of it developed within the context of labour laws or general laws on anti-discrimination. The question is whether this is sufficient to cover people's needs in an emergency.

Existing legally binding human rights treaties, for example, oblige the state to respect, protect and fulfil women's human rights. Ideally, this means the state is responsible for plans that ensure violence against women and other forms of discrimination are prevented before, during and after a disaster. However, this is not made explicit in international law.

As noted in Chapter 5, discrimination against women is a human rights violation that applies to acts committed in both private and public spheres. Therefore, the law covers acts or decisions made by the state – and also by non-state actors such as humanitarian aid agencies, non-governmental organizations (NGOs), families and so on.

The UN Convention on the Rights of Persons with Disabilities says states should take all necessary measures to ensure the protection and safety of persons with disabilities in conflicts, humanitarian emergencies and natural disasters.

But there are difficulties over terms such as 'disability' and 'minority'. There is no internationally recognized definition for either, and countries interpret them differently. For example, the United States has a much broader definition of disability than many developing countries.

Again, it is older people who are arguably the least protected. No international treaty is devoted to the rights of people over 60, and this lack of focus on their needs inadvertently compounds their discrimination. As discussed in Chapter 3: "A specific legal treaty would raise awareness of older people's rights within the human rights system… Currently, governments frequently fail to address older people's rights in their periodic reporting on the implementation of the human rights convention that they have already ratified."

Even when substantial international legal protection exists in theory, it is not always there in practice. The UN Convention on the Rights of the Child covers discrimination, but only 2 per cent of the world's children are legally protected from violence in all settings, according to the United Nations. Moreover, children's unique needs in disasters continue to be marginalized in disaster responses.

International human rights standards can be used to clarify steps that need to be taken to eliminate discrimination in all contexts. But the question remains: Do we need international legislation specifically addressing discrimination in an emergency situation? (See Box 1.3.)

The following overview of the issues covered in the report highlights some of the challenges in this field.

Minorities: listening is essential

Discrimination against minority groups, both in disaster planning and in society, can multiply the effects of an actual disaster on minority groups.

As described in Chapter 2, the vast desert and semi-desert expanses of northern Kenya are home to 3 million people – most of whom are pastoralists. The region has, according to the World Food Programme, one of the highest levels of poverty and vulnerability to food insecurity in Kenya.

In 2006, three years of crippling drought were broken by severe floods that washed away the only road to the worst-affected area. Aid workers in Garissa, the largest town in the region, could not get health kits to people who needed them. Communities lacked clean water. Diarrhoea and malaria increased, and an outbreak of Rift Valley Fever decimated livestock.

While the scale of the floods may not have been foreseen, the drought certainly could have been. The United Nations now has a sophisticated early warning system that can predict well in advance when critical food shortages are likely to arise. The government was accused of failing to put in place the infrastructure necessary to head off suffering.

Why did the Kenyan government not act? One answer lies in its attitude towards the pastoralist community. Often geographically distant from the big cities, pastoralists are sidelined politically, lacking the influence to press their case in the corridors of power. Without the effective participation of pastoralists themselves in the policy-making process and recognition by the authorities of the urgent need for preventative measures, these communities are likely to become ever more dependent on disaster relief assistance.

The International Convention on the Elimination of All Forms of Racial Discrimination (ICERD), the first enacted, modern, international human rights law, defines the term racial discrimination as "any distinction, exclusion, restriction or preference based on race, colour, descent, or national or ethnic origin which has the purpose or effect of nullifying or impairing the recognition, enjoyment or exercise, on an equal footing, of human rights and fundamental freedoms in the political, economic, social, cultural or any other field of public life".

The only international law with legal binding effect that directly mentions the rights of minorities is Article 27 of the International Covenant on Civil and Political Rights (ICCPR).

There is also the UN Declaration on the Rights of Persons Belonging to National or Ethnic, Religious and Linguistic Minorities (UN Minority Declaration).

But no universally accepted definition of the term 'minorities' exists. The word is interpreted differently in every society.

In some cases, governments are aware of the issues of minorities and act accordingly to protect their rights. But such action can also raise questions (see Box 1.4).

Chapter 2 also considers the plight of survivors of the 2004 Indian Ocean tsunami. Following the disaster, the Tamil Nadu state government in India provided segregated facilities and camps for Dalit survivors on the grounds that it was the only way to ensure those at the bottom of the Hindu caste system were not abused. *The Indian*

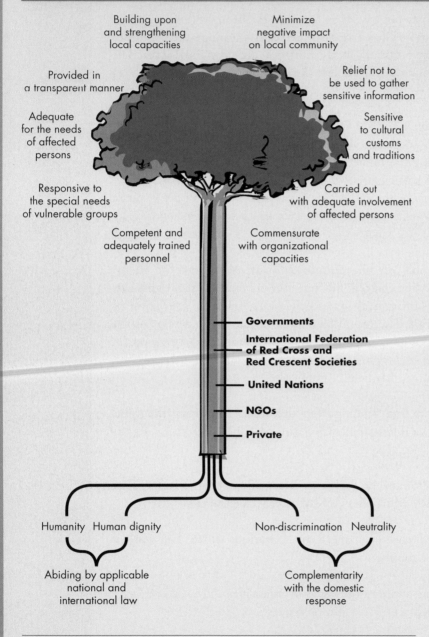

Building upon and strengthening local capacities

Minimize negative impact on local community

Provided in a transparent manner

Relief not to be used to gather sensitive information

Adequate for the needs of affected persons

Sensitive to cultural customs and traditions

Responsive to the special needs of vulnerable groups

Carried out with adequate involvement of affected persons

Competent and adequately trained personnel

Commensurate with organizational capacities

Governments

International Federation of Red Cross and Red Crescent Societies

United Nations

NGOs

Private

Humanity   Human dignity

Non-discrimination   Neutrality

Abiding by applicable national and international law

Complementarity with the domestic response

Source of these core responsibilities: UN General Assembly Resolution 46/182, Red Cross/NGO Code of Conduct, Fundamental Principles of the Red Cross and Red Crescent Movement, Principles and Practice of Good Humanitarian Donorship, the Sphere Humanitarian Charter and Minimum Standards, 1999 Food Aid Convention, International NGO Accountability Charter, Principles and Rules for Red Cross and Red Crescent Disaster Relief, Balkans National Societies Recommended Rules and Practices, Draft Guiding Principles for Philanthropic Private Sector Engagement in Humanitarian Action.

IDRL programme Mission statement: the International Disaster Response Laws, Rules and Principles (IDRL) programme seeks to reduce the vulnerability and suffering of people affected by disasters by raising awareness, promoting the implementation, and strengthening the laws, rules and principles that ensure a timely, adequate and efficient international response to disasters where international assistance is needed. The International Federation of Red Cross and Red Crescent Societies received an official mandate from the 28th International Conference of the Red Cross and Red Crescent in 2003.

The IDRL programme advocates for legal preparedness for disasters, without which international actors providing assistance, as well as domestic actors receiving it, consistently encounter legal challenges. Therefore, with a view to minimizing these legal challenges,

International Federation of Red Cross and Red Crescent Societies

the IDRL programme emphasizes the need for comprehensive, national legal frameworks that incorporate how international assistance will be initiated, facilitated, coordinated and regulated.

Examples of these legal challenges are:

■ for domestic actors: irrelevant or culturally inadequate aid from international actors, the latter's use of untrained or unqualified personnel, lack of adherence to quality and accountability standards, as well as humanitarian principles and values, and the non-utilization of local response capacities and skills

■ for international actors: delayed entry of foreign relief workers or goods and equipment, lengthy procedures for gaining legal status to operate in the disaster-affected country

IDRL guidelines for domestic legislation

The purpose of the Guidelines for the Domestic Facilitation and Regulation of International Disaster Relief and Initial Recovery Assistance, as submitted to the 30th International Conference of the Red Cross and Red Crescent of November 2007, is to contribute to national legal preparedness by providing guidance to states interested in improving their domestic legal, policy and institutional frameworks concerning international disaster relief and initial recovery assistance.

Content: while affirming the principal role of domestic authorities and actors, the guidelines recommend minimum legal facilities that should be provided to assisting states and to assisting humanitarian organizations that are willing and able to comply with minimum standards of coordination, quality and accountability. The guidelines will enhance the quality and efficiency of international assistance in order to better serve disaster-affected persons.

Core responsibilities of assisting actors: non-discrimination as a cornerstone

All assisting actors (for example, states – including their military personnel when accepted by the affected state – humanitarian and development organizations, private sector, religious groups and individuals) should abide by core responsibilities, the pillars of which are:

■ respect for the human dignity of the disaster-affected persons at all times

■ humanity: allocation of aid solely in proportion to needs, as part of the overall aim of preventing and alleviating human suffering

■ non-discrimination: provision of assistance without any adverse distinction (such as with regard to nationality, race, ethnicity, religious beliefs, class, gender and political opinions) to all persons in need

■ neutrality: provision of assistance without seeking to further a particular political or religious standpoint or to obtain commercial gain

■ abiding by applicable national and international law

■ complementarity of international assistance with the domestic response and necessary coordination with the responsible authorities of the affected state ■

Express reported that, when asked how the government could endorse the segregation of relief work by caste and communal affiliation, the Nagapattinam senior officer, Dr Umanath, said that having segregated camps was a conscious and practical decision. "There are real divisions and distrust between communities. A crisis like this is no time to experiment with casteist and religious amity."

Box 1.4 Ethiopia's pastoralists at a turning-point

Louren Nakali Loyelei passes his hand across his eyes as he talks – as if he still cannot believe what he saw in August 2006 when severe floods devastated his home region in south-west Ethiopia. In one month, the flood killed 364 people and swept away around 3,200 cattle.

"The whole land was covered with water," he says. "There was nowhere to pass and we rowed for an hour. We usually cross two rivers on this journey and during this flood we crossed four." Louren, 28, is a pastoralist. He grew up herding cows across the borders of Kenya, southern Sudan and Ethiopia.

Even though he is accustomed to the hardships of the nomad's life, the events of 2006 were exceptionally severe. Louren says: "The government and NGOs provided supplies and mosquito nets. They did helicopter drops where the people were displaced. After three weeks, the government sent trucks with maize and wheat, but they have not yet replaced animals."

Months later, people in Louren's home area are still recovering from the devastation. But he predicts it will not be long before the next disaster strikes. "Before this flood, there was a long drought, and people suffered. When drought comes again, they will suffer again."

Already, the long-term effects of prolonged and more frequent droughts – widely attributed to climate change – are being felt. Haji Mussa Gara, a pastoralist elder from the Oromiya region, is a veteran of many harsh seasons. "I have a herd of 30 cattle. It is less than before," he says. "The lowland only grows grass – not cereal. We cannot grow crops. We have only our cows... Our lives are in our livestock."

Dwindling natural resources have already led to an upsurge of fighting among the pastoralist peoples in the border lands of Ethiopia, Somalia, Kenya and Uganda. The situation in southern Ethiopia is further complicated by the overspill from the war in neighbouring Somalia – and the ready availability of small arms in the region.

This insecurity has had an impact on the provision of emergency relief. A spokesman for an international non-governmental organization (INGO) says: "Local government officials are afraid for their security. International aid agencies have also pulled out of certain regions. It is hard to provide assistance in insecure areas and, thus, certain groups suffer."

But the violence has also had the effect of reinforcing discriminatory stereotypes of pastoralist peoples. Widely seen as backward by mainstream African societies, the intertribal fighting is written off as typical of 'primitive' tribes. But an Ethiopian NGO activist has a different interpretation: "People think pastoralist areas are breeding centres for conflict. But it is not true. Pastoralists live in conflicting situations."

Official efforts to introduce disaster-prevention measures have been hampered by ignorance of the pastoralists' culture. Their lifestyle and the intricate civil systems they have developed to survive in Ethiopia's lowlands – one of the world's harshest environments – have been little understood by successive governments.

The current Ethiopian government is dominated by Tigrayans, from the highland area of northern Ethiopia. Dr Zerihun Mabaye, of the Ethiopian Pastoralist Research and Development Association (EPaRDA), an Ethiopian NGO, says: "Do not expect high-

International Federation
of Red Cross and Red Crescent Societies

level people in important positions to understand the discrimination and neglect. They are highlanders, they think like highlanders and their solutions are not the right solutions for pastoralists."

He went on to describe watering holes that were provided for cattle with no other services around them, clinics being built where barefoot doctor schemes would be more appropriate, and schools that were hard to reach, with lesson times that coincide exactly with the time that men and boys tend to the herds and women and girls cannot leave the home.

In a similar vein, Haji Mussa Gara says the government tried to build stock ponds to counter the effect of drought, but added that: "This can cause us to settle. We do not want to settle with the cattle: it is inappropriate for cattle to stay in one place. They need to move." When it comes to food aid, his assessment was that: "There is support, but it is on and off. It is here today and gone tomorrow." In any case, he reckoned it was not good for pastoralist communities to become dependent on food aid.

Despite the difficulties, there have been some improvements in recent years. An early warning system for lowland pastoralist areas has been established, while the infrastructure has been improved. There is now a new road to Jinka – a drought-affected area in the southwest – which has cut the time it takes to reach the capital, Addis Ababa, from six days to one. In 2002, a department for pastoralist development was established as part of the Ministry of Federal Affairs.

Three years ago, the government also officially recognized Pastoralist Day – an event that NGOs had been marking for six years – as a national event. On this day, Ethiopian society as a whole has a chance to familiarize itself with the issues pastoralists are facing. It also gets a chance to understand the pastoralists' rich traditions and the positive contribution they make to Ethiopian life.

Sisay Tadesse, spokesman for the Ethiopian government's Disaster Prevention Preparedness Agency (DPPA), says: "Awareness creation is very important; we have to break traditional thinking." He adds: "I highlight pastoralist issues at various forums and I have seen encouraging changes in the last five years – even in the last two."

Dr Mabaye recognizes this change in attitude, saying: "The government is now thinking about water development in pastoralist areas. If we have enough wells, we could solve 50 per cent of the problems." But he stresses that aid agencies and governments must draw on the expertise to be found at the grass-roots level. He says: "Officials must sit down and discuss genuinely and critically with the communities where such wells should go." For Dr Mabaye, the genuine participation of local people is the key to long-term sustainable development.

Pastoralist communities themselves are also taking the initiative. In a project supported by Minority Rights Group International and Pastoralist Forum Ethiopia (an umbrella forum that connects 27 INGOs and NGOs), a pastoralist elders' council made up of men and women from Uganda, Ethiopia, Tanzania and Kenya has been established. The council will work with local government and will lobby at national level to raise the profile of pastoralist issues. It will also have a peacemaking role by attempting to mediate in the conflicts that are tearing apart pastoralist communities.

There are no guarantees that any of these measures will work. But there is no doubt about the urgency. Emergency relief is only ever a short-term solution. If the pastoralists' lands in Ethiopia are always in a state of emergency, their unique way of life may be lost forever. ■

Some Dalits wanted to be housed separately because they feared attack from dominant communities. But in at least one reported incident in Tarangambadi in Tamil Nadu, 513 Dalits in a separate camp found they received less help than other tsunami victims.

Older people: growing isolation

Chapter 3, which focuses on the elderly, begins with an account of how one survivor fared after the Indian Ocean tsunami. When relief was being distributed after the tsunami, 75-year-old Perumal stood alone in the remains of his thatched hut in Tamil Nadu, refusing to join the hungry crowds jostling for aid.

"Some cars came by and just threw the packets," he said. "The fastest get the food, the strong one wins. The elderly and the injured don't get anything. We feel like dogs."

Governments and aid agencies often assume that older people are looked after by their community or family and, therefore, that mass distributions will reach them. However, this is not necessarily the case.

The chapter describes how indirect discrimination often creates additional problems for older people in emergency situations. They may find it difficult to travel to distribution sites and often do not have the strength to carry the goods back to their shelters. This is especially the case when sites are placed on high points away from populated areas for security reasons. But this process discriminates against the elderly and the housebound. Mobility is also a problem when people have to flee a conflict or flooding, for example.

The United Nations defines an older person as being aged 60 or over. Every year, an estimated 26 million older people are affected by natural disasters, and this figure is set to double by 2050. Older people are often disproportionately affected by a crisis. According to the UN refugee agency, UNHCR, those over 60 comprise 21 per cent of people displaced by war in Serbia and Montenegro. This is probably because many young adults had already migrated in search of work, fled or been killed.

There are six key misconceptions about older people that affect their treatment in an emergency situation (see Chapter 3, Box 3.2).

Perhaps the most glaring is the idea that the extended family and community will protect them at all times. Not all have families and, even when they do, older people are not always treated equitably.

Another crucial misconception is that needs can be covered by general aid distributions, whereas in fact older people have particular nutritional, cultural and other requirements that are often not met by general relief programmes. Clothes distributed in response to the Darfur crisis in July 2004, for example, were culturally inappropriate for older people, and medicines did not cater for their illnesses.

There is often an assumption that a specialist agency will look after older people, but there are no UN agencies and very few INGOs dedicated to the elderly.

Many agencies assume older people only have themselves to worry about. In fact, displacement, conflict and HIV and AIDS mean that, increasingly, they are responsible for their children and grandchildren. Over half of older people living in southern African countries severely affected by HIV care for orphaned and vulnerable children.

The elderly are often deemed helpless, whereas in fact many are used to providing for themselves and want to contribute to the welfare of the community as much as possible. When the Iranian city of Bam was destroyed by an earthquake in December 2003, killing over 26,000 people, disaster response experts were helped by local elderly men of influence who organized community responses across the city.

Finally, there is often the assumption that the elderly are too old to work, which means they are excluded from schemes to help people recover their livelihoods after a disaster.

Chapter 3 goes on to describe how these misconceptions are compounded by other factors. Since there is no UN agency and few INGOS dedicated to older people, their specific needs are often left out of pre-disaster planning. Linked to this is a lack of funding for older people. The *Sphere Humanitarian Charter and Minimum Standards in Disaster Response*, which seeks to promote minimum standards for relief agencies, recommends that 7 per cent of humanitarian funds should be channelled to help older people. HelpAge International says that, in practice, just 1 per cent of funds or less is used for this purpose.

Countries usually have little official data on older people, and emergency assessments often fail to identify their needs and abilities, which means they become invisible and excluded during the emergency planning and response.

Their exclusion is aggravated by the fact that there is no legal treaty devoted to protecting their human rights, and guidelines regarding their special needs are rarely put into practice.

Research carried out by HelpAge International in 2005 with 16 leading INGOs found that organizations do not actively exclude older people, but neither do they address their particular needs. "Yes, we had forgotten about them," one INGO director in West Darfur told the researchers.

A specific legal instrument would help to address discrimination, raise awareness of older people's human rights and help pinpoint specific contexts where those rights are violated.

Persons with disabilities: putting them on the map

Disasters and emergencies can leave a huge legacy of injury. As highlighted in Chapter 4, for every child killed as a result of violent conflict it is estimated that three more are permanently injured. And those who are already disabled before a crisis may become further marginalized and excluded because of their disability.

In Bangladesh, 6 per cent of the population has a disability. This group suffers by far the most during the country's recurrent floods (see Chapter 4, Box 4.2).

This woman was lucky enough to have received food aid from the Swaziland Red Cross during the food crisis in October 2005. Aid agencies need to ensure that older members of the community, particularly women, are not overlooked when it comes to the distribution of food.

© Yoshi Shimizu/ International Federation

International Federation of Red Cross and Red Crescent Societies

Setara Begum, whose husband had been paralysed in an accident, gave a vivid account of their experience in 2001. After their home was washed away, they had to move to a flood shelter. "But moving such a big man is difficult," she said. And when they got there they encountered more problems. The toilets were too far away. "Now when he defecates in bed, the other families suffer from the stench, and so they have tried to throw us out. It seems that the authorities here are also thinking along the same lines."

Their experience was by no means unique. One recent survey of persons with disabilities living in Bangladesh's cyclone-prone coastal belt found that many were excluded from humanitarian aid because of inaccessible shelters and food distribution mechanisms.

According to the *IASC Operational Guidelines on Human Rights and Natural Disasters*, exclusion can be the result of "inappropriate policies or simple neglect" (see Chapter 4). This was borne out by a 2006 global survey by the UN Special Rapporteur on Disability, which found that persons with disabilities have been largely overlooked in emergency relief programmes. It suggested that states, in conjunction with relevant UN agencies, should develop specific policies and guidelines for emergency situations.

After years of brutal war, many young people in Liberia are now permanently injured (see Chapter 4, Box 4.3). Members of the general public often assume they are ex-soldiers who 'deserved what they got'. Whatever the cause of their injuries, very few disarmament, demobilization and reintegration programmes implemented by the United Nations and other international organizations made any provision for large numbers of young, disabled former combatants. So now they are stigmatized and neglected, with no option but to beg on the streets of the capital, Monrovia.

Not being 'seen', being off the radar, is part of what puts persons with disabilities at risk. Many are stigmatized by families and communities, kept hidden from view and sometimes left out of official registration processes. This is one of the main reasons why those with disabilities are rarely included in disaster programmes, despite the existence of guidelines and policies.

But even when they are officially registered, they may be sidelined by the government and by NGOs.

The tsunami has become a catalyst for agencies and planners to rethink their methods, but many organizations that try to provide special services tend to plan from the top down – *for* persons with disabilities but not *with* them. Many of these people can help prepare for a disaster and are a useful source of expertise.

Women: a woman's place in disasters

Whether disabled or not, young or old, of whatever colour or race, women remain the most vulnerable and discriminated category. They do more and suffer more than anyone else in a disaster.

This is visible from the outset. Frequently, the first local response comes from women, as was seen once again in Indonesia after the tsunami. Over 70 per cent of staff of local NGOs delivering relief in Banda Aceh were women.

As the South Asia earthquake of October 2005 showed, women often have little or nothing to say on who has a right to what, and who should benefit from aid. In Pashtun-dominated areas of Pakistan's North West Frontier Province, women were strictly forbidden to express their needs or negotiate assistance (see Box 1.5).

Then there is violence against women. Alongside contraventions of women's rights, disaster after disaster produces irrefutable evidence that with displacement – be it as a result of natural hazards or conflict – the risks of physical abuse to women and girls rises substantially. The World Health Organization has suggested that the stresses brought on by disasters is behind the increase, and around the world millions suffer the consequences.

As discussed in Chapter 5, violence and violation are extreme manifestations of gender discrimination, while many experts agree it is one of the most difficult challenges faced by humanitarian workers in crisis settings.

The nature of the discrimination varies but commonly includes sexual violence, exploitation and abuse, forced prostitution, domestic violence, trafficking, forced and early marriage and widow inheritance. Men and boys can also be victims, but the impact is greatest on women and girls.

Again, brutality and marginalization do not occur suddenly in crises. They are reflections of the 'norms' in women's lives and prevention must begin long before emergencies happen. It is a recurring theme in the search for solutions to discrimination in disasters.

Such 'norms' can be invisible to aid agencies and are therefore not included in their planning.

In Africa, HIV affects women disproportionately. More than half of those infected are female. It is often left to women to nurse the sick and to feed, educate and agonize over the future of their soon-to-be-orphaned children.

Box 1.5 Pakistan: discrimination in disasters

Some disaster-prone communities, groups, households and individuals are, in addition, also prone to various forms of discrimination. Disaster can reinforce social discrimination in a hierarchical society, where opportunities and resources are not fairly distributed between and among various social, ethnic, religious, gender, political, geographical and community groups. However, disaster can also provide an opportunity for social transformation that can result in the neutralization of existing disparities, depending on the level of rigidity and flexibility in the dynamics of the prevalent power structure in a given society and community.

Following the South Asia earthquake in October 2005, various forms of discrimination were noted in the affected areas of Pakistan's North West Frontier Province (NWFP) and in Pakistan-administered Kashmir. The nature of discrimination, however, varies according to the social location.

For instance, in the Pashtun-dominated areas of the Mansehra, Abbottabad, Battagram, Kohistan and Shangla districts of NWFP, women were strictly forbidden to articulate their demands and negotiate with the relief and recovery administration. In contrast, in the Hindko-speaking areas of NWFP and Pakistan-administered Kashmir, women were relatively assertive and active in accessing resources and subsidies provided by the Pakistani government and other organizations.

"In Pashtun-dominated areas, the male-female interaction is restricted only to *mehram* [immediate family relations]," explains Mushtaq Gadi, an anthropologist based in the Pakistani capital, Islamabad. According to this cultural tradition, women are stigmatized if they engage in any social interaction with strangers. Yet, during the crisis, such cultural boundaries prevented women from accessing their entitlements as the relief administration was largely dominated by male workers. "We had hardly seen a woman at the distribution points during the emergency period of the earthquake," says Yasir Saleem, who was working at the Allai unit of the International Federation of Red Cross and Red Crescent Societies. "Women did not come in public; they designated some male member of their family to receive relief goods on their behalf."

Ghulzar Khan, from the Kaghan Valley, claims: "A woman cannot be the head of the family; the security of [the] woman is the responsibility of her family." This attitude led to discrimination against female-headed households that lost male members of their family in the wake of the earthquake. Access to relief and recovery packages was denied or made difficult for such women, who were prevented from participating in public life due to religious-cum-cultural customs. Elderly and single women therefore had to suffer multiple discrimination as a result of their inability to assert their rightful demands for relief and reconstruction.

Fatima Jan, a widow whose husband was injured in the earthquake and who died after ten months of medical treatment, is now living in a makeshift camp in Hafizabad, near Balakot, NWFP. Her damaged house was not assessed as she was attending to her wounded husband in hospital in Abbottabad during the survey process. "We got only one tent and a cheque for 25,000 rupees. Most of the money was spent on the medical treatment for my husband, who died later," Fatima recalls. When asked whether she had rebuilt her house, Fatima replied that she could not get a housing subsidy despite the fact that they were living on their own land. "I am worried who would help me to get money from the government to rebuild my house," she says.

Widowed, elderly, disabled and tenant women had to endure multiple discrimination when they tried to access information, relief assistance and reconstruction subsidies. The majority of such women could not pursue their claims, for various reasons. At a procedural level, particularly in the case of tenant women, they could not provide documentary evidence as to their identity and eligibility to prove their claims. Mukhtar Bibi, from Garhi Habibullah, is one such case. Her parents bought the land from a local *khan* (lord) but the property transfer order was not handed over to her parents. After the earthquake, she was asked to pay 50 per cent of the reconstruction subsidy to the *khan* if she wanted the property transfer order to register her claim with the Earthquake Rehabilitation and Reconstruction Authority (ERRA). However, she could not raise the money and is still struggling to obtain a housing reconstruction subsidy.

Geographical location can be another factor in discrimination. The earthquake-affected area consists of inaccessible, mountainous terrain, with high- and low-altitude areas. Settlements are scattered across the area and access to the main towns is difficult. In addition, high-altitude areas are particularly vulnerable to health hazards due to a lack of medical facilities and services. In the aftermath of the earthquake, the base camps of medical service and other relief assistance providers were mainly established in urban centres further down the valley. It was difficult for people living in high-altitude areas to carry patients down to lower-lying areas for emergency medical treatment. In order to address

these gaps, the Pakistan Red Crescent Society and the International Federation established mobile medical units in high-altitude areas in Mansehra district.

Communities living in high-altitude areas complained of discrimination resulting from ERRA specifications for building materials. ERRA made compliance with its specifications a condition for the disbursement of financial aid. However, the cost of transporting materials to high-altitude areas was significantly more than the materials themselves. Communities living in areas above 5,000 feet in Kahori, Pakistan-administered Kashmir, described how sand worth 700 rupees cost 1,800 rupees to transport from the nearest ERRA construction materials hub. The reconstruction process was therefore hampered in these areas due to the high cost of carriage.

Local power relations at community level also played a part in spreading discrimination in the wake of the earthquake. In tribal and semi-tribal localities in NWFP, local *khans* were reported to be influencing the relief distribution decision-making process. For example, the water and sanitation team working with the International Federation was not allowed to talk to communities in Allai without the presence and permission of the local *khan*. Elected representatives and the non-elected local elite acted as self-appointed interlocutors between affected communities and the governmental and non-governmental relief administration. Influential local figures were reported to have intercepted relief trucks and to have diverted supplies to their own kith, kin and constituencies, which resulted in conflict at community level.

It appears that caste was also a factor in the distribution of aid. This was noted by a joint research report launched in March 2007 by ActionAid and Shirkat Gah, which claimed that the Sawati castes were discriminated against by the Syeds, who received the bulk of relief material in the village of Charan Gada, in Muzaffarabad district, Pakistan-administered Kashmir. A focus group discussion with residents of Ratta Chanja, in the Kaghan Valley, NWFP, revealed that about 66 households were not given corrugated galvanized iron (CGI) sheets because of their political affiliation to a certain party, which was opposed by the local elite. Syed Qasim Shah, an International Federation field officer, noted that sectarian affiliations also played a role in relief distribution in the villages of Shot and Meera, in Chakothi district, Pakistan-administered Kashmir.

A joint study by Church World Service Pakistan/Afghanistan and Duryog Nivaran Secretariat revealed cases of religious-based discrimination following the earthquake. It reported that, at the time of the October 2005 earthquake, about 37 Christian families had been living in Muzaffarabad. During the relief and recovery phase, these families were discriminated against as they were not allowed to share shelters with Muslim survivors. Despite the fact that these families had been living there for 25 years, they had not been registered as citizens and voters, nor had they been issued with national identity cards. They faced problems burying their dead as no place had been specified as a graveyard for the Christian community.

In another example in Bagh, members of the Christian community had erected their tents on land belonging to the forestry department, which subsequently dismantled them, leaving them without refuge. Local social activists later took up their case and organized protests, demanding equal rights for religious minorities affected by the earthquake. It was only then, and with the intervention of a government minister, that the Christian community was allowed to set up its tents again on the same land.

Disaster Alert, a newsletter published by the Islamabad-based Rural Development Policy Institute (RDPI) and Sri Lanka's Practical Action South Asia, reported a unique case of 'strategic disadvantage' in areas close to the Line of Control (LoC) between India and Pakistan. The case concerns Khalana Union Council, situated some 64 kilometres from Muzaffarabad on the Muzaffarabad-Chakothi-Srinagar road. Because of its location in a high-security zone, Khalana Union Council remained neglected by government organizations and INGOs. This is mainly because access to the area for 'outsiders' is restricted, while the local population did not receive assistance and support in relief and recovery compared with other earthquake-affected areas, where the aid flow remained unhindered and no security clearance was required to enter.

The South Asia earthquake not only exposed institutional inefficiencies in the response to a large-scale disaster; it also re-activated dormant conflicts and allowed latent discriminatory factors to come into play against politically, socially and culturally marginalized communities, households and social groups in the affected areas. ▪

Busisiwe, a 37-year-old mother of five whose husband had died of AIDS in Swaziland, fell foul of agency criteria during a food security intervention in southern Africa in 2003. Busisiwe had tuberculosis and was HIV-positive. Her health and strength were waning and she was struggling to feed her children.

On her homestead the maize was already high, but the impression was misleading. Unable to afford seed or to work her fields properly she, like many other widows, leased them to neighbours for a share of the crop. So even after the coming harvest she would retain only a few bags of maize.

She was eating into them already. Short of food, she was cutting and grinding the unripe crop, and those bags would be depleted further. Her children's school fees were in arrears and, come the harvest, she would have to sell some maize to pay them or the youngsters would be unable to attend school.

Help was at hand, but not for her. The agencies active in her district had excluded landowners from relief.

The needs assessments had failed. Landowners as a group did not need assistance, but many women widowed by AIDS did. It raised fundamental questions about how humanitarian agencies assess emergency needs, who they involve in the process and on what they base their criteria.

Recommendations

Each of the chapters that follow assesses and analyses discrimination as it relates to different groups and lists recommendations specific to that group. There are, however, some clear changes and initiatives that overarch the whole:

- Individual countries need to be encouraged, enabled and supported to conduct an accurate and reliable census of their population in order to identify all those who, through vulnerability or marginalization, could or might be at risk of discrimination in an emergency.
- The international community needs to agree on clear definitions of all potential minority groups to prevent opposing interpretations and to ensure a common understanding of the vulnerability of minorities.
- Aid agencies need to improve initial needs assessments by sharing information, learning from experience and developing common indicators on the impact of discrimination.
- Community-based organizations for minority groups need to be encouraged and enabled in times of stability in order to build capacity, empower the groups involved and reduce potential vulnerability in an emergency.
- Minority and vulnerable groups need to be supported and enabled to participate in the planning, design and implementation of all emergency and non-emergency programmes.
- Agencies need to advocate within communities to change existing negative attitudes towards minority and vulnerable groups. Government and non-governmental agencies must also identify and address obvious and hidden discrimination within their own organizations.

Conclusion

The first steps in addressing discrimination in disaster situations should occur before emergencies happen. Risk reduction and preparedness are as much a part of the process as any aspect of disasters. Preventing discrimination – and changing attitudes – has to be the first priority. Advocacy and community development are needed to make vulnerability more visible. Greater efforts must be undertaken to map discrimination in crises, and guidelines need to be shared through the humanitarian system.

The participation of the marginalized is essential in disaster management, both in planning response and in implementation. Empowerment is a powerful remedy.

Disaster can be an opportunity for change. Following the Indian Ocean tsunami, former US President Bill Clinton called for the recovery programme to "build back better". This goal is equally relevant to all efforts to eliminate discrimination: what existed before can be replaced by an environment conducive to social justice.

This chapter was contributed by John Sparrow, an independent writer and communications consultant currently working on disaster risk reduction issues, who also contributed Box 1.2; Tim Large and Alex Whiting, journalists with Reuters AlertNet, a web-based, humanitarian news network. Box 1.1 was contributed by Yvonne Klynman, Senior Officer, Disaster Policy at the International Federation. Box 1.3 was contributed by Dr Katrien Beeckman, Senior Officer, International Disaster Response Laws, Rules and Principles at the International Federation. Preti Taneja, a journalist working with Minority Rights Group International, which works to secure the rights of ethnic, religious and linguistic minorities and indigenous peoples worldwide, contributed Box 1.4. Box 1.5 was contributed by Amjad Bhatti, a development journalist specializing in the political economy of disasters and development in South Asia.

Sources and further information

Carr, Robert. 'On 'Judgements:' poverty, sexuality-based violence and human rights in 21st century Jamaica' in *The Caribbean Journal of Social Work*, volume 2, pp. 71-87, 2003.

Chew, Lin and Ramdas, Kavita. *Caught in the Storm: The Impact of Natural Disasters on Women*. The Global Fund for Women, San Francisco, 2005. Available at www.globalfundforwomen.org/cms/images/stories/downloads/disaster-report.pdf

European Roma Rights Centre (ERRC). *Women, Housing Rights and Pariah Minorities*. Position paper of the ERRC in the context of the Europe/Central Asia regional consultation on women and housing, UN Special Rapporteur on Adequate Housing. European Roma Rights Centre, Budapest, 2006.

Harper, Erica. *Guardianship, Inheritance and Land Law in Post-Tsunami Aceh*. International Development Law Organization, Rome, 2006.

CHAPTER 1

Hines, Horace. 'Mob beats cross-dresser', *The Jamaica Observer*, 28 April 2007. Available at www.jamaicaobserver.com/news/html/20070428T020000-0500_122324_OBS_MOB_BEATS_CROSS_DRESSER.asp

Human Rights Watch (HRW). *Hated to Death: Homophobia, Violence and Jamaica's HIV/AIDS Epidemic*. HRW, New York, 2004.

International Committee of the Red Cross (ICRC) and the International Federation. *Tolerance, non-discrimination, respect for diversity*. ICRC and the International Federation, Geneva, 2003. Available at www.ifrc.org/docs/pubs/values/ 2003-council-delegates.pdf

International Development Law Organization. *The stories of Aisha, Rauda and Ainun: Protecting Women's Legal Rights Post-Tsunami*. Educational film. Aceh, Indonesia: International Development Law Organization, 2007.

International Federation. *Guidelines on working with vulnerable Roma and other marginalized groups in Europe*. International Federation, Geneva, 2007.

International Federation. 'Saving the elderly's lifelines' in *The Bridge*. International Federation, Geneva, Autumn 2002.

International Federation. 'Tide of TB troubles Central Asia' in *The Bridge*, special issue on Central Asia. International Federation, Geneva, 2004.

International Federation. 'Special Focus on the Rwandan Refugee Crisis' in *World Disasters Report 1994*. International Federation, Geneva.

National Authority for Disabled People. *Equal opportunities for persons with handicap: towards a non-discriminatory society*. National Authority for Disabled People, Bucharest, 2005.

UN Children's Fund (UNICEF). *The State of the World's Children 2007*. UNICEF, New York, 2006. www.unicef.org/sowc07/docs/sowc07.pdf

UN Development Programme (UNDP). *At Risk: Roma and the Displaced in Southeast Europe*. UNDP Regional Bureau for Europe and the Commonwealth of Independent States, Bratislava, Slovakia, June 2006.

UN High Commissioner for Refugees (UNHCR). *Italian media heeds UNHCR call to set up code of conduct for refugee issues*. Rome: UNHCR, 2007. Available at www.unhcr.org/news/NEWS/45df04ea4.html

Web sites

European Roma Rights Centre **www.errc.org**
Global Fund for Women **www.globalfundforwomen.org**
International Development Law Organization **www.idlo.int**
International Federation Reference Centre for Psychosocial Support
   http://psp.drk.dk
ReliefWeb **www.reliefweb.int**
Reuters AlertNet **www.alertnet.org**
UN Children's Fund **www.unicef.org**
UN Development Programme **www.undp.org**
UN High Commissioner for Refugees **www.unhcr.org**
UN Office for the Coordination of Humanitarian Affairs
   http://ochaonline.un.org

CHAPTER 2

International Federation
of Red Cross and Red Crescent Societies

Overcoming multiple disasters: discriminating against minorities

Disasters do not discriminate. They strike indiscriminately, affecting minorities and majorities alike. However, do minorities and majorities experience the same hardships? Are minorities always treated fairly by those delivering a humanitarian response? As this chapter illustrates, there have been many reported cases of discrimination during disaster operations around the world and humanitarian workers are often faced with difficult decisions in times of emergency. Previous experience, however, has allowed humanitarian organizations to develop tools and approaches to identify social vulnerability which are then reflected in appropriate response. Before a disaster strikes, minorities are often already vulnerable people in terms of their struggle for political, social, cultural and economic rights. Both humanitarian workers and minority rights activists are working towards the elimination of discrimination and the reduction of vulnerability. It should therefore be indispensable for them to collaborate in order to develop additional disaster risk reduction strategies by analysing discrimination against minorities in natural disasters.

What is discrimination against minorities and why does it happen?

For certain groups in the international community, discrimination has mainly been discussed in the context of prejudice both in public perception as well as within institutions, particularly following the introduction of apartheid in South Africa and the civil rights movement in the United States. In both cases, the international community welcomed the ending of institutionalized segregation. The elimination of discrimination has been the primary purpose of international cooperation for the protection of human rights (see Box 2.1). The International Convention on the Elimination of All Forms of Racial Discrimination (ICERD), the first enacted, modern, international human rights law, defines the term racial discrimination as "any distinction, exclusion, restriction or preference based on race, colour, descent, or national or ethnic origin which has the purpose or effect of nullifying or impairing the recognition, enjoyment or exercise, on an equal footing, of human rights and fundamental freedoms in the political, economic, social, cultural or any other field of public life". Therefore, even in disaster management and relief works, discrimination is a much wider concept which includes social exclusion and restrictions resulting from marginalization and vulnerability, as highlighted in the *World Disasters Report 2006*.

Box 2.1 Minority peoples and minority rights

Despite the fact that issues surrounding discrimination against minorities have been raised during discussions on the international and regional regime for the protection of human rights, there is no universally-accepted definition of the term minorities. In fact, the word is interpreted differently in each society. The United Nations (UN) has failed to agree on a definition of what constitutes a minority – as referred to in Article 27 of the International Covenant on Civil and Political Rights (ICCPR), the only international law with legal binding effect, which directly mentions the rights of minorities – or beyond that implied in the title of the UN Declaration on the Rights of Persons belonging to National or Ethnic, Religious and Linguistic Minorities (UN Minority Declaration). Attempting a more precise statement has been fraught with difficulty: in some cases, the motivation for a tighter definition has been to deny certain rights to certain peoples.

Numbers: Francesco Capotorti, United Nations Special Rapporteur on Minority Rights, states that "the minority is numerically inferior to the rest of the population of a state". But Patrick Thornberry, a member and rapporteur of the UN Committee on the Elimination of Racial Discrimination (CERD), rejects this definition as it excludes dominant minority groups where there is a dominant majority, i.e. the white minority and the black majority in South Africa. Felix Ermacora, who was a leading human rights expert and Austrian parliamentarian, explained them as a 'racial-political minority'. According to Thornberry, however, it can also be a matter of self-determination to enhance their political rights rather than minority rights, and points out that apartheid should be regarded somewhat differently from minority issues in general.

Nationality/citizenship: Both Capotorti and Jules Deschênes, who succeeded Capotorti as UN Special Rapporteur on Minority Rights, refer to the requirements of nationality or citizenship by describing "a group…[of] nationals of the state" (Capotorti) and "a group of citizens of a state" (Deschênes). Thornberry claims the distinction between national and non-national is hardly relevant in terms of human rights protection in modern international law. However, another CERD member, Luis Valencia-Rodriguez, states that international human rights standards are ineffective in dealing with the issue of equality between nationals and non-nationals. In view of the human rights situation of non-citizens worldwide, CERD issued General Recommendation XXX – Discrimination against Non-Citizens – which clarifies the responsibilities of states parties to the International Convention on the Elimination of All Forms of Racial Discrimination (ICERD). With this general comment, non-national minorities and non-citizen minorities, including foreign residents in a country, are guaranteed their rights, including economic, social and cultural rights (Chapter VI).

Community aspects: Despite being described as rights, some minority rights cannot be claimed by individuals. But how, exactly, is membership of a minority group determined? Most countries, according to Thornberry, use subjective criteria, while the Austrian courts use both objective and subjective criteria – or they give priority to subjective factors in case of doubt. This means that, in most cases, the state party recognizes the existence of a minority community based on features such as common language and culture. However, people belonging to a minority may also exercise their rights individually, as well as collectively with other members of their group, without discrimination. (Paragraph 53, Commentary of the UN Working Group on Minorities to the UN Minority Declaration).

Indigenous peoples: Indigenous peoples enjoy additional special rights. As a result of having been subjugated by others, indigenous peoples retain indigenous rights in addition to minority rights. Indeed, they are able to claim land rights to indigenous lands. This is reflected in the clear distinction in the nature of the solution taken by the state party. For example, after examining the situation in India, in 2007 the UN Committee on the Elimination of Racial Discrimination recommended that the Indian government ensure the land rights of tribal (indigenous) peoples in Manipur to lands that they traditionally occupied (Article 19). The committee also urged the state party to secure land access rights for Dalits, India's lowest social caste (Article 20). With regard to cultural matters, indigenous peoples assert their collective rights to decide on issues that affect them, within a framework in which all cultural groupings have a right to exist. Indigenous peoples, therefore, frequently reject the application of minority rights to their group, and demand indigenous rights and self-determination.

What kinds of rights are contained in the package of minority rights in general? Minority Rights Group International, an international non-governmental organization (INGO), believes minority rights should consist of the following elements:

- non-discrimination
- the protection of existence
- the protection and promotion of identity
- effective participation

In practice, however, these are interrelated. For example, discrimination can emerge as a form of ignorance or of inferiority/vulnerability of particular groups in disaster management, through the non-incorporation of indigenous spiritual concepts in disaster-related land management, and in the exclusion of their participation in disaster preparedness programmes (including the non-preparation of hazard maps).

Finally, what kind of institutions can be introduced in order to overcome disadvantages of minorities in general? The unique mechanism, which is quite typical for minority rights, could be the special measures undertaken for the solution of discriminatory status. These special measures are sometimes referred to as positive action or affirmative action. Article 27 of the ICCPR does not call for the mandatory introduction of special measures by states parties, but instead requires states that have accepted the covenant to ensure that all individuals under their jurisdiction enjoy their rights (Fact Sheet Number 18 of the UN Office of the High Commissioner for Human Rights). In fulfilling this requirement, the state party may be asked to take action to correct inequalities. The type of measures vary from place to place and from community to community: for instance, the provision of scholarships, quotas in higher education, the employment of civil servants, employment in private enterprises, parliament, or the launching of community development projects, including the development of infrastructures. ∎

In disaster relief operations, prejudice towards specific groups is often the main cause of discrimination. When Romania suffered severe flooding in 2005 – ruining farmland and property, and driving thousands from their homes – the Roma were doubly affected, facing not just the flood waters but also entrenched attitudes (see Box 2.2). Instead of receiving sympathy for their desperate plight, they faced censure. *The Sofia Echo*, one of Bulgaria's English-language newspapers, reported: "Floods have also brought a considerable increase in infectious diseases to the city… Health officials said that the rate of infection among Roma was higher, because of the minority's 'disregard for personal hygiene'." Such prejudiced remarks may negatively influence response activities, lead to an inadequate identification of problems, create additional trauma for survivors, and prejudice the distribution of resources in relief and recovery activities.

Box 2.2 Romania's Roma: bringing them in from the cold

The village of Rast in Romania's Dolj county was destroyed by the Danube in 2006. The worst flooding in 140 years caused much of it to simply collapse, and what was left was dangerous and irreparable. The village had to be resited.

Today, new neighbourhoods are springing up, land has been allocated and homes handed over. A large number of Roma, maybe 30 per cent of the population in the village, have been part of the relocation and, when the waters receded, some long-hidden social challenges surfaced – for the community, the authorities and for aid organizations.

Like most neighbourhoods, the Roma were located on the edge of the village and were the first area to be inundated. Evacuation occurred in the middle of the night and people got out with very little, losing what they left behind. The rest of the village followed suit and soon the whole population was sheltered under canvas.

For the Dolj branch of the Romanian Red Cross, dealing with floods all along the Danube, trust was important in helping the Roma and, with no branch in Rast, contacts there had been minimal. Early distributions were stressful. Roma crowded in on volunteers dispensing relief from the back of vehicles. When the cars moved on, the Roma moved

with them and hassled for more whenever they stopped to distribute.

Such incidents give the Roma a reputation and aid agencies can become wary. As a result, some stay away. But Romanian Red Cross volunteer Camelia Voinea is quick to quash the stereotyping. "They were not trying to cheat. They were afraid of being excluded, so they put us under pressure. When they realized we were helping them in just the same way as we were helping other Romanians, they stopped reacting like that."

The director of the Dolj branch, Maria Vintila, says a young Roma man helped Romanian Red Cross operations enormously. A councillor appointed by the mayor, he established dialogue and understanding. "He asked us to let him do the talking," she says, "and from there on in we did not have problems. When people got upset he would calm them. It was so important. Trust builds when someone like that is with you, and people express themselves more openly."

Where the floods struck, the Romanian Red Cross created sub-branches. All have Roma links today and one has a Roma woman president. "She is respected within the community," Vintila says, "and we are more effective because of it. It's all about empowering people." A sub-branch is planned for Rast

International Federation of Red Cross and Red Crescent Societies

as well – a mixed one of Romanians and Roma.

Reaching the Roma is one thing, bringing them in from the cold another. Some players believe local authorities just do not understand what marginalization means. "Sometimes I have the feeling," Vintila says, "that the authorities think they know what's wrong. They believe they understand and act accordingly." The floods had opened eyes, and, certainly in Rast, had brought the authorities and the marginalized closer.

Whether the problems of a 21-year-old mother of six were fully understood was doubtful. She hardly understood them herself. Libia had a new, two-roomed house because Mayor Iulian Slisteanu was doing his best. But the young woman was still in trouble. It was not just her poverty, the lack of furniture and the one bed with a mattress of protruding springs where everyone slept. She was totally outside the system. She had no idea how it worked.

Her husband had no job and they survived on casual labour – the only regular income being a modest state allowance for her youngest child. It was enough to buy beans and potatoes, but not enough for bread.

Next year, her eldest child is due to start school, aged seven. But then again, he may not. To go to school he has to be registered. None of her children has been. None of her children has documents.

Maria Vintila took the case to social services because Libia needed help and advice. Ironically, it may have taken a disaster to finally get her some.

Helping the Roma to register, to get identity cards and access to services to which they are entitled has occupied Red Cross National Societies in several European countries, before and after disaster. Unless they are on the map, they will continue to live on the margins.

Mihaela Steriu, former director general of the Romanian Red Cross, says: "We have a job to do advocating on behalf of all the marginalized. We can raise the awareness of authorities about people with special needs. Disasters and how we respond to them provide us with opportunity." ∎

In addition to this overt prejudice, indirect discrimination in the disaster relief operation and policy implementation proved to be equally crippling for the Roma. When it came to rehabilitation following the floods, the government put in place conditions that the Roma found impossible to fulfil. Marian Mandache, head of the human rights department at Romani CRISS, a non-governmental organization (NGO) in Romania, said: "After the floods, the Romanian government offered financial and material support for rebuilding houses, but it was conditional on having property papers. Most Roma don't have such papers and are excluded from the benefits of rehabilitation."

According to the European Roma Rights Centre (ERRC), the typical government response to flooding in Roma communities is to build temporary housing which then becomes permanent. ERRC adds that it is common for the authorities to refuse to legalize settlements or to provide adequate dwellings or infrastructure. Roma who previously lived in mixed communities may also find themselves rehoused in predominantly Roma areas during the recovery process. Marian Mandache says that after the 2005 floods, his organization documented a case where Roma, whose homes were spread across a locality, were all rehoused in the same street. The Romanian government had responded to the floods in a way that effectively increased segregation.

A lack of understanding of minorities' socio-economic and cultural position can lead to discrimination. Mount Ruapehu is situated in Tongariro National Park, located in the centre of New Zealand's North Island. Mount Ruapehu is regarded as sacred by the Maori, who make up 40 per cent of the population in Ruapehu district. The mountain is the largest cone volcano in the country and has been active for many years. Approximately 60 lahars (volcanic mudslides) have occurred over the past 150 years. The volcanic activities of the late 1990s and the first years of the 21st century raised the crater lake's water level and created a seven-metre-high barrier of debris which blocked the lake's outlet.

By 2001, the need to be prepared for a lahar – a major occurrence is expected in the next few years – had increased significantly. One option, to reduce the risk of a lahar, was to dig through the volcanic ash dam on the rock lip of the crater and to drain water from the crater lake – the easiest option, with an estimated cost of between NZ$ 150,000 and NZ$ 200,000. The New Zealand government, however, decided not to proceed with this course of action and, instead, to implement an electronic early warning system – the Eastern Ruapehu Lahar Alarm and Warning System (ERLAWS) – at a cost of about NZ$ 300,000.

Even though Mount Ruapehu poses a significant risk, its location within a world heritage national park means that interference in the volcano's natural processes is restricted by law, even when human life and property are at risk. In addition to these legal limitations, human intervention would also be limited out of respect for Maori spiritual values. The government's decision, however, was much criticized for compromising public safety. The government was accused of playing Russian roulette with people's lives by investing in an early warning system and by abandoning risk prevention measures around the crater lake. The National Party conservation spokesman, Nick Smith, accused the government of placing environmental sensitivities and the mountain's spiritual significance for the Maori before public safety. On 18 March 2007, a moderate lahar broke, but there were no reports of any injuries as ERLAWS worked effectively, thanks to the efforts of staff from the central government, the regional council, the district council and scientists.

Even when disaster management work is able to save human lives and property, it is not necessarily an option free from controversy.

In the cases described above, discrimination against minority groups can, in itself, spell disaster for minorities, and the effects of an actual disaster can be doubled or

International Federation
of Red Cross and Red Crescent Societies

multiplied with the structural discrimination in disaster management as well as in society. In addition, the difference between discrimination against Roma during the Romanian floods and Maori-related issues in the lahar response in New Zealand demonstrates the different ways in which discrimination against minority groups in disaster management manifests itself. In the case of the Roma, the main demands from the discriminated community might be to be treated fairly and to be offered the same benefits as other affected communities. On the other hand, the Maori in New Zealand might ask to be treated differently, as far as their beliefs are concerned, and for special priority to be given to their spiritual values.

To respect minorities, it is clear that simple equality is not enough. Discrimination is so much more than just about treatment or attitude, and should also be considered from a structural and contextual point of view.

Who are the perpetrators of discrimination against minorities?

Governments often discriminate against minorities, especially when government bodies identify and meet the needs of the majority. Minorities may simply be excluded. Governments may also discriminate through their administrative processes, as well as through government institutions, which may be inaccessible to minority communities. Launching disaster preparedness education in schools, for example, can exclude minority communities when their children are unable to attend school, whether it be for reasons of poverty, language or something else. Similarly, humanitarian organizations can become perpetrators of discrimination when launching disaster preparedness initiatives, distributing aid and in their recovery programmes. International agencies, as outsiders, might be considered to be in the best position to sidestep prejudice and negative attitudes and ensure equitable distribution of help and support. However, various key factors militate against this. These are: a lack of priority given to discrimination issues; a lack of knowledge of the context in which they are operating; the sensitivity of relations between national governments and international aid organizations, especially where there is confrontation between majority and minority groups. In addition, international agencies are also in a delicate position in that they depend on government permission to carry out their work and are, therefore, reluctant to be drawn into criticizing them over issues such as the treatment of minority groups.

The perpetration of discrimination, however, is not just restricted to governments, organizations or institutions. In times of emergency, tensions between communities can erupt. A notable example from history are the events that followed the Kanto earthquake of 1923, which hit Tokyo and the surrounding cities, including Yokohama. The *Asahi Shimbun* newspaper described the widespread discriminatory attitude towards the Korean minority – as well as the atrocities committed against them – as follows:

"The day after the earthquake, a rumour that Koreans had become violent spread through Yokohama. In retribution, vigilantes killed Koreans in Hodogaya, Totsuka and Tsurumi. There was another rumour that Koreans had poisoned wells. The chief of the Tsurumi police station, Tsunekichi Okawa, took more than 300 Koreans and Chinese into protective custody at the station. An armed mob demanded the Koreans be handed over."

The media can also play a very important role in spreading rumours – even false or discriminatory ones. Of course, when it comes to disaster management, it is widely accepted that the media has an important role to play by publicizing information as well as by raising public awareness. Following the Kanto earthquake, however, the media, particularly the non-Tokyo-based newspapers, effectively spread false rumours regarding the Korean minority, with a report in the *Hokkai Times* claiming: "Ferocious Koreans mix poison and petrol in food. They carry bombs disguised as tin cans."

The truth is, however, that everyone has the potential to discriminate against specific minority groups. This can even apply to members of minority groups themselves. Although being unlikely to discriminate against other members of the same group, due to a shared ethnicity, an individual of the group can discriminate against other members for other reasons. Solidaritas Perempuan, an Acehenese women's NGO, noted that a camp for internally displaced persons (IDPs) established in the aftermath of the 2004 Indian Ocean tsunami had a lack of washing, bathing and latrine facilities. Men and women had to use the same bathing area, while sexual harassment and violence against women was commonplace. Although male IDPs at the camp belonged to a minority group – and therefore ran the risk of being oppressed by non-IDPs – they also committed violations against fellow minority members. In general, minority women are one of the most vulnerable groups, being discriminated against because of their ethnicity, status, and their gender. Vulnerability to discrimination is not simply a distinction between majority and minority, but a multi-layered vulnerability within the social structure.

The grounds, or reasons, for discrimination can vary. As has already been shown, discrimination can occur unintentionally. Therefore, every action taken by disaster management specialists should be critically assessed; failure to carry out reviews can develop into a root cause of discrimination. However, disaster managers can take steps to prevent discrimination. As is the case with indigenous peoples, the real roots of discrimination towards them are the deprivation of land rights, which results in a struggle for indigenous rights. For minority women who suffer multi-layered discrimination, the root causes can be found in a combination of patriarchy (in culture and social ideology) and a perceived inferior social status.

What is the impact of discrimination against minorities?

When disaster strikes a region, the effects can be much more serious than anticipated, and the form of the effects is variable. The vast desert and semi-desert region in northern Kenya is home to 3 million people – most of whom are pastoralists. It is the most underdeveloped part of the country – a stark illustration of this is in a 2007 Christian Aid report which says that "there are only ten kilometres of tarmac road in the entire region. Much of the remaining road network is only passable in the dry season". The population lives on the edge. It has, according to the World Food Programme (WFP), one of the highest levels of poverty and vulnerability to food insecurity in Kenya.

By 2006, there had been a three-year drought in the region. In Wajir in north-eastern Kenya, visiting journalists reported that many grazing cattle had died by March and that two-thirds of the people were dependent on food aid. The crippling drought was then followed by floods. The appalling infrastructure seriously hampered the food and medical aid distribution programme, as the only road to the worst-affected area had reportedly been washed away. Health kits were stuck in the largest town in the region, Garissa. Clean water shortages meant humans and cattle were forced to drink from polluted sources. Diarrhoea and malaria increased, and an outbreak of Rift Valley Fever (RVF) began, decimating livestock.

While the scale of the floods in the area may not have been foreseen, the drought certainly could have been. The United Nations now has a sophisticated early warning system in place, based on factors such as expected rainfall and crop yield, which can forecast when critical food shortages are likely to arise well in advance. A representative of an INGO in Nairobi accused the government of not putting the infrastructure in place to ensure that people do not suffer, despite the fact that droughts can now be predicted.

Why then, does the Kenyan government not act? One answer lies in the attitude of the government towards the pastoralist community. As in many other countries in Africa, Kenya's political elite regard the pastoralist way of life as an anachronism. Ali Wario – an MP from a Kenyan pastoralist community – summed up the quandary facing his community in comments reported in the respected *East African* newspaper in 2006. He said: "Most governments and policy planners view pastoralism as a way of life that is not viable." According to Wario, there are only two legally-recognized land systems in Kenya – farming and town planning. Despite the fact that 80 per cent of Kenya is arid and semi-arid, pastoralism is not recognized as a land-use system.

Often geographically distant from the capital cities, pastoralists are also sidelined politically, lacking the influence to press their case in the corridors of power. But with the effects of climate change already being felt in desert areas across Africa, it is clear that the consequences of long-term neglect are going to be increasingly catastrophic. Without the effective participation of pastoralists themselves in the policy-making process, the organization of effective preparedness activities, and the recognition by governments of the urgent need for preventative measures, these communities are likely to become ever more dependent on disaster relief assistance, delivered by international aid agencies, to survive from season to season.

In addition to the issue of 'territorial exclusion' (see *World Disasters Report 2006*), preparedness work on discrimination is indispensable when it comes to dealing with cultural sensitivity. Discrimination against specific groups means that there is often a lack of information about the very communities likely to be affected by natural disaster. In 2005, Hurricane Stan struck south-west Guatemala, a region containing the country's highest concentration of indigenous populations. More than 650 people were killed in the mudslide triggered by the storm. The Economic Commission for Latin America and the Caribbean (ECLAC) illustrated, regarding Guatemala, the "evident lack of information disaggregated by gender and ethnicity" of the area severely affected by the hurricane. Ramiro Batzin, a spokesman for Sotz'il, a

Minority women are one of the most vulnerable groups and often suffer multiple discrimination because of their ethnicity, status and gender.

© Claudia Janke/
British Red Cross

International Federation
of Red Cross and Red Crescent Societies

Guatemalan indigenous organization that works with the Guatemalan Red Cross, claims the tragedy would not have had such an impact if plans had existed that considered the particularity of indigenous communities and cultures. The *World Disasters Report 2006* also describes the shortage of disaggregated information as crucial, as the region most seriously affected by the hurricane is populated by many indigenous communities from which many of the men have emigrated to the United States, leaving behind a high proportion of households headed by women.

Discrimination also prevents participants in response work from conducting appropriate activities when problems arise. Stereotypical views of a specific group can overwhelm the scientific methods employed to prioritize the order of relief works, even if some of those involved are professionally trained, such as disaster managers and relief workers. New Orleans City Councilman Oliver Thomas says, about Hurricane Katrina which struck Louisiana in 2005, that people were too afraid of black people to go in and save them. He claimed rumours of shooting and riots were making people afraid to take in those who were being portrayed as alleged looters. In the name of security, these rumours and stereotypical views of specific communities can be rationalized, and frequently hamper relief efforts.

Discrimination can also be reflected in every single action carried out by relief workers at the shelters or camps. Shocking examples continue to come to light in India – disaster after disaster. Following the earthquake in Gujarat in 2001, camps were organized on the basis of caste, and camps of lower caste peoples were marginalized from the relief support. After the Indian Ocean tsunami Dalits, who are treated as 'untouchables' in the Hindu caste system, were forbidden by other castes from drinking water from UNICEF water tanks because sharing with Dalits would, in their view, pollute it. Minority Rights Group International reported that in other camps, members of the Fisher community excluded Dalits altogether and much of the relief materials – such as family relief kits, rice packets and donated clothes – failed to reach them. The report of the National Campaign on Dalit Human Rights (NCDHR) quoted Father Gunalan, a local pastor of the Asian Protestant Church in Tamil Nadu, as saying it was "appalling to see the Fisher people stopping relief trucks on the road and diverting them to their own community".

Following the tsunami, the Tamil Nadu state government provided segregated facilities and camps for Dalit victims on the grounds that it was the only way that it could ensure Dalits were not abused. *The Indian Express* reported that, when asked how the government could possibly endorse the segregation of relief work by caste and communal affiliation, the Nagapattinam senior officer, Dr Umanath, said that having segregated camps was a conscious and practical decision. "There are real divisions and distrust between communities. A crisis like this is no time to experiment with casteist and religious amity." Some Dalits wanted to be housed separately because they feared attack from dominant communities. But in at least one reported incident in

Tarangambadi in Tamil Nadu, 513 Dalits in a separate camp found they received less help than other tsunami victims.

Discrimination can be deep-rooted, not just for operational relief work but also for recovery and further rehabilitation work. For Dalits, discrimination also affected their involvement in the relief efforts. One told a researcher from ActionAid, the international anti-poverty agency: "I was employed as a scavenger [to carry out the manual cleaning of drains and toilets, and all such work considered as dirty] by the local authority. When the tsunami hit, they told us to go pick up the dead bodies on the shore, but they wouldn't give us protective gloves and masks." Other NGOs confirmed this treatment was common. Of course, collecting dead bodies is work that needs to be carried out by someone, but despite maintaining a caste-neutral approach in other areas of the operation, the government employed Dalits to collect the bodies.

Moreover, their working conditions were poor. The Dalits were not even offered enough money to buy a cup of tea and they were repeatedly threatened by higher caste survivors, who saw it as dirty work. Those carrying out this distressing task also failed to receive any counselling.

But problems with resource distribution during rehabilitation affect many minority groups around the world – not just Dalits (see Box 2.3). The treatment of the Dalits

Box 2.3 Guest workers in the Lebanese crisis

For a month in July-August 2006, the conflict between Israeli and Hezbollah forces in Lebanon destroyed much of the country's infrastructure and resulted in around 1,000 civilian deaths; some 1,000 were wounded and half a million displaced. The Israeli invasion also created a crisis for guest workers in the country. Around 60 foreigners were reported to have been killed or injured, including nationals from Argentina, Australia, Brazil, Canada, Germany, India, Indonesia, Iraq, Jordan, Kuwait, Nigeria, the Philippines, Sri Lanka, Syria, Ukraine and the United States. Some 17 Syrians were killed by Israeli air attacks – mostly agricultural workers and truck drivers in the Bekaa Valley.

The number of migrant domestic workers in Lebanon varied between 120,000 and 200,000, serving a population of 4 million prior to the recent crisis. By far the largest groups of domestic workers were Sri Lankan women (80,000–120,000), followed by Filipinas (20,000–25,000) and Ethiopians (20,000–30,000). The key to understanding the plight of these particular guest workers is their lack of access to information and social services, partly because of language problems and partly because they are secreted in homes and in apartment buildings that were targeted in southern Lebanon and in the heart of the Shia suburbs of Beirut.

The governments of Sri Lanka, the Philippines and Ethiopia had neither the financial means nor the organizational capacity to arrange for evacuations of their citizens. They relied heavily on the collaboration of

International Federation
of Red Cross and Red Crescent Societies

the Catholic non-governmental organization, Caritas Lebanon Migrant Center, and the International Organization for Migration (IOM) to pay for and arrange relief, accommodation and repatriation. A trilingual booklet in Sinhalese, Amharic and Tagalog was produced by the Ministry of Justice and Caritas Lebanon, which warned domestic workers about possible traffickers as they tried to leave.

Under a sponsorship system, Lebanese employers withhold the passports of migrant domestic workers as security against them absconding and the loss of their payment to the agencies. While many employers delivered their employees to their respective embassies for safety and repatriation, many also refused to let them leave. Many simply ran away, claiming they were escaping from abusive employers and left without papers or money. Others chose to stay because they did not want to lose their income, because they had not been paid or because they did not consider their situation back home to be any better. Reports indicate that around five or six women died, while others were injured while attempting to escape from high-rise apartment buildings.

Several hundred Sri Lankans camped around their embassy in the foothills of Beirut (many feared to go there because it is near a major Lebanese military post that came under Israeli air attack). The many that arrived at the embassy without travel documents were issued with an emergency *laissez-passer*, which was then ratified by General Security, the body responsible for all foreigners in Lebanon. Playing a crucial role in addressing the situation, General Security also released hundreds of migrant domestic workers from prisons and a detention centre, declaring an amnesty for all illegal migrant workers on the condition that they leave the country and not return for at least five years.

The IOM received around US$ 11 million earmarked for the evacuation of migrants from developing countries, in part as a security issue. Facilitating the repatriation directly to their home countries would ensure that they did not seek safety in Europe. More than 13,000 foreign nationals were evacuated by the IOM – mostly Asian and African domestic workers. Bus convoys transported them on a three-hour journey to Damascus, where they were given 48-hour visas, housed and placed on charter flights to their respective countries. By contrast, Spain and Italy provided ships and the British government provided navy ships and helicopters. The United States government provided a number of warships and helicopters for its citizens, levying a charge on evacuees; although, after intense criticism, the charge was later rescinded, the tardiness of the US to act prompted a number of Americans to take a 500-dollar taxi ride to Damascus. Some 5,000 Swedish nationals in Lebanon were the first to be evacuated, with the precise arrangements sent to them by mobile phone text messages.

The relief and evacuation arrangements during the Lebanese crisis were, for the most part, ad hoc and largely left to citizens' and foreigners' own resources. Despite the fact that more Lebanese and those of Lebanese descent live outside the country, Lebanon has not ratified the International Convention on the Protection of the Rights of All Migrant Workers and Members of their Families. Nor has it signed the 1951 Refugee Convention. It requires all embassies of foreign nationals in countries under risk of conflict or invasion to have evacuation plans in hand at all times. In this case, the sophistication of the IOM meant being able to move thousands with relative safety because of their coordination with the Israeli military. Evacuees in other circumstances may not be so fortunate. ■

in the aftermath of the tsunami illustrates the dilemma of rehabilitation professionals. In a 2005 Human Rights Watch report, *After the Deluge*, a local official for the state government of Tamil Nadu, C.V. Shankar, reportedly addressed a Tsunami Relief Rehabilitation Coordination meeting in Chennai, on 26 January 2005. He admitted that Dalits were not immediately included on lists of those eligible for aid. But he said: "We are conscious of the fact that the calamity has affected other communities. But 70 to 80 per cent were from the fishing communities, so naturally, initially more attention was given to them." When interviewed earlier this year, he added that "Dalits are poor not only because of disaster, but for other reasons". The policy-makers try to distinguish vulnerability caused by calamity from other types of vulnerability. The reality, however, is that vulnerability is well structured in each community. It is impossible to separate one from the other; rather, social vulnerability can also be a factor in vulnerability resulting from a disaster during the rehabilitation process. Just as it is important to incorporate a vulnerability assessment in the disaster preparedness process, disaster managers should also include a social vulnerability assessment in the rehabilitation programme by combining disaster recovery programmes and rehabilitation programmes with other social projects.

The cases discussed earlier in this section also highlight the misery that results when minority peoples and minority residents are excluded from response activities. These stories are, however, quite passive stories. Any disaster relief operation involves a variety of stakeholders; namely, administrators, experts and, of course, the communities themselves. There are also three types of help: public help provided by the government, mutual help conducted in the community and self-help executed by the residents themselves. The activities by the Buraku community in the aftermath of the 1995 Kobe earthquake provide a positive example of mutual help carried out in and around the community (see Box 2.4). The Buraku could be successfully empowered to participate in additional disaster relief works with the mutual support of the community. The mutual help provided by the Buraku could also extend beyond work with minorities. Thanks to special measures introduced, some Buraku communities acquired public human rights centres, which were mainly dedicated to working to eliminate discrimination against the Buraku, as well as acting as multi-purpose community halls. While rarely accommodating people from outside, the centres also offered temporary shelter for all. Cooperation between the Buraku and non-Burakus provided a good opportunity to get to know each other, as well as furthering emancipation on human rights issues in the region. Similarly, the promotion of community resilience through the operation can surely contribute to the elimination of discrimination. A greater awareness of discrimination issues by all the stakeholders, including, of course, resident peoples, should be the key for minority-friendly disaster management.

Box 2.4 Japan: Buraku discrimination and resilience during the 1995 Kobe earthquake

On 17 January 1995, at 5.46 am, a huge earthquake struck the Kansai area of Japan, killing 6,434 people. The modern city of Kobe, home to over 1 million people, suffered significant damage. As the images broadcast around the world illustrated, even the most modern, developed and well-coordinated countries in the world are vulnerable when faced with disasters. The earthquake is, so far, the costliest natural disaster ever to befall a single country. Kansai, the area most affected by the earthquake, is an area that had experienced radical redevelopment for the Buraku minority based on the 1969 Law on Special Measures for Dowa Projects.

The Buraku people – or Burakumin – are discriminated against on the basis of their social status and lineage. They are the most discriminated-against population in Japan. They are not a minority based on either race or nationality, but a caste-like minority among the ethnic Japanese. The discrimination faced by today's Burakumin is the result of a rigid social stratification created in 17th-century Japan, when the Buraku were segregated and given menial labour as leather workers, slaughterers and executioners. They were effectively placed on the bottom rung of society's ladder, classed as either *eta* (extreme filth) or *hinin* (non-human). In 1871, the Meiji government promulgated the Emancipation Edict, which abolished the feudal caste system. However, in modern-day Japan, ongoing discrimination against Buraku, particularly in marriage and employment, still exists and discriminatory remarks made by non-Burakumin, including public officials, are not uncommon.

According to a 1993 government survey, there were about 1.2 million Buraku living in 4,442 Buraku communities across Japan.

These figures, however, only cover those areas classified as *dowa* assimilation districts by government administration. The actual figures are estimated to be much higher. According to the Buraku Liberation League, one of the biggest Buraku non-governmental organizations, there are as many as 6,000 Buraku communities and a total Buraku population of over 3 million.

Historically, Buraku communities were formed as a result of enforced migration to the wetlands, to the intersection of rivers. In fact, to anywhere isolated from the rest of society. As a result, Buraku communities have always been vulnerable to natural disasters. To compound the geographical isolation, there has always been a wide socio-economic gap between Buraku and non-Buraku. To close this gap, the government introduced projects to improve standards of living, education and to resolve unemployment problems in *dowa* districts.

In the town of Akiko, the Buraku were once housed in wooden barracks. Just one year before the earthquake, however, the housing projects were completed. The wooden dwellings were replaced with reinforced concrete apartment blocks. A journalist, Hiroshi Yano, mentions that Buraku communities, particularly in Kobe, Nishinomiya and Takarazuka, where *dowa* projects had not been well implemented, were severely affected. Ashiya, located between Osaka and Kobe, was at the epicentre of the earthquake, with 400 deaths and half the buildings either totally destroyed or damaged. Buraku communities in Ashiya suffered no deaths and little damage to buildings. Non-Buraku communities were affected significantly more than the Buraku.

Surviving the earthquake did not leave the Buraku worry free. The Kami Miyagawa Cultural Centre was established for Buraku people. The director, Yukio Nakao, admits he was concerned about discrimination after the earthquake. The centre was opened as a shelter: 200 Buraku and 200 non-Buraku shared it but it was rare to have non-Buraku in the centre. Yukio felt anxious; there was not enough food to go round.

As relief materials from Buraku communities throughout Japan started to arrive, one woman from the Buraku community said: "Don't exclude non-Buraku people. Distribute the relief equally. If there is a shortage, give priority to the non-Buraku." She explained that after years of exclusion from classmates and teachers, she had learnt the need to be kind to others. In return, the Buraku community could expect greater kindness from non-Buraku volunteers. Buraku survivors, non-Buraku survivors and volunteers talked and got to know each other better. The recovery programmes may have long finished, but the centre remains a place for interaction between Buraku and non-Buraku people.

Mutual cooperation between two disparate groups does not always result in a positive outcome, as one university student discovered. Before the earthquake, he had been offered a position in a large company. After the earthquake, he was subjected to discrimination because of his lineage. Staff members from the company were sent to Kobe to volunteer in the disaster operation. They discovered that their future colleague's mother belonged to the Buraku community. This piece of information was quickly relayed back to headquarters and the new recruit was advised to limit contact with his home town. He decided to withdraw his application and now works as a labourer.

These two examples show the light and dark side of mutual cooperation in a disaster operation. The great earthquake highlighted the two faces of discrimination: the solution and the problem. ▪

Identifying and addressing discrimination against minorities

Meanwhile, how can we detect the potential of discrimination or the signs of it during the disaster management process? There are no specific methods for detecting discrimination. While some institutions are developing indicators to measure discrimination, or the impact of anti-discrimination – such as UNESCO's initiatives for organizing indicators for racism and discrimination in cities – it can vary from one community to the next. This is because it has a variety of forms, perpetrators and victims. But, at least, its occurrence can be presumed with the analysis of background information on discrimination. The UN Committee on the Elimination of Racial Discrimination (CERD) examined reports on the implementation of the International Convention on the Elimination of All Forms of Racial Discrimination (ICERD) submitted by the governments that ratified ICERD. The report from governments, as well making recommendations, also includes important information for understanding discrimination issues. There are also regional and domestic bodies whose role is to combat racial discrimination, such as the European Commission against Racism and Intolerance (ECRI), as well as human rights institutions in many countries. As for multiple discrimination, that is, the intersectionality of ethnicity, gender, age and disability, reports on each of these areas from UN institutions – such as the Committee on the Elimination of Discrimination against Women (CEDAW) and the Committee on the Rights of the Child (CRC) – could also provide useful resources.

Despite the existence of a large number of documents and instruments on human rights and discrimination, it is vital to identify any signs of discrimination on site. In order to do so, it is important to incorporate strategies to prevent and mitigate discrimination into disaster management work. To correct discriminatory situations, governments are encouraged to adopt special measures when dealing with target communities, such as providing scholarships, introducing quotas in employment and launching community development projects. For disaster management professionals, it might be sufficient to include staff from minority communities in the team (see Box 2.5). Even when it is not easy to identify such experts, there might be an alternative option: for instance, calling for the participation of or asking for independent consultancy from human rights specialists. As well as including human rights specialists in the team of disaster relief workers, it is also crucial for humanitarian workers to commit to human rights work in order to redress any situations of injustice based on ethnicity.

In addition, what is more important is to target minority peoples or regions affected by racial tension in the work of a vulnerability and capacity assessment (VCA). As discrimination is strongly linked to vulnerability, VCA may be useful in helping to identify discrimination against minority groups. For example, the Canadian Red Cross Society discovered that its existing VCA was not meeting the needs of all the at-risk groups in the region including aboriginal (indigenous) peoples and refugees. The Canadian Red Cross Society has, therefore, introduced training on social justice aimed at volunteers, staff members and organizations that conduct similar activities. By being made aware of cases of discrimination affecting communities in the region, staff can be well prepared to deal with any sudden occurrences. The social justice workshops should also take statistics on social vulnerability based on ethnicity – or any other factor. Despite the lack of common indicators for measuring the impact of anti-discrimination, these statistics can provide a clearer picture of vulnerability and the needs of minority peoples.

Further challenges

In addition to conducting a VCA, it is important to provide disaster education for children from vulnerable minority communities. As well as being the potential disaster management experts of the future, these children can also act as teachers on disaster management within the family. In the event that the minorities concerned use a different language from the rest of the population, this would then result in a

Box 2.5 Paradise lost: migrant workers in the Maldives

Paradise: blue skies, beautiful beaches and azure waters. Hundreds of thousands of tourists every year take back treasured memories of their time in the Maldives but, for migrant workers sent to post-tsunami reconstruction sites around the Maldives, it is a paradise lost.

The construction industry in the Maldives employs low-cost migrant labour from Asia due to a shortage of Maldivian nationals willing to work in construction. The low status and pay of construction work in the Maldives deters local workers, whose higher socio-economic status affords them greater choice.

The magnitude of assistance and goodwill to assist those affected by the 2004 tsunami was great, as was the pressure for humanitarian agencies to respond quickly. In the early stages, the Red Cross Red Crescent focused on assisting tsunami-affected populations. Initially, little attention was given to the highly vulnerable position of migrant labourers who would undertake reconstruction work, as it was assumed contractors would enforce adequate standards.

Red Cross Red Crescent-funded programmes in the Maldives have successfully implemented Sphere standards in transitional shelters for beneficiaries, and the new houses being constructed are of very high quality. However, migrant workers building Red Cross Red Crescent-funded houses were not initially afforded the same standards to safeguard their dignity, health and security as those affected by the tsunami. Sphere standards quantify what it means to live with dignity, outlining minimum requirements in health, security, shelter, food and non-food items, as well as access to water and sanitation facilities. The contractors paid to manage post-tsunami

reconstruction work are driven by profit and not by humanitarian imperatives. On the ground, this can result in beneficiaries being treated without dignity, and the migrant workers building houses for the beneficiaries living in sub-standard conditions.

Mindful of this, and in response to the sub-standard conditions, the British Red Cross and the French Red Cross initiated a set of labour/living standards (adapted from Sphere standards) for inclusion in all current and future contracts to ensure that Sphere standards should apply, without discrimination, to safeguard the dignity of those involved in Red Cross Red Crescent-funded programmes. Jill Clements, head of mission for the British Red Cross, said the initiative stems from a belief that: "The use of labour for any humanitarian endeavour, whether it is distributing food packages or rebuilding houses, must respect and protect the safety, health and dignity of staff, volunteers and contracted workers – wherever we work."

Another initiative to address health and safety concerns has been to conduct first-aid training on Red Cross Red Crescent-funded construction sites, in order to improve the capacity of construction site supervisors to respond to workplace injuries.

As highlighted by *In support of the Millennium Development Goals: Activities of the International Federation of Red Cross and Red Crescent Societies*, protecting and enhancing livelihoods directly addresses income poverty. Ensuring workers on reconstruction projects are paid appropriately and on time, ensuring that they are protected from the likelihood of worksite injury or disability, and that they are provided with dignified living conditions all contributes to the Millennium

Development Goals in the eradication of extreme poverty.

Concerns for migrant workers are known, discussed and recognized by governments and non-governmental organizations in South Asia. Much of this discussion focuses on wages, terms and conditions, and appropriate housing and medical facilities. Providing basic rights at work, reducing discrimination and providing a healthy and safe working environment for workers and/or migrant workers is considered a means of reducing poverty.

"The situation for Bangladeshi workers in the Maldives, well, it is sad news for humanity," says Mr Abul, a site engineer working on a French Red Cross-funded reconstruction site in Laamu Gan. He explains how many workers sell their land or their wives' jewellery and borrow from moneylenders to pay brokers who facilitate their employment in the Maldives.

Turning from the interpreter, Jamaal Hussain spoke of his feelings in English: "I do not feel very well here, how can one under these conditions?" Jamaal is a 23-year-old Bangladeshi migrant worker working on a Red Cross Red Crescent-funded, post-tsunami reconstruction site in the Maldives. He explains nervously, but with a certain pride, that he is a carpenter trained in fine cabinet making. He is the major income earner for his family and, as the eldest, he is responsible for providing for his siblings, including saving enough money for his sister to marry. What causes him great stress and worry is the money he owes to the moneylender he used in order to pay the employment broker who came to his village, offering lucrative work abroad.

The fee he paid the broker was US$ 2,000 before interest. In return, the broker advised that he would earn US$ 300 a month. However, on arrival in the Maldives, he learnt that as a skilled worker his salary would be US$ 140 a month. Jamaal explains that the big company man is in Malé and he does not always come with the money on time. When the end-of-month pay is late or does not come his family has nothing to eat, and his five other younger siblings have no money to buy rice or cloth.

Although not technically bonded Jamaal, by his very circumstances, is not free to return to his country of origin. Due to his socio-economic dependence there are limited opportunities for him to make choices about his tenure. Jamaal says that he feels isolated and unhappy in the Maldives but must stay to pay his debt.

Jamaal's situation illustrates how migrant construction workers can be victimized by unregulated and dishonest recruitment practices and how this impacts on the worker and the worker's family. These practices prevent migrant workers from the poorest countries from breaking their cycle of poverty. Among foreign workers – who often arrive without any knowledge of their new environment, local customs or language – there is often a very poor understanding regarding the contracts or agreements they have signed and confusion over visa status. This limits the worker's ability to seek redress or to negotiate terms and conditions.

Issues related to the recruitment processes of foreign workers and their onsite management are a complex, global issue. Global advocacy and cooperation is required to address issues of exploitation and discrimination of migrant construction workers. Humanitarian and development organizations can work to raise awareness of these issues and find practical measures within their respective mandates to improve the health, safety and living conditions of migrant workers.

By applying Sphere standards to the living conditions of construction workers, the Red Cross Red Crescent has brought improvement to the health and well-being of workers on Red Cross Red Crescent-funded construction sites. This practical experience needs to be captured and made part of future reconstruction procedures to protect construction workers' rights in disaster relief and recovery operations. Further advocacy and research is required to ensure that the lessons learnt in the Maldives recovery operation are incorporated into future programming. ■

shortage of awareness-raising materials. It is, therefore, crucial to develop ways of involving families and communities in disaster education at school and to provide other opportunities. Disaster education can contribute greatly to the ability of minorities to help themselves in time of disaster.

When developing disaster risk reduction strategies, it is also necessary to tackle the causes of discrimination. Disaster managers, in particular, can improve the situation of some minorities – such as those who are discriminated against because of their nomadic lifestyle, or whose occupation is linked with the concept of impurity, or who are forced to live in disaster-prone areas. Their physical vulnerability should be assessed and recommendations made to the authorities concerning the introduction of special measures.

It is also important to share experiences with policy-makers and the public. Are VCA guidelines only applicable to National Red Cross and Red Crescent Societies? Is the discrimination experienced by relief workers only shared with disaster managers? Both relief workers and disaster managers should cooperate with human rights workers and activists in order to contribute to the decision-making process of higher authorities. For example, by lobbying parliament, debriefing officials, and submitting reports to UN human rights institutions.

Incidents of discrimination against minorities in disaster management around the world indicate that there are many possibilities for mitigation. In addition, the example of the New Zealand lahar response, as well as relief work conducted by Buraku and non-Buraku peoples in Japan, show that there are opportunities for disaster managers to do more to help protect the rights of minorities. As the aim of disaster relief and disaster management is to reduce and avoid losses from hazards, it might also be important for disaster managers and other stakeholders to help reduce and avoid the loss of dignity of minority peoples during disasters. If humanitarian workers take a participatory approach in their work – that is, by securing the participation of majority and minority communities – community-based strategies for preparedness against natural disaster can provide a great opportunity to eradicate discrimination against minorities.

International Federation of Red Cross and Red Crescent Societies

Recommendations

For humanitarian organizations:

- Include minority peoples in the team. Ideally, the ratio of minority peoples in the organization should equal the ratio of minority peoples among the public.
- Educate minority peoples, with the aim of developing community resilience as well as obtaining professionals from the communities.
- Develop at least a basic understanding of discrimination against minorities in each country. Using VCA to identify vulnerability, which is often linked to discrimination, and collecting data by ethnicity could be useful in reviewing humanitarian work in the light of discrimination towards minorities.
- Be aware of discrimination against minorities in humanitarian work, by self-examination as well as through consultations with people from the community and human rights specialists.
- Participate in advocacy in domestic, regional and international forums. Humanitarian organizations can also play a vital role in human rights advocacy.
- Develop indicators on the impact of discrimination against minorities in disaster management with the cooperation of human rights specialists.

For human rights organizations:

- Try to collaborate with humanitarian organizations by providing the whole picture on the minority (or minorities) of the country concerned.
- Learn more about the disaster management process by participating in the process – not just at the time of response and recovery, but also during the preparedness phase.
- Develop indicators on the impact of discrimination against minorities in disaster management with the cooperation of disaster management experts and humanitarian organizations.

For governments and donors:

- Put more value on the issue of discrimination in humanitarian operations. Disaster relief and discrimination are inseparable issues.
- Examine the possibility of introducing special measures for minority groups, particularly those who do not have access to basic materials.
- Understand the vulnerability of minorities, especially those who are prone to being affected by disasters. If the region has a history of disasters, then there is an absolute need for disaster preparedness.

For the media:

- Be more sensitive to minority issues. Discriminatory remarks from the media can have a seriously negative impact on minorities.
- Try to share disaster-related information with minority communities – ideally in their own language.

- Try to include members of minorities in the team.
- If available, check minority-oriented media outlets as well.

For communities:

- Know that you are the stakeholder for the disaster operation.
- Without mutual help, you cannot survive.
- Cooperation in disaster relief can broaden networks among peoples, which could be valuable for further disaster resilience as well as for community harmony.
- Learn about the background of minority peoples and understand the need for special measures.

This chapter was contributed by Preti Taneja, a journalist working with Minority Rights Group International, which works to secure the rights of ethnic, religious and linguistic minorities and indigenous peoples worldwide; Hayato Nakamura, a researcher at the Crisis and Environment Management Policy Institute, Tokyo, and international assistant for the Tamil Nadu Women's Forum in Chennai, India, who also contributed Boxes 2.1 and 2.4. John Sparrow, an independent writer and communications consultant who is currently working on disaster risk reduction issues, contributed Box 2.2. Dr Ray Jureidini, Associate Director of the Forced Migration and Refugee Studies programme at The American University in Cairo, contributed Box 2.3. Elizabeth Loeber, Regional Advocacy Delegate for the South Asia Regional Delegation of the International Federation of Red Cross and Red Crescent Societies, contributed Box 2.5.

Sources and further information

Anaya, S. James. *Indigenous Peoples in International Law.* Oxford: Oxford University Press, 2000.

Asia Pacific Forum on Women, Law and Development (APWLD)/The National Secretariat of Solidaritas Perempuan. *Tsunami Aftermath: Violations of Women's Human Rights in Nanggroe Aceh Darussalam, Indonesia.* APWLD, 2006. Available at www.apwld.org/pdf/tsumai_vwhr.pdf

APWLD/Tamil Nadu Dalit Women's Movement (TNDWM). *Tsunami Aftermath: Violations of Human Rights of Dalit Women, Tamil Nadu, India.* APWLD, 2006. Available at www.apwld.org/pdf/Tsunami_India.pdf

CBS. *Race an issue in Katrina response,* CBS News, 3 September 2005. Available at www.cbsnews.com/stories/2005/09/03/katrina/main814623.shtml

Centre for Research on the Epidemiology of Disasters (CRED). *Risk Factors for Mortality and Injury: Post-Tsunami Epidemiological Findings from Tamil Nadu.* Brussels: CRED, 2006. Available at www.em-dat.net/documents/Publication/RiskFactorsMortalityInjury.pdf

Christian Aid. *Life on the Edge of Climate Change: The Plight of Pastoralists in Northern Kenya.* Christian Aid, 2006.

Eisenstein, Zillah. *Katrina and her Gendering of Class and Race*, WHRnet (Women's Human Rights net), 12 September 2005. Available at www.whrnet.org/docs/issue-katrina.html

Gill, Timothy. *Making things worse: how 'caste blindness' in Indian post-tsunami disaster recovery has exacerbated vulnerability and exclusion.* Dalit Network Netherlands with People's Watch Tamilnadu, 2007. Available at www.ohchr.org/english/bodies/cerd/docs/ngos/tsunami_report.pdf

Habitat International Coalition-Housing and Land Rights Network (HIC-HLRN) and People's Movement for Human Rights Learning (PDHRE). *International Human Rights Standards on Post-disaster Resettlement and Rehabilitation.* Bangalore: Books for Change, 2005.

Hughes, Alexandra. Poverty Reduction Strategy Paper (PRSPs), *Minorities and Indigenous Peoples – An Issues Paper.* Minority Rights Group International, 2005. Available at www.minorityrights.org/ admin/Download/pdf/MRG-PRSP.pdf

Humanitarian Policy Group (HPG). *Humanitarian Response to Natural Disasters: A briefing paper prepared by the Humanitarian Policy Group for the International Development Committee inquiry into Humanitarian Response to Natural Disasters.* Overseas Development Institute (ODI), 2006. Available at www.odi.org.uk/HPG/papers/ODIparliament_briefing_disasters.pdf

International Federation. 'Hurricane Stan lifts the lid on Guatemala's vulnerability' in *World Disasters Report 2006.* Geneva: International Federation, 2006.

International Movement Against All Forms of Discrimination and Racism (IMADR), Buraku Liberation League (BLL) and Buraku Liberation and Human Rights Research Institute (BLHRRI) (eds.). *Reality of Buraku Discrimination in Japan: History, Situation, Challenge.* Tokyo: IMADR, 2001.

Kostadinova, Galina. *Substantive Equality, Positive Action and Roma Rights in the European Union.* Minority Rights Group International, 2006. Available at www.minorityrights.org/admin/Download/pdf/MRG_RomaBriefing2006.pdf

Makoloo, Maurice Odhiambo. *Kenya: Minorities, Indigenous Peoples and Ethnic Diversity.* Minority Rights Group International, 2005.

Minority Rights Group International. *State of the World's Minorities: Events of 2006.* Minority Rights Group International, 2007. Available at www.minorityrights.org/admin/Download/pdf/SWM2007.pdf

National Campaign on Dalit Human Rights (NCDHR). *Caste Discrimination in Tsunami Relief and Rehabilitation.* NCDHR, 2005.

NGO Committee for the Reporting on the ICERD. *Collective Report among Japan-based NGOs on the International Convention on the Elimination of All Forms of*

Racial Discrimination: The Implementation of the Convention in Japan and the Problems of Japan's First and Second Report. IMADR-JC, 2001.

Salomon, Margot E. (ed.). *Economic, Social and Cultural Rights: A Guide for Minorities and Indigenous Peoples.* Minority Rights Group International, 2005. Available at www.minorityrights.org/admin/Download/Pdf/MRG-ECOSOC.pdf

Tanaka, Atsuko with Nagamine, Yoshinobu. *The International Convention on the Elimination of All Forms of Racial Discrimination: A Guide for NGOs.* Minority Rights Group International and IMADR, 2001. Available at www.minorityrights. org/admin/Download/Pdf/ICERDManual.pdf

The New Zealand Herald, 'Madness not to drain Crater Lake', 23 December 2003. Available at www.nzherald.co.nz/section/1/story.cfm?c_id=1&objectid=3540731

Thornberry, Patrick. *Indigenous Peoples and Human Rights.* Manchester: Manchester University Press, 2002.

University of Chicago, Center for the Study of Race Politics and Culture. *2005 Racial Attitudes and the Katrina Disaster Study: Initial Report.* Chicago: University of Chicago, 2006.

Watkins, Tracy. 'Ruapehu risk: Government rejects call to act over lahar risks', *The Dominion Post*, 10 March 2004.

Web sites

ActionAid International **www.actionaid.org**

European Roma Rights Centre (ERRC) **www.errc.org**

Humanitarian Accountability Partnership (HAP) International
www.hapinternational.org

International Work Group for Indigenous Affairs (IWGIA) **www.iwgia.org**

Minority Rights Group International **www.minorityrights.org**

National Campaign on Dalit Human Rights (NCDHR) **www.dalits.org**

Office of the United Nations High Commissioner for Human Rights (OHCHR)
www.ohchr.org

OHCHR Committee on the Elimination of Racial Discrimination
www.ohchr.org/english/bodies/cerd/index.htm

Reuters AlertNet **www.alertnet.org**

Romani CRISS **www.romanicriss.org**

The Sphere Project **www.sphereproject.org**

Tsunami Response Watch **www.tsunamiresponsewatch.org**

UNESCO International Coalition of Cities against Racism
www.unesco.org/shs/citiesagainstracism

CHAPTER 3

Older people and discrimination in crises

"Some cars came by and just threw the packets. The fastest get the food, the strong one wins. The elderly and the injured don't get anything. We feel like dogs."

Perumal, 75, Tamil Nadu, India

When relief material was being distributed following the Indian Ocean tsunami, Perumal stood alone in the remains of his thatched hut, refusing to join the hungry crowds jostling for aid. Asked why he did not join in, Perumal shook his head and said: "It's no use. I've been pushed out before and have fallen on the ground. I know I'll get nothing this time around, too."

This chapter focuses on how older people are discriminated against during humanitarian emergencies (for a definition of older people, see Box 3.1). It examines the ways in which this discrimination – at the hands of governments, humanitarian organizations and communities – exacerbates the inherent vulnerability of age and prevents older people from realizing their rights to disaster response and resources for recovery.

Limitations of mobility, chronic poor health, isolation and poverty are difficulties common to older people across the world. But such physical and economic constraints are greatly aggravated by prejudices and false assumptions which this chapter seeks to explore.

> ## Box 3.1 Defining older people
>
> The UN defines an older person as being aged 60 and over. As with other age groups, the diversity of older people must be recognized and captured in age-disaggregated data. The internationally defined categories for research and advocacy purposes are:
>
> - Young old (60–70)
> - Old old (70–80)
> - Oldest old (80+)
>
> *Source: The International Plan of Action on Ageing adopted at the first World Assembly on Ageing (Vienna, 1982) used "aged 60 years and older" for defining "older persons". This was endorsed by the Second World Assembly on Ageing (Madrid, 2002).*

Most humanitarian agencies assume – wrongly – that generalized emergency aid will reach older people or that family members will look after their interests. Only a handful of organizations implement programmes that consider their specific needs and actively engage them.

The lack of a United Nations (UN) agency dedicated to ageing issues; the failure of many humanitarian agencies to develop a clear rationale for reaching older people; the lack of specific data and information on this group; and the assumption that older people will be covered by general response provisions – all these factors add up to discrimination which, whether intentional or not, has a life-threatening impact on the lives of older people.

Photo opposite page: One of the village elders of Bubisa, Marsabit District, Kenya, who met to discuss how to distribute food delivered by the Kenya Red Cross Society. The region was affected by a severe drought in 2006.

Daniel Cima/ American Red Cross

The chapter argues that creating greater awareness of older people's specific vulnerabilities and capacities can help redress the false assumptions that lie behind prejudicial attitudes towards the over-60s. It presents good practice to combat discrimination in emergency response. And it proposes a new UN convention on the rights of older people, to complement similar provisions for children, women, minority groups and people with disabilities.

Ageing world triples while children stay static

Between 2005 and 2050, the global population aged 60 or above will triple from 673 million to over 2 billion, while the number of children (0–14 years of age) will remain largely static at around 1.8 billion, according to the UN's *World Population Prospects, 2006* (see Figure 3.1). Today, two-thirds of the world's older people live in developing countries. By 2050, this will increase to 80 per cent.

As a proportion of populations within developing countries, older people will leap from 8 per cent in 2005 to 20 per cent by 2050. Over the same period, the proportion of children will drop from 31 to 21 per cent. So, by the middle of the century,

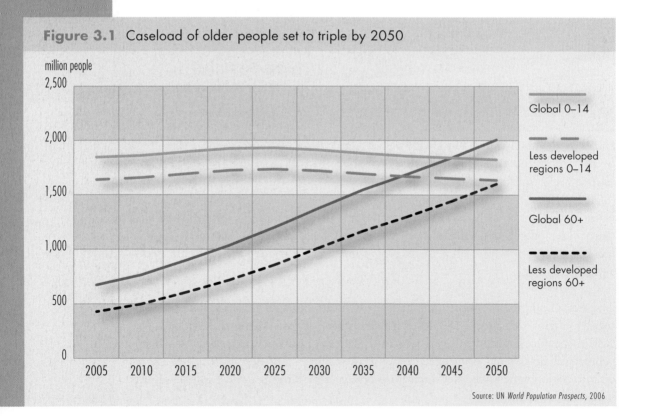

Figure 3.1 Caseload of older people set to triple by 2050

million people

Global 0–14

Less developed regions 0–14

Global 60+

Less developed regions 60+

Source: UN *World Population Prospects, 2006*

✚C International Federation of Red Cross and Red Crescent Societies humanitarian organizations are likely to be assisting as many older people as children (see Figure 3.2).

Between 1997 and 2006, an average of 260 million people worldwide were affected by natural disasters per year, according to the Belgium-based Centre for Research on the Epidemiology of Disasters (CRED). Given that roughly one in ten people is aged over 60, this means that around 26 million older people were likely to have been affected by natural disasters each year over the past decade.

However, the number of older people affected by disasters or displaced by crises is often measurably higher than their proportion in the general population. The 2003 heatwave in France claimed nearly 15,000 lives, 70 per cent of whom were older than 75 years (see *World Disasters Report 2004*, Chapter 2). According to the UN refugee agency, UNHCR, those over 60 comprise 21 per cent of people displaced by war in Serbia and Montenegro. This is probably because many young adults had already migrated in search of work, fled or been killed.

Yet data on populations affected by disasters and crises, disaggregated by age and gender, are very limited. Collecting and presenting such data would help humanitarians to identify and reach vulnerable populations far more accurately.

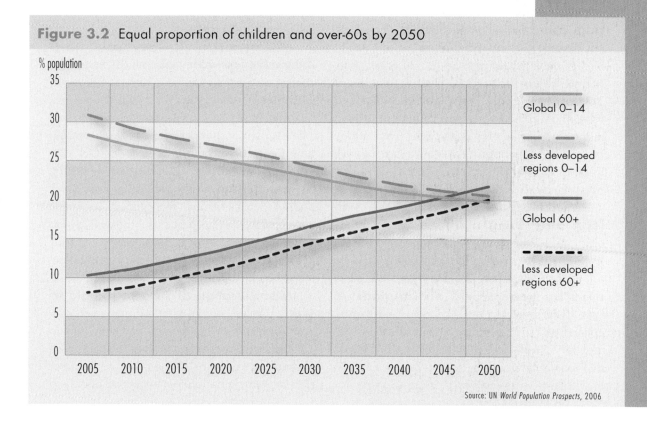

Figure 3.2 Equal proportion of children and over-60s by 2050

% population

Global 0–14

Less developed regions 0–14

Global 60+

Less developed regions 60+

Source: UN *World Population Prospects*, 2006

Misconceptions about older people perpetuate discrimination

At the root of discrimination against older people lies a range of prejudices and false assumptions, grounded in older people's physical, mental and economic vulnerability. These prejudices are held by communities in which older people live as well as by people in governments and aid organizations seeking to serve them (see Box 3.2).

Older people are often less mobile than younger people – or perceived to be less mobile. They may suffer from chronic poor health – or are perceived to be always ill. They may not contribute to decision-making and the local economy – or their potential to contribute may be ignored. Such perceptions and attitudes, whether grounded in reality or not, can create a stigma around older people that they are weak, useless or worthless. As a result, their needs, contributions and rights are neglected. They are left battling with not only their own objective physical, mental and financial barriers, but also with the subjective, attitudinal barriers in the minds of people around them.

Box 3.2 Six misconceptions about older people in emergencies

Misconception 1: The extended family and community will protect them at all times. Not always true, especially not in exceptional situations (e.g. disaster situations). After the Indian Ocean tsunami of 26 December 2004, HelpAge India identified more than 9,000 older people who had been missed in the rush for assistance. Even if they have families, older people are not always treated equitably and may be denied the opportunity to contribute.

Misconception 2: An agency will look after them. There are no UN agencies and very few international NGOs (INGOs) dedicated to older people.

Misconception 3: They can be covered by general aid distributions. In fact, older people have particular nutritional, cultural and other requirements that are not met by a general relief distribution. Clothes distributed in response to the Darfur crisis in July 2004 were culturally inappropriate for older people, and medicines did not cater for their chronic illnesses.

Misconception 4: They only have themselves to worry about. Displacement, conflict and serious diseases such as HIV mean that increasing numbers of older people are responsible not only for themselves, but also for their children or grandchildren. In Darfur, nearly a third are caring for orphans.

Misconception 5: They're waiting to be helped. The reality is that older people want to be recognized for their capabilities. Accustomed to providing for themselves, they want to regain control of their lives and contribute to the welfare of the community as much as they are able to.

Misconception 6: They're too old to work. Older people often still contribute economically to their households and may remain the key decision-makers in times of crisis. Supporting the recovery of their livelihoods after disaster is an important but neglected priority. ∎

International Federation of Red Cross and Red Crescent Societies

Relief organizations often assume that older people's needs and rights are met within community support networks or through generalized emergency response. Discrimination is the result, not through intentional exclusion but because a one-size-fits-all response is not always appropriate for older people. Nor are they always assisted through the household.

Agencies may wrongly assume that specialist organizations are focusing on older people's issues (as there are agencies whose focus is on children or women). And they may fail to appreciate the value of older people's contributions – as carers and coordinators and decision-makers.

In 2005, HelpAge India observed a massive gap in post-tsunami service provision: there was no specific component for older people in the relief operations of state governments, non-governmental organizations (NGOs) or multilateral agencies. Older people make up over 7 per cent of the population, but they were not singled out as a vulnerable group and were unable to access food, health care and cash due to discrimination and a lack of information or support mechanisms.

In Sri Lanka, older people received no monetary compensation to help them restart their livelihoods after the tsunami, if they were living with adult children. One older man complained that his son received all the relief material and he got nothing. The pervasive assumption by aid organizations that all relief materials (including food) will be shared equally within multi-generational families often leaves older people without the material support they need to reassert their economic and social independence.

False assumptions perpetuate discrimination against older people. Exploring such misconceptions is vital to reduce the unnecessary suffering of some of society's most vulnerable people.

Age discrimination in emergency relief

Edith Moore, a 70-year-old survivor of Hurricane Katrina, said: "It was the worst thing I've ever witnessed in my life… Nobody ever told me anything… This is America, but they didn't think enough of [older people here] to get them out." Her experience epitomizes that of many older people in emergencies throughout the world.

Those who suffer most during crises are vulnerable populations who remain largely invisible, who are overlooked in the design and provision of emergency services, and whose potential to contribute is not tapped. Some older people face discrimination at the hands of individuals, while at the same time the failure of governments and aid organizations to provide older people with assistance that takes into account their situation also amounts to discrimination.

CHAPTER 3

Within the context of emergency relief, the following factors can, among others, lead to discrimination against older people:

1. limited agency mandates
2. lack of data
3. few specific laws or policies
4. inadequate resources

1. Limited agency mandates: humanitarian organizations carry different, specific mandates of response on which their programmes are focused. There is no UN agency solely dedicated to ageing issues.

Agencies with specific mandates rarely engage in integrated interventions that include vulnerable populations beyond their immediate target groups. There are some instances of child-focused agencies recognizing the role of older people as carers of children, such as the United Nations Children's Fund (UNICEF) and Save the Children, working in conjunction with HelpAge International in Darfur, Sudan. However, this work is just getting underway and remains the exception.

Older people's lack of representation within the humanitarian system means their specific needs are often omitted from pre-disaster planning. This is as much a challenge for the developed world as for the developing world.

2. Lack of data: there is a lack of official baseline data on the demographic representation of older people prior to an emergency. This is compounded by a failure to identify their needs and capacities during emergency assessments. As a result, older people become invisible and excluded from emergency planning and response.

Following the tsunami, estimates of the displaced 60-plus population across the region were almost non-existent and the number of those killed was extrapolated from country censuses up to five years out of date.

During initial emergency response, humanitarian agencies tend to undertake rapid assessments tailored to their own skills, mandates and resources. Comprehensive assessments that provide a total picture of needs are unusual – even in well-resourced operations such as the tsunami response. This results in indirect discrimination during subsequent relief and recovery. There are very few references to older people in the Tsunami Evaluation Coalition's (TEC) synthesis report of July 2006, other than to note: "TEC studies found that in general the needs of vulnerable groups (women, the elderly and children) tended to be overlooked."

Indicators in needs assessment manuals focus on measurements of under-five mortality, morbidity and malnutrition – with few indicators for older people. Data are rarely disaggregated by sex and age. Yet collecting such data is essential – not just

International Federation
of Red Cross and Red Crescent Societies

on the over-60s, but in decade intervals up to 80-plus years. Older people are not one homogenous group: those aged 61–70 or 71–80 may have substantially different capacities and vulnerabilities to the over-80s.

The failure to include older people in assessments can have devastating effects. A survey of nine camps for internally displaced people (IDPs) in West Darfur revealed that 8 per cent of IDPs were older people. Of these, 12 per cent lacked ration cards issued by the World Food Programme (WFP). They might have been physically unable to reach WFP's registration points or, because of their relative invisibility within communities, they might simply have been excluded from the camp population lists submitted to WFP. This meant that roughly 700 IDPs and 4,700 extended household members had been missing out on vital food aid until they were identified at a later stage.

By addressing older people's invisibility through better data collection during needs assessments and monitoring, humanitarian organizations can avoid discriminating against them – and, by extension, the households in which they live.

3. Few specific laws or policies: few legal instruments or policy frameworks relate specifically to older people as a distinct category (see Box 3.3). The rights of over-60s are not legally protected by international instruments in the same way as other vulnerable groups, such as children, women, minorities and people with disabilities – all of whom are the subject of specific UN conventions.

Older people tend to be covered implicitly through the universality of certain fundamental rights, including the right of all people to non-discrimination, enshrined in international humanitarian and human rights law. They may also be covered by way of their gender, refugee status or membership of a minority.

However, the absence of a specific legal treaty devoted to older people and the corresponding lack of focus on their needs and concerns inadvertently compounds their discrimination. A specific legal treaty would raise awareness of older people's rights within the human rights system and catalogue the specific contexts where older men and women's rights are violated. Currently, governments frequently fail to address older people's rights in their periodic reporting on the implementation of the human rights conventions that they have already ratified.

There are some policy trends towards recognizing older people as a vulnerable group: the *Sphere Humanitarian Charter and Minimum Standards in Disaster Response 2004* calls on agencies to pay special attention to their nutritional and care needs. But the humanitarian response illustrates that such policies are rarely put into practice. Research carried out by HelpAge International in 2005 with 16 leading INGOs found that, while organizations do not actively exclude older people

Box 3.3 **Humanitarian policy for older people**

United Nations Principles for Older Persons, 1991: the first intergovernmental initiative to recognize the importance of focusing attention on the situation of older persons. It encourages governments to address the "independence, participation, care, self-fulfilment and dignity of older persons". In 2001, the UN refugee agency, UNHCR, developed a policy on older refugees – the only separate policy for this age group within the UN system.

Madrid International Plan of Action on Ageing (MIPAA), 2002: this international agreement explicitly commits governments to include ageing in social and economic development policies and devotes several key articles to older people in emergencies. For example, MIPAA demands that there is:

"Equal access by older persons to food, shelter and medical care and other services during and after natural disasters and other humanitarian emergencies" and "enhanced contributions of older persons to the re-establishment and reconstruction of communities and the rebuilding of the social fabric following emergencies".

While not a legal treaty, MIPAA was endorsed by the UN General Assembly and, therefore, all 192 member states have a moral and political obligation to ensure its implementation.

IASC Operational Guidelines on Human Rights and Natural Disasters, 2006: the Inter-Agency Standing Committee (IASC) is the primary mechanism for coordination between UN and non-UN humanitarian organizations. Its guidelines emphasize "the need to ensure non-discriminatory humanitarian assistance" and mention older people among those whose physical security may be most at risk during displacement.

The issue of ageing is addressed in several other humanitarian policy frameworks, usually by including older people as one of a list of vulnerable groups. However, the specific needs of older people are not comprehensively articulated and the policy texts relating to them are not widely known. This is in stark contrast to policy on other vulnerable groups such as children – a key reason for discrimination against older people in disasters.

In 2007, HelpAge International is leading an IASC review of policy and practice relating to older people. This will focus on developing policy guidance in the health and protection clusters as part of the humanitarian reform process. Once clearer policies are in place, the challenge will be to develop capacity on ageing issues within humanitarian organizations. ∎

from their programmes, they do not explicitly address their needs. As the director of one INGO in West Darfur admitted in 2005: "Yes, we had forgotten about them."

4. Inadequate resources: funding to support older people represents a fraction of the overall sums directed through humanitarian organizations. Research by HelpAge International reveals that such funding accounts for 1 per cent or less of individual country responses – significantly short of the 7 per cent recommended by the Sphere Project.

Bridging the gap between perceptions of older people's lives and the reality of their rights, needs and potential contributions is a key challenge for the humanitarian community. Meeting this challenge means first tackling the false assumptions and prejudices that lead to discrimination. Creating greater awareness of ageing issues is one way to start changing such attitudes.

Impact of discrimination on older people

The chapter will now focus on five areas in which the over-60s are particularly vulnerable, explore how discrimination exacerbates these vulnerabilities and propose possible solutions:
1. lack of mobility
2. chronic poor health
3. nutritional needs
4. isolation
5. abuse and sexual violence

1. Lack of mobility

"When they attacked I couldn't run. Some neighbours helped me to the fields and hid me under the trees. I stayed there for four days because I was scared," relates Halima Ahmed Hissein, an older woman who lives alone in Goker camp, Darfur. Not everyone was as lucky as Halima: some older people who did not flee had ropes put around their necks and were dragged around by horses until they died.

For those who can flee from crises, extended periods travelling with inadequate food and shelter take their toll. Some older Darfurians are unable to make it to reception centres and simply die along the way. Those who remain are often unprotected and less likely to receive aid due to limited access and provision.

Of the 4,000 older Darfurian IDPs surveyed in 2005, 61 per cent had limited mobility. In a population of 2 million IDPs, this equates to 140,000 people. Of these, one-quarter could not move without a guide, one-fifth had impaired vision and 7 per cent were housebound.

Across a wide range of emergencies, age-related mobility problems affect the ability of older people to access humanitarian services. Older people find it difficult to travel to relief distribution sites. On arrival, they often lack the strength to carry heavy goods (including vital supplies of food and water) back to their shelters. Distributions are frequently located at high points away from inhabited areas: this helps aid workers to visually gauge the number and movement of people seeking aid. It enables agencies to transfer relief items directly to the majority of recipients in a controlled, secure way. This process, however, discriminates against older people and those who are housebound.

Research undertaken by HelpAge International in Colombia in 2006, where 9 per cent of IDPs are over 60, confirmed that many older people are the last to leave dangerous and isolated areas and suffer the greatest upheaval and isolation on arrival in new places. In the Pailin area of western Cambodia, over 40 per cent of war-affected, older IDPs surveyed in late 2006 cited difficulty performing physical tasks such as crouching, lifting heavy objects and walking. These challenges were more difficult for older women than men.

HelpAge International's findings confirm this, noting that limited mobility was a critical issue for older people throughout tsunami-affected areas. Older Indians told of being pushed out of the way by younger, more physically able people during relief distributions. Aid workers observed that the receipt of relief packages was down to "the survival of the fittest". Older people often had to rely on a child, grandchild or neighbour to help carry relief goods to their shelters.

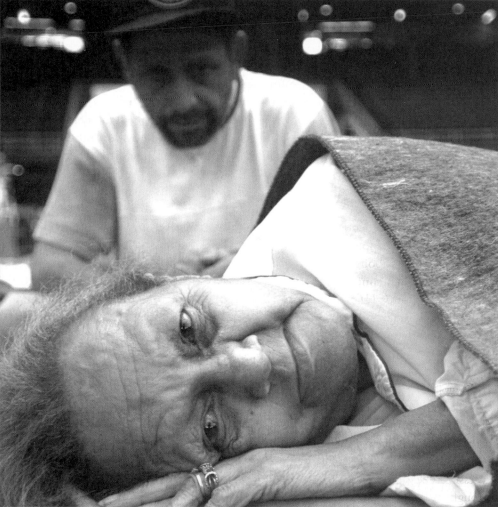

Weary elderly evacuees rest in the Houston Astrodome following Hurricane Katrina, which struck in August 2005.

Daniel Cima/ American Red Cross

International Federation of Red Cross and Red Crescent Societies

The outreach programmes and referral systems needed to get to housebound, immobile older people are extremely limited – but there are some examples of good practice. Networks of older people, community-based staff and volunteers capable of following individual cases from assessment through to addressing nutritional, non-food and psychosocial needs have succeeded in Darfur.

Older people's ability to overcome immobility and access lifesaving services can be enhanced by:

- moving distribution points to more level, accessible locations, while ensuring that these distribution points do not pose added security risks to people receiving aid
- ensuring that food and non-food items are packed in containers sufficiently small and light for older people to transport, as well as easy for older hands to open
- enabling older people to use a proxy to collect relief goods
- setting up a committee of older people to assist with aid verification and distribution
- providing simple aids commonplace in wealthier countries, such as walking sticks or frames, spectacles, hearing aids and transport tailored to older people's needs
- greater community participation and consultation

2. Chronic poor health

Older people cite health as the most important issue affecting their ability to live with dignity. For many, the immediate health issues during crises are characterized and compounded by the effects of pre-existing chronic ailments, as well as by discrimination at the hands of health staff and the lack of accessible, appropriate response services.

By failing to consider the impact of chronic, age-related health issues, health staff assume that older people are not ill, but rather just old. Health staff operate within cultural prejudices about the kinds of services older people seek to access as well as the health issues which concern them. In South Africa, clinic staff do not routinely offer people aged 49-plus HIV tests, because data are only collected nationally for people up to the age of 49, after which they are considered sexually inactive.

Interventions for chronic illnesses – such as mobile eye clinics, physiotherapy and the provision of mobility aids – may not be lifesaving, but they are life-*changing*. Treatment for chronic arthritis or a cataract operation would enable an older person to work again or to move unaided around their community. Fetching water, collecting firewood, preparing food and cultivating a garden are some basic, daily activities that are possible for older people receiving treatment and mobility aids.

Accessing health services is more difficult for older people. This can be addressed through networks of community health workers who are trained to care for older people, to refer them to health clinics when necessary and to follow up on their return home. In Darfur, several international medical NGOs have allotted specific hours during which older people are given priority for consultations. Donkey-cart ambulances transport older people for referrals. Following the tsunami and South Asia earthquake, HelpAge India established mobile medical units providing chronic and acute health care to older people and their communities.

Older people also experience mental trauma stemming from the shock of a crisis. It may not be the first time they have experienced disaster, or lost the accumulated memories and assets of a lifetime. It can be physically and emotionally devastating. Apart from the loss of household members and community networks, they are overwhelmed by the lack of support available.

Research conducted by the World Health Organization (WHO) has detected a global shift from communicable to chronic disease patterns which will increase as populations age. To avoid discriminating against vulnerable older people during emergencies, interventions must include long-term support for these health issues. Equally, educational and awareness training for health staff and humanitarian service providers should be a priority.

3. Nutritional needs

In a rapid survey carried out in Darfur in 2006, HelpAge International researchers found nearly 40 per cent of older people were at risk of malnutrition. Yet, apart from isolated surveys, little is known about rates of malnutrition for older people globally. Research by WHO in 2002 into emergency situations in Africa found that the nutritional requirements of older people were overlooked and that dependable systems for measuring adult malnutrition were woefully inadequate.

But the number of people dying from nutritional deficiencies in low-income countries is more than 50 per cent higher among the over-60s than among children under 14, according to WHO. Emergency food rations, when available, are generally the same as for younger adults, with no allowance made for the difficulty older people might have in chewing, digesting and absorbing sufficient micronutrients. Nor do agencies give sufficient thought as to whether older people can collect enough water with which to cook the food.

As a result, HelpAge International, in partnership with WFP, began distributing supplementary food baskets to older people at risk of malnutrition or caring for several dependants. In one camp, a 'social nutrition centre' was piloted, providing freshly cooked meals to vulnerable older people three times per week. After a few months, a significant impact was evident: older people became more willing to access health services and their overall well-being showed a marked improvement.

International Federation
of Red Cross and Red Crescent Societies

4. Isolation

"These thousands of elderly victims didn't die from a heatwave as such, but from the isolation and insufficient assistance they lived with day in and out." So Stéphane Mantion, a French Red Cross official, told *Time* magazine in an article on the 2003 heatwave which claimed nearly 15,000 lives and caused an outcry in his country.

But why was the loss of life considerably lower in other European countries, despite similar temperatures that summer? "The French family structure is more dislocated than elsewhere in Europe, and prevailing social attitudes hold that once older people are closed behind their apartment doors or in nursing homes, they are someone else's problem," Mantion said.

Similarly, in his study of the Chicago heatwave of 1995, Eric Klinenberg found that death rates depended significantly on social ecology. "The areas of the city that had high concentrations of deaths are areas that had lost the viable public spaces, the busy sidewalks, the commercial streets. Those are the things that draw people out of the home and into social contact."

Isolation is now the norm for many older, war-affected Darfurians. A house-to-house survey of over 4,000 IDPs aged 55 and over, carried out by HelpAge International in six camps in West Darfur in late 2005, found 80 per cent of respondents citing limited social interaction. Once the most respected group in the community, they are now sidelined by most social programming and are invisible to the majority of humanitarian actors. The hopelessness and abandonment they express affect not only their emotional health but also their physical well-being.

Older people in Georgia cite social isolation as one of five main issues characterizing their lives, along with a lack of income, poor health, food security and shelter (see Box 3.4). The collapse of the Soviet social welfare system has left many older Georgians abandoned, isolated and plunged into destitution. Researchers found that older people had minimal opportunities to interact socially.

For those affected by the 2005 South Asia earthquake, mental health concerns were more prevalent among people aged 60 and over, including "increased isolation, feelings of being a burden more than an asset, inter-generational conflict, and the reality of major losses that will not be able to be restored in their lifetimes", according to the author of a psychosocial needs assessment conducted in September 2006.

Social programmes for older people during crises can help combat isolation. Evaluations carried out by HelpAge International in Darfur of the impact of establishing centres for older people to come together for a meal or to produce local

Box 3.4 Elderly Georgians cope with extended emergency

For 17 years, much of Georgia has endured an extended humanitarian emergency. Civil war ended over ten years ago, but people displaced by civil war continue to live in collective centres. The wider population remains impoverished from the post-Soviet, socio-economic collapse. The official subsistence minimum in 2006 was 165 Georgian lari (US$ 85) per month. Over a third of the population lives on less than this. Pensions are around 38 lari (US$ 20).

In 2004, the Red Cross Society of Georgia and its international partners embarked on a research project with the active participation of older people in western Georgia. The aim was to identify support options for Georgia's most vulnerable people – with a view to consolidating ongoing coping mechanisms rather than just meeting immediate needs. The research painted a stark picture of daily crisis.

Older people were among those most disorientated by the collapse of the Soviet social welfare system. The entitlements they had accumulated throughout their working lives suddenly became inaccessible. Family networks broke up as children moved away to find work. Older people were left struggling to access what were now hostile transport and health services. Their pensions were sufficient for only the most frugal diet. As a result, older people socialized less and left their homes less frequently. Many slipped into very hidden lives, ever receding in influence and scope.

Discussions in focus groups with older people revealed stories of great hardship. "It is so embarrassing to talk about this," one participant said. "In the past, we never had to think about food, and now food has become our greatest concern." Another said: "Sometimes, when my neighbours are cooking, I have to shut all the doors and windows so that I am not tortured by the smell." Participants spoke of eating one or, at the most, two meals a day, and never eating meat or fish.

Many suffered from chronic health problems and were distressed by the difficulties of accessing health care. One participant told us: "My insurance policy finally got me admitted to hospital and allocated a bed. But the hospital had no food and so I couldn't stay." Most participants related tales of humiliation in the face of rudeness in hospitals and polyclinics.

Initially, there was some reluctance to talk about 'coping strategies'. One participant claimed: "It is no good asking us how we cope in the winter. We stay wrapped up in bed for months. That's how we cope." Yet four strategies did emerge:

- using neighbourhood support networks (borrowing from shops, reciprocal favours between neighbours)
- addressing ill-health through self-medication
- selling capital assets (although most participants had already exhausted this option by the time research was conducted)
- staying at home to avoid hunger, cold and unnecessary contact with people

Of these, the first strategy was always the most important.

What quickly became evident was the strength and dignity that emerged within the focus groups once participants began to share ideas, concerns and experiences. These were doctors, engineers, factory directors and teachers that had become isolated and excluded by the impact of a 17-year socio-economic crisis.

What they wanted was not handouts, but better access to quality health services where they would be treated with dignity. They wanted

International Federation
of Red Cross and Red Crescent Societies

to be able to influence decision-makers so that the everyday realities of older people – such as the inadequate size of their pension and the way it is distributed – could be understood and reflected in policy and budgets. And they wanted opportunities to socialize, to contribute and to break the cycle of isolation and loneliness. As one participant said: "I would get up in the morning if I only had somewhere to go."

It was with these comments in mind that the Red Cross Society of Georgia began to design social rooms for older people, to provide:

■ some service delivery, supporting access to entitlements and basic health advice

■ a platform for advocacy and sensitization work between older people, service providers and policy-makers

■ a place for older people to engage in the social and civil activities most important to them

The transformation among those older people who are now regular visitors to these social rooms is remarkable. The two pilot centres attract around 400 regular visitors a month. Another 140 homebound older people are visited by volunteers from among the 400. Demand to visit the centres is far higher, but financing and space are limited.

Both centres are guided by a pensioners' advisory committee to ensure that ownership remains in the hands of older people. Visitors regularly claim that now they have an incentive to get up in the morning and once again feel that they are needed.

Regular visits from doctors and other health workers mean that providers of health services are becoming more aware of the needs of older people. And when older people do report problems in accessing health care, the health visitors are quick to take action to address the issue. An entitlement officer at each centre follows through on individual cases of access to entitlements.

Perhaps the greatest contribution has been psychological. The warmth of the centres keeps older people visiting for long hours in the winter; the light snacks are no small incentive, given the day-to-day struggle to find enough to eat; and the opportunity to have entitlement claims dealt with is of fundamental importance to many visitors. But it is the opportunity to meet, to help each other, to volunteer and to influence visiting health workers and politicians that is restoring older people's dignity and motivation.

The external environment has not improved since the research was conducted in 2004. Pensions have increased, but at the same rate as the price of utilities and basic products, so purchasing power is as weak as it was three years ago. The quality of life and coping mechanisms of those older people who do not visit the centres has, therefore, remained unchanged.

For now, the pilot centres are having a positive impact on the quality of life of regular visitors. Encouragingly, there has been private and government interest in copying the model in other parts of Georgia. Further centres could contribute to the wider goal of empowering older people to influence national service provision and social policy. ■

handicrafts show that the activities have gone beyond the centres: many older men and women now meet in the evenings and visit each other in their homes.

In northern Pakistan, a joint Pakistan Red Crescent Society/Danish Red Cross programme is benefiting from older women's involvement: 41 older women in Kashtara village support field officers in encouraging younger women and the youth to participate in psychosocial education sessions. In Hissari village, 25 older women conduct sewing and embroidery classes for younger women, giving them an opportunity to pass on useful skills and to support younger women on a range of issues.

Socially or physically isolated older people need to be identified in advance for disaster preparedness measures. This will help agencies provide them with the kind of swift, targeted disaster response which is vital to ensure their own survival and well-being – as well as the survival of those for whom they care.

To achieve this, humanitarian organizations need to adopt a more cross-generational approach to programming (see Box 3.5). For agencies mandated to address the needs of specific groups such as children, women and older people, this means integrating all vulnerable groups in their interventions and building stronger operational links with other agencies.

5. Abuse and sexual violence

Kaltouma lives with her family in one of West Darfur's largest IDP camps. When a HelpAge International worker found her she had a chain tied around her ankle to stop her wandering outside the family shelter. She was crying for a key and the plate of food left by her side had not been touched.

In her sixties, Kaltouma was suffering from dementia and her family did not understand her condition or how to care for her. HelpAge International staff visited the family to work out a plan to care for Kaltouma. Finally, the padlock was opened and the chain discarded.

The crisis in Darfur contradicts the widely-held but false assumption that older people are not victims of abuse and sexual violence. They have taken on the task of foraging for wild food and collecting firewood outside the relative safety of the camps in order to protect younger women from rape, despite putting themselves at risk. In other crises where older women have been forced to live close to men, there have been instances of rape, for example in Bangladeshi flood shelters.

Elder abuse, which includes physical, sexual, psychological and financial abuse, neglect and abandonment, is under-reported and is more likely to occur when resources are stretched and older people are perceived to be unproductive. It is vital that more is done to protect people of all ages from this abuse. One way of minimizing the risks is to tackle the isolation in which older people find themselves.

Clearly, unlocking Kaltouma is simply addressing the symptom rather than the cause of discrimination. How to enable her and others like her to live a life of dignity is an

Box 3.5 Contributions across generations

"We older people have no future, so we have no status here. Even children have a higher status, because they can be useful in the future." Halima, Sisi camp, West Darfur

Older people often play key roles in their communities and households that are not sufficiently recognized. They contribute significantly to caring for children, particularly when conflict and disease take their toll on middle-aged population groups.

In the face of the HIV pandemic, grandparents struggle to look after their own dying children, as well as the orphans left behind. UNAIDS data from eight countries in sub-Saharan Africa found that up to 60 per cent of orphans live in households headed by grandparents, particularly by older women.

Older people maintain traditional knowledge and survival strategies of benefit to others. They may know how to collect, preserve and prepare wild foods. They may understand complementary medicine or act as traditional birth attendants. Studies by HelpAge International in sub-Saharan Africa have shown that the presence of a grandmother in the household reduces infant mortality and improves nutritional status and child development.

Older people are often preservers of cultural and social identity through oral history, storytelling and songs. They can help solve problems and advise younger people. They can pass on to children skills learnt from decades pursuing their profession or trade. They often contribute to the income and food security of their families. By not consulting older people or considering them in livelihood interventions, aid organizations reinforce the perception among younger people that older people no longer serve a useful purpose.

In Darfur, where older people have traditionally been highly esteemed by society, there is a growing gap between the older and younger generations. Child-friendly spaces created by agencies with protection mandates for children place little emphasis on involving older people. This contributes to a growing sense of older people's alienation from youth. Older Darfurians expressed feeling a sense of shame among adolescents who would once have looked to them for help and guidance.

"Here in the camp I have not seen any respect from the youth towards old people," says Muhammed. "This is because of the changing of many things – community and culture and thoughts. Instead, the youth laugh at us because they think the older person is not useful for the community."

Muhammed, aged 65 and blind, lives alone with his 13-year-old grandson. He was a well-respected former sheikh in his home village for 27 years, but now begs in the market to support them both. In turn, he relies on the boy to undertake chores and guide him, which means the boy cannot attend school.

Inter-generational programming is key to recognizing that older people need not exist in isolation from their communities and can play important roles that will earn respect and support. This programming may:
- involve adolescents in older people's social centres, to provide young people with a place for interaction with their elders
- develop livelihood activities based on young and older people sharing the work in cooperative gardens and livestock regeneration
- include older people as storytellers and animators in child-friendly spaces operated by child protection agencies in camps. ■

altogether tougher challenge, which starts with changing societies' attitudes towards older people.

Older people's contributions overlooked

One vital way of dispelling the negative attitudes that underpin discrimination against older people is to spread a broader understanding of the positive contributions they make to their households and communities – both during disasters and 'normal' times.

"Before I got credit, people were afraid of me. They thought I was just coming to beg. Now that they see me selling things outside my house, they are no longer afraid of me," says Alfonse Mwindo. "People laugh more at older people, because they believe that we are unable to support ourselves."

Mwindo, a retired headmaster from Pinga in the Democratic Republic of the Congo, had made provision for his old age. But in 2000, heavy fighting by rival militia forced him to flee with his grandchildren to Goma, Zaire. Then, in 2002, a volcanic eruption destroyed everything and he was reduced to begging on the streets. He used the credit he received to purchase household items for sale. It was a long way from being a headmaster, but a first step towards regaining his self-respect.

It is a useful reminder of the role that older people play at various levels of society – crisis or otherwise. At least half the global population aged over 60 is economically active, while a third of 70- to 74-year-olds and a fifth of those over 75 still work. Maintaining independence as long as possible is crucial for older people and for society. When resources are scarce, their active economic participation becomes even more urgent.

Because older people are not a homogenous group, they need specific and targeted support in rebuilding their livelihoods – based on an awareness of the contributions they make to the household economy as both providers and decision-makers.

Older people contribute to household security through their accumulated knowledge of disasters, traditional foods, coping strategies and other forms of livelihood support during times of crisis. Evidence shows that older people are more likely to be aid givers than receivers.

In communities hit by conflict, migration and disease, older people take on additional childcare responsibilities. Over half of older people living in southern African countries severely affected by HIV and AIDS care for orphaned and vulnerable children. In Darfur, 29 per cent of the 4,000 older people surveyed by HelpAge International looked after orphans – most of them caring for two or more.

International Federation
of Red Cross and Red Crescent Societies

Older people and their associations are also active in disaster response. When the Iranian city of Bam and surrounding villages were destroyed by an earthquake in December 2003, killing over 26,000 people, it was not just disaster response experts who rushed to the rescue. They were helped by local 'notables' or 'white beards' – five or six men of influence who, centred on the mosques, organized community responses across the city.

One way of supporting older people and building on their capacities is to establish community-based older people's associations (see Box 3.6). When the tsunami struck Sri Lanka, Hinnihmina lost the home she shared with her daughter and son-in-law. The 84-year-old widow from Matara was worried for her family's survival. With no income coming in, she felt she was a burden on the household's already stretched finances.

However, through a local older people's association, Hinnihmina received a grant of 50,000 rupees (US$ 490) to open a shop with her daughter. The shop sells biscuits, rice, soap and other household items and now provides the family with an income of 200 rupees (US$ 2) a day. This helps buy food and pay towards rebuilding their house. "The older people's association has been a great help to me and my family by providing a cash grant to help us establish a livelihood," says Hinnihmina.

Older people's associations aim to:
- enable older people to participate in decisions that affect their lives
- provide a channel for communication between older people, their families, their communities and external agencies and authorities
- identify those who need specific support
- promote mutual support through the development of healthy social networks
- provide learning opportunities to increase knowledge and skills
- create opportunities for income generation and greater financial independence
- increase older people's awareness of access to services and entitlements

Most importantly, such associations empower older people.

Conclusion

Older people throughout the world are poorly served in terms of disaster preparedness and response. Far more needs to be done to tackle the false assumptions and discrimination that blight their chances of survival and recovery.

They have consistently asked to be seen, heard and understood. They need equal access to essential services. They want their potential and contributions to be valued and supported. When this does not happen older, vulnerable people feel worthless and powerless – as well as deteriorating physically and mentally. The full participation

Box 3.6 Older people take initiative in South Asian disasters

Relief: in August 2006, unprecedented floods hit the normally drought-affected Barmer district of the Thar Desert in north-western India. Older people were not given any preferential treatment during governmental evacuation, relief and rehabilitation efforts. In relief camps, there was no separate provision for older people to receive food or medicines. However, four village-based older people's associations (OPAs) took the initiative and organized community kitchens to provide hot meals for 2,250 flood-affected people during the initial days of the crisis, before food aid arrived. The meals were available at the community kitchen sites and were also taken to those who could not get to the kitchen. OPA members used village funds to buy supplies and coordinated a team of volunteers to help. They also took a lead in consoling affected families and were actively involved in beneficiary selection.

In Bangladesh, following floods in Pubail district in September 2004, older citizen monitoring groups identified poor, older people who needed assistance, developed a list of relief items to be distributed and packaged and delivered those items once they had been procured by a local aid organization. One member said: "This is the first time in such a crisis I have the feeling I am not alone. There are many fellow older people around me to share and do something collectively."

Rehabilitation: in tsunami-affected areas of Tamil Nadu and Kerala, India, older people joined self-help groups established exclusively for older people. The primary role of these groups is to provide income-generation and savings activities for poor, older tsunami survivors. The elder self-help groups are often organized around particular livelihood activities, for example fish vending or basket weaving, to enable members to share experiences and expertise as well as to advocate with authorities

on specific issues of concern. Individuals are able to access loans though the group.

Senior citizen committees have been established in tsunami-affected areas of southern and eastern Sri Lanka to provide livelihood support for older people. Puthukudierupu, in Batticaloa district, is a village where many people lost family, belongings and property. It is famous for cane craft and, although older people felt they could not collect the cane themselves, they were confident that by working as a group they could buy cane to restart their activities.

One committee member, Mr Markandu, said: "We could not work alone but we could work together in groups and start a saving system to provide loans for self-employment."

Mitigation: since 2003, village-based OPAs have been established in the chronically drought-affected Barmer and Jodhpur districts of western Rajasthan, India, where traditional family networks were breaking down. The OPAs are actively consulted by the local community and government officials and are involved in implementing disaster mitigation activities such as constructing traditional water-harvesting systems, setting up and running community-based fodder and seed banks, and maintaining village ponds.

OPAs encourage older people's participation and promote dignity and respect. They are found in South and South-East Asia, (e.g. India, Bangladesh, Viet Nam, Cambodia, China, the Philippines), Africa (Sudan) and eastern Europe. In Cambodia, they have existed for over ten years and they are spreading. Most have been established by HelpAge International members, but other humanitarian organizations are building on this methodology. The Sri Lankan government is now establishing OPAs. Often, older people form their own groups after seeing successful groups operating nearby. ■

International Federation
of Red Cross and Red Crescent Societies

of older men and women in disaster management – as in development – is both an operational imperative and a matter of basic human rights.

Over the past decade, an estimated 26 million older people were affected each year by natural disasters alone. By mid-century, this figure could more than double, as the proportion of older people overtakes that of children under 14.

These changing demographics of ageing combined with the increasing number of disasters will exert a disproportionate impact on the world's oldest and poorest. Ageing issues need to be integrated into all humanitarian programmes, from preparedness and relief to recovery and risk reduction. All stages of the project cycle, including planning, assessments, implementation, monitoring and evaluation, must include the active participation of older people to ensure effective, sustainable targeting.

Failure by governments, humanitarian organizations and communities to perceive older people as a group with specific needs and capacities compounds discrimination. It delivers a clear, if unintended, message that efforts to support the most vulnerable members of society need not be a priority. Conversely, integrating older people in humanitarian efforts will reduce vulnerability and discrimination.

Lasting solutions to the problem of discrimination are as difficult and elusive to find as the root causes – but they revolve around changing the attitudes of individuals, societies and governments towards older people. While this may be beyond the scope of disaster response organizations, there are many solutions that agencies can adopt to tackle the symptoms of discrimination. And adopting such measures may, in turn, help create a greater awareness of the needs – and rights – of older people in disasters.

Humanitarian organizations and governments need to take the following steps:

1. Protect older people through relevant legislation
- Understand how older people are currently covered by human rights law and ensure these rights are upheld and protected in emergencies.
- Take a proactive stance to prohibit discrimination by age.
- Create a specific legal treaty or UN convention on the rights of older people.

2. Mainstream older people's concerns into policies and practice
- Banish false assumptions – that older people will be covered through general aid provision or that they are the responsibility of a specialized agency.
- Develop a clear rationale for reaching older people, by recognizing their unique vulnerabilities and contributions.
- Train disaster relief staff to recognize older people's needs and rights.

■ Pay particular attention to those who are less mobile and housebound – establish outreach services.

■ Collaborate with other agencies to develop inter-generational programmes, boosting the place of older people in society.

3. Provide more resources

■ Increase funding for community-based older people's organizations – and for those agencies that support them.

■ Increase the global funding for older people via humanitarian organizations from the current 1 per cent to the 7 per cent recommended by the Sphere Project.

4. Improve data and delivery by increasing older people's participation

■ Include older people in emergency needs assessments, targeting, planning, implementation, monitoring and evaluation.

■ Disaggregate data by age and gender.

■ Carry out more research into the impact of disasters on older people.

■ Record older people's views through evaluations.

■ Assess the impact of humanitarian aid on older people.

Principal contributors to this chapter and Boxes 3.1, 3.2 and 3.6 were Jane Scobie, communications manager at HelpAge International, a global network of not-for-profit organizations which works with, and for, disadvantaged older people worldwide; Susan Erb, research manager at HelpAge International. Boxes 3.3 and 3.5 were contributed by Jo Wells, emergency policy coordinator at HelpAge International. Box 3.4 was contributed by Alexander Matheou, head of the regional office for Russia, Ukraine, Belarus and Moldova at the International Federation of Red Cross and Red Crescent Societies.

Sources and further information

Bramucci, G. *Rebuilding lives in longer-term emergencies.* HelpAge International, November 2006.

British Red Cross, Red Cross Society of Georgia, ICRC, Social Welfare Department of Kutaisi, the Municipalities of Ukimarioni and Avtoplant and community representatives. *Participatory Action Research with Older People in Western Georgia*, June/July 2004, Kutaisi, Georgia.

Cooperation Committee for Cambodia. *Growing Old in the Former Khmer Rouge Stronghold of Pailin: Analyzing Development Issues, Trainees (Round 17) and Team*, November 2006.

DIFD. *Not just a numbers game: ensuring the excluded get counted in poverty monitoring.* Report of a side event held during the 44th Commission on Social Development, United Nations, New York, 10 February 2005.

Dodge, Gordon R. *Kashmir Pakistan Earthquake Psychosocial needs assessment report and programme plan. Report to HelpAge International,* September 2006.

HelpAge India. *Older People in the Tsunami.* 2005.

HelpAge International. *Addressing the nutritional needs of older people in emergency situations in Africa: Ideas for action.* Nairobi, HelpAge International, 2001.

HelpAge International. *Ageways: Ageing and Emergencies.* Issue 66, December 2005.

HelpAge International. *Older people in disasters and humanitarian crises: guidelines for best practice.* HelpAge International, 2000.

HelpAge International. *The Impact of the Indian Ocean Tsunami on Older People.* HelpAge International, 2005.

HelpAge International. *The mark of a noble society: human rights and older people.* HelpAge International, 2000.

IASC. *Protecting persons affected by natural disasters.* IASC Operational Guidelines on Human Rights and Natural Disasters, 2006.

IASC. *Synthesis of commissioned research.* Humanitarian Work Programme, undated.

Physicians for Human Rights (PHR). *Darfur assault on survival: a call for security, justice, and restitution.* Cambridge, MA: PHR, 11 January 2006.

The Sphere Project. *Humanitarian Charter and Minimum Standards in Disaster Response.* The Sphere Project, Geneva, 2004.

Thomas, Anisya. 'Linking preparedness and performance: the tsunami experience' in *Humanitarian Exchange,* No. 32, December 2005.

United Nations. Political Declaration and Madrid International Plan of Action on Ageing, *Second World Assembly on Ageing,* 2002.

United Nations High Commissioner for Refugees (UNHCR). *2005 Global Refugee Trends.* Geneva. UNHCR, 6 June 2006.

United Nations Population Division. *Population Ageing 2006,* wall chart.

United Nations Population Division. *World Population Prospects,* 2004 revision.

Wells, J. *Protecting and assisting older people in emergencies.* HPN Network Paper, No. 53, December 2005.

World Health Organization. *Health and Ageing.* Discussion paper, 2002.

Web sites

HelpAge International **www.helpage.org**

Madrid International Plan of Action on Ageing, 2002
www.un.org/esa/socdev/ageing/madrid_intlplanaction.html

World Health Organization (Ageing and life course section)
www.who.int/ageing/en

World Population Prospects **http://esa.un.org/unpp**

CHAPTER 4

  International Federation
of Red Cross and Red Crescent Societies

Disability and disasters: towards an inclusive approach

According to the World Health Organization (WHO), there are over 600 million persons with disabilities worldwide – between 7 and 10 per cent of the global population – 80 per cent of whom live in developing countries. Their number is increasing through population growth, greater longevity and advances in medical technology.

Disability and poverty are linked in a vicious cycle. Across the world, persons with disabilities (see Note) are disproportionately poor because of barriers, discrimination and exclusion from opportunities to escape the unending poverty that they face. Marginalized by laws, customs, practices and attitudes, in addition to having a difficult physical environment, they are excluded from educational and livelihood opportunities. Poor people have limited access to health care, shelter, food, education and employment, and are more likely to work in hazardous conditions – all factors that increase the risk of illness, injury and impairment.

Persons with disabilities are doubly vulnerable to disasters, both on account of impairments and poverty; yet they are often ignored or excluded at all levels of disaster preparedness, mitigation and intervention. They are particularly at risk of marginalization and discrimination in such situations due to exclusionary policies and practices by communities and the agencies involved in providing humanitarian aid and intervention.

This chapter will explore why they have been excluded from these processes; the mechanisms now in place to redress this, including the recent UN Convention on the Rights of Persons with Disabilities; and what they are doing to make themselves more resilient to disasters.

Context

There is no single agreed definition of disability, while there are many local understandings of who is disabled and what disability constitutes. There is also little internationally comparable information. Higher-income countries tend to demonstrate higher rates of people registered as disabled, which seems to be in part because of broader definitions of what disability is and the availability of welfare structures and resources.

Photo opposite page: Many people suffered fractures during the earthquake which struck Pakistan in October 2005. In the field hospital at Abbottabad, provided by the Norwegian Red Cross, children learnt to use crutches to walk after becoming disabled.

Olav A. Saltbones/ Norwegian Red Cross

The UN Convention on the Rights of Persons with Disabilities does not define disability. However, it notes that:

> "Disability is an evolving concept and results from the interaction between a person's impairment and obstacles such as physical barriers and prevailing attitudes that prevent their participation in society. The more obstacles there are, the more disabled a person becomes. Persons with disabilities have long-term physical, mental, intellectual, or sensory impairments such as blindness, deafness, impaired mobility, and developmental impairments. Some people may have more than one form of disability and many, if not most people, will acquire a disability at some time in their life due to physical injury, disease or ageing."

The 'social model' perspective currently forms the basis of many disability policies and practices. This model focuses on discrimination and exclusion rather than impairments – and provides a tool to analyse the barriers to persons with disabilities that prevent full participation, inclusion and access to their rights. These barriers can be social, economic, physical, institutional, attitudinal and cultural. One or all of them may present themselves to persons with disabilities across the world, and can result in poverty, discrimination and social exclusion. Disability is therefore best understood as a multidimensional concept.

Disasters create disability

Disasters and emergencies can leave a huge legacy of impairment and injury, although the actual injury rate and numbers depend on the context and type of disaster. For example, an earthquake in Armenia in 1988 killed 25,000 people but injured 130,000 of whom 14,000 were hospitalized. It is estimated that for every child killed as a result of violent conflict, three are injured and permanently impaired. Inevitably, there are difficulties obtaining such data in the immediate aftermath of a disaster or conflict, and many organizations do not collect disability-related data in the immediate needs assessments. Following an initial assessment of the situation in post-conflict southern Sudan, Handicap International and its partners in the field estimated that over 11 per cent of the population were disabled, but that this number only actually reflected those visible to the team.

While those injured as a result of the disaster or conflict may be very visible, it is important to remember that many other people living in the affected areas may already be disabled, and may then become further marginalized and excluded on the basis of their disability in the aftermath.

To avoid such exclusion following a disaster or emergency, it may be helpful to consider persons with disabilities in different groups, such as:

- those with an injury that may be at risk of developing into an impairment (for example, injuries such as bone fractures not properly treated or followed up after discharge)
- people whose injuries result in (permanent) impairment (for example, spinal cord injuries, amputations etc.)
- people who were already disabled prior to the emergency or disaster
- people with chronic diseases (including HIV, epilepsy, diabetes etc., which can all deteriorate without medication)

Despite the obvious direct correlation between disability, disasters and conflicts through injuries or accidents, there are also more indirect effects such as inadequate health care, poverty, and malnutrition, loss of support structures and change of environment. If the health care system is disrupted, as it often is in such situations, and relief organizations have limited capacity to follow up or include people with chronic illnesses, then there is a risk of further disability. The loss of family members, homes and livelihoods in the aftermath of a disaster means that recovery may be slow. Families may have to adapt to new structures and seek alternative means of income. In some instances, those who are seen to be 'victims' of a disaster or emergency may receive the most input and services.

Policy and discrimination

In 1991, as a contribution to the UN Decade of Disabled Persons, the UN Standard Rules on the Equalization of Opportunities for Persons with Disabilities (Standard Rules) were adopted, based on existing international human rights legislation. Yet in 2006, a global survey by the UN Special Rapporteur on Disability found that persons with disabilities still faced discrimination in many areas of life. For example, even if they were employed, they were not always entitled to the same privileges as persons without disabilities. Children with disabilities still faced many barriers in accessing education across the world – in both developing and developed countries. These two factors alone contribute significantly to ongoing economic marginalization and, as the report notes, "…explain why persons with disabilities are the poorest of the poor". This is compounded by a lack of government action to ensure income maintenance and support.

The survey also drew attention to disasters and emergencies, in particular to ways in which persons with disabilities have been largely overlooked in relief programmes. To this end, it suggested that states, in conjunction with relevant UN agencies, should develop inclusive policies and guidelines for persons with disabilities in emergency situations.

The Standard Rules were a precursor to the UN Convention on the Rights of Persons with Disabilities, which was adopted by the General Assembly of the United Nations in December 2006. The formal ratification process began on 31 March 2007 in New York. The convention comprises 50 articles, covering a wide range of issues including education, health, international cooperation, equality and non-discrimination. Particularly relevant to this discussion are Article 32, International cooperation, and Article 11, Situations of risk and humanitarian emergencies (see Box 4.1).

Discrimination in emergencies

Persons with disabilities encounter many problems before, during and after disasters and emergencies, which are not necessarily due solely to their impairment but also to the inadequacy of disaster risk reduction and response systems in meeting their particular needs. In addition, these specific needs may vary according to the time of the intervention: pre (mitigation), during (immediate) and after (intermediate and long-term). In general, the needs of persons with disabilities are often overlooked by disaster planners and they have little or no input into disaster risk reduction planning.

Box 4.1 Articles 32 and 11 of the UN Convention on the Rights of Persons with Disabilities

Article 32: International cooperation
1. States Parties recognize the importance of international cooperation and its promotion, in support of national efforts for the realization of the purpose and objectives of the present Convention, and will undertake appropriate and effective measures in this regard, between and among States and, as appropriate, in partnership with relevant international and regional organizations and civil society, in particular organizations of persons with disabilities. Such measures could include, inter alia:
a. Ensuring that international cooperation, including international development programmes, is inclusive of and accessible to persons with disabilities;
b. Facilitating and supporting capacity-building, including through the exchange and sharing of information, experiences, training programmes and best practices;
c. Facilitating cooperation in research and access to scientific and technical knowledge;

d. Providing, as appropriate, technical and economic assistance, including by facilitating access to and sharing of accessible and assistive technologies, and through the transfer of technologies.
2. The provisions of this article are without prejudice to the obligations of each State Party to fulfil its obligations under the present Convention.

Article 11: Situations of risk and humanitarian emergencies
States Parties shall take, in accordance with their obligations under international law, including international humanitarian law and international human rights law, all necessary measures to ensure the protection and safety of persons with disabilities in situations of risk, including situations of armed conflict, humanitarian emergencies and the occurrence of natural disasters. ■

An example of this comes from Bangladesh, a low-income country frequently affected by disasters and flooding, and with an estimated 12 million persons with disabilities (see Box 4.2). One recent survey of them in the cyclone-prone coastal belt found clear differentials in the distribution of relief and rehabilitation aid between families that had members with disabilities and the rest of the community. Only 3 per cent of the sample had received any targeted support for persons with disabilities from flood relief and rehabilitation programmes. The survey found that many persons with disabilities were widely excluded on the grounds of inaccessible shelters and food distribution mechanisms. The survey also found that even some of the materials widely used in the reconstruction phase, such as corrugated iron sheets for roofing, had the potential themselves to cause serious injury and even impairment to people repeatedly affected by disasters.

However, these problems are not confined to any one country or region. The general problem of exclusion has been demonstrated by the experience of major events such as Hurricane Katrina, and by research in such diverse locations as California, New Zealand and South Asia, as well as by extensive anecdotal evidence.

According to the *IASC Operational Guidelines on Human Rights and Natural Disasters*, this exclusion is mainly a result of "inappropriate policies or simple neglect". To this, we would add discrimination. As the guidelines note, the longer the situation of displacement continues, as a result of a disaster, the greater the risk of discrimination and human rights violations. There is evidence that persons with disabilities are particularly at risk of marginalization and discrimination in such situations due to exclusionary policies and practices by communities and the agencies involved in providing humanitarian aid and intervention. Persons with disabilities, especially women and children, are particularly vulnerable to violence, exploitation and sexual abuse in such situations. Anyone affected by disasters or conflict is more vulnerable to mental health and psychological problems – which may result in misunderstandings and further isolation and social exclusion for families and communities.

The *IASC Operational Guidelines* specifically mentions persons with disabilities in a number of areas:
- camp security (location and layout of camps and settlements)
- safe and non-discriminatory access to available humanitarian assistance
- available, acceptable and adaptable provision of goods and services without discrimination
- inclusion in long-term planning of resettlement and reconstruction
- inclusion in livelihood measures, such as microcredit opportunities
- appropriate mechanisms for feedback regarding relief, recovery and re-construction responses

Box 4.2 Bangladesh: discrimination during floods

Following an accident about eight months back, my husband, a truck driver, lost his right hand, two lower limbs, and became paralysed from below his neck. We haven't yet learnt how to cope with this loss. We have never seen floods in our village before. There were no boats around when the flood waters rushed in. We sat on the roof for three days. Then our house was washed away, so we had to move here. But moving such a big man is difficult. The toilets are also too far away. Now when he defecates in bed, the other families suffer from the stench, and so they have tried to throw us out. It seems that the authorities here are also thinking along the same lines.

Setara Begum, 45, in a flood shelter at Jessore, 2001

Bangladesh is one of the most flood-prone countries in the world. Essentially, it is a flood plain criss-crossed by 230 rivers. When the rivers flood, so does Bangladesh. In addition, frequent cyclones can drive millions of tonnes of sea water over coastal areas. For a country with about 1,000 people per square kilometre, this can spell catastrophe – particularly for people in rural areas.

But of all Bangladeshis, those with disabilities – who constitute 6 per cent of the population – suffer by far the most during recurrent floods. As well as facing challenges of mobility, sight, hearing, speaking, sensing or rationalizing, they face additional barriers of discrimination from the non-disabled community in their day-to-day lives – discrimination which gets worse during disaster.

As part of their flood response, only a handful of organizations operate flood shelters. The rest generally organize relief programmes. Depending on the budget and human resources available, they vary from large numbers of relief teams with comprehensive aid packages to very small responses. Whatever the scale, in most cases persons with disabilities are usually left out of the effort. This is not done intentionally but because relief teams do not know where to find them – and because relief efforts tend to focus on the most accessible areas.

Even if families can evacuate with their disabled members in time to find relief distribution points, they find it almost impossible to stand in queues for the long hours needed to access aid. So here, too, they do not get their fair share. Mothers of children with disabilities and wives of disabled husbands are torn between the moral duty to remain by the side of their loved ones or standing in long queues to fetch the scant relief that is available. They may send their other children to fetch aid, but a child usually gets given a far smaller packet which is not enough for the whole family.

Those persons with disabilities who make it to flood shelters face discrimination from other survivors inside. Most shelters are overcrowded, while toilets and water sources are inadequate and inaccessible. Families with mobility-restricted adults find it extremely difficult to pacify the people around them, especially when the paralysed persons have no option but to defecate in their makeshift beds. Since many shelters are in closed warehouses with limited ventilation, other families blame persons with disabilities for adding to the stench and often gang up on them to leave.

Accompanying family members with disabilities to the toilet brings its own risks, as Mariam Bewa, 40, a blind widow in a flood

International Federation of Red Cross and Red Crescent Societies

shelter at Netrokona in 1998, explained: "By the time flood waters became knee-deep in our village, our neighbours began to leave. I didn't know what to do with my two daughters, aged 13 and 15. The only way we earn our living is by begging. But then our tiny hut got washed away. Now at this shelter, in the evenings, if one has to go to the toilet, we all need to go together. But then the relief goods that we get, and our little possessions at the tiny space that we have here, are at risk of being stolen. I wonder how long we will have to cope with this."

Poor lighting after dusk makes the shelters unsafe for single women – especially if the shelters are open-air. And if a family has an intellectually-impaired adult daughter with limited communication skills, they need to deal with additional safety concerns. "My 19-year-old sister is mentally very ill," said Abdul Latif, 25, in a flood shelter at Satkhira in 2001. "She rarely keeps clothes on. It wasn't too much of a trouble at home, as we could always keep her indoors. We live in a joint family, so everyone knew and took care of her collectively. When the flood waters began to rise, our extended families left one by one to better shelters. We stayed at home for four days. But since there was no food and also our house had been flooded, we had to leave. We don't yet know where our close relatives are. Now here out in the public, my mother, my younger brother and I have to keep a constant watch on her for her safety. Every night, we keep awake and watch over her by turns."

Floods can also inflict injuries on people – but greater awareness among relief organizations could reduce the risk. Jahanara Begum, 35, from Bogra village, explains: "After the flood waters receded in 1998, we returned to our homestead. We had to rebuild all the houses in the entire neighbourhood. So the adults remained busy all day, and didn't mind their children playing in the stagnant waters. My younger son was only about eight then. With the situation improving, all medical help had also left the place. Being illiterate and poor, we didn't know that ear infections could be so bad for the children. Now my son is completely deaf in both ears. There are at least five of his friends who have suffered similar deafness. I wish someone had told us back then that simply cleaning and drying their ears could prevent this problem."

The National Forum of Organizations Working with the Disabled (NFOWD), a network of Bangladeshi non-governmental organizations (NGOs), has consistently raised these concerns with the government and relevant disaster management bodies – as well as issuing guidelines on how to make disaster relief more accessible to persons with disabilities.

In 2000, the government issued special instructions to all district administrators to ensure that persons with disabilities are given priority in evacuation, relief and rehabilitation measures. In 2005, the DER, a disasters and emergency response group of international non-governmental organizations (INGOs) and large national NGOs, hosted workshops looking at disasters and diversity. The DER agreed that, if a response were fully accessible to persons with disabilities, it would become automatically accessible to elderly people, children, pregnant women and people suffering from debilitating illnesses. This has prompted many INGOs to support disability-friendly disaster response plans.

Fortunately, the country has not suffered a major disaster since then. But when floods inevitably inundate the country again, it remains to be seen how effective this planning will prove for persons with disabilities. ∎

However, there is still a large gap between policy, guidance and implementation – even in countries with highly-developed disaster policies. In the United States, which is a leader in research and policy in this field, there is still plenty of evidence of exclusion and discrimination. The key question is why, despite the existence of guidelines and standards, persons with disabilities are rarely mainstreamed into disaster and emergency programmes. There are a number of answers that might explain this.

Many agencies and organizations working in the field consider disability to be a specialized subject, requiring technical skill and knowledge, often of a medical nature. This means that when they encounter persons with disabilities in their programmes, they are automatically referred to a specialist agency dealing with disability. These assumptions by agencies and practitioners perpetuate discrimination and exclusion. Within most mainstream humanitarian aid and development organizations, disability has been addressed either as a cross-cutting issue or as part of a vulnerable group.

However, many of the needs of persons with disabilities are exactly the same as everyone else in a disaster or emergency (water, sanitation, shelter, food), but it is how they are provided that matters. Many activities can be undertaken in order to ensure that they and their families access the same benefits and relief as other people. This is not to say that persons with disabilities (and other vulnerable people) may not have particular needs, but to treat them merely as in need of special attention disempowers them and denies them a voice in planning and implementation. It also denies that persons with disabilities have any role to play in disaster relief, disaster risk reduction and recovery. This perpetuates discrimination.

Another exclusionary factor is perceived expense. Constructing accessible buildings, for example, is seen as expensive, even though evidence suggests that it only adds minimal extra cost initially compared to having to alter buildings later on to comply with regulations. Moreover, all of these adaptations benefit the wider community. Time is also a constraint: in many post-disaster situations, there is considerable pressure on governments and donors to complete rebuilding work to allow people to return home.

Other aspects of discrimination in disaster response and recovery are less clear, or less well understood. One of these is the long-term effect of a disaster on a community: how it affects families, income, poverty levels and so on. We need to know much more about the impact on persons with disabilities. There is also very little work on how they reintegrate into communities in the aftermath of a disaster or conflict. However, such situations can also be a catalyst for change and, in a number of countries, have resulted in their forming organizations and lobbying to get disability issues onto the government's agenda; this was certainly the case in

International Federation
of Red Cross and Red Crescent Societies

Sierra Leone and Liberia. It is also true that there are few other alternatives for persons with disabilities other than to form self-help groups if there is minimal welfare provision.

Also in the aftermath of an emergency or disaster there is inevitably an influx of organizations and services, so, conversely, persons with disabilities may find themselves receiving better services and care than they did beforehand: for example, rehabilitation services are developed, and assistive devices may be distributed. Despite this, it may be difficult for many people with impairments acquired as a result of the emergency or conflict to adjust to their situation.

Another area that requires consideration is the difference in treatment for those perceived as victims or heroes, and those seen as ordinary persons with disabilities. In many countries, for example in Afghanistan, people seen as martyrs or war heroes are compensated and fêted by others in the community, whereas those not injured as a result of war are marginalized and excluded. In Sierra Leone, those who become disabled as a result of disrupted immunization campaigns during violent conflict are not considered for any kind of war-related compensation (see Box 4.3).

Invisibility and identity

One of the biggest factors in the exclusion of persons with disabilities from many humanitarian responses is a paucity of data: as they are not 'seen', they are assumed not to be there and are not included. However, evidence from disabled people's organizations (DPOs) around the world has shown that adults and children with disabilities are often hidden from view, stigmatized by families and communities. They may not be included in national censuses or other registration mechanisms.

For example, in Prakasam District, south of Andhra Pradesh, an area badly affected by the Indian Ocean tsunami in December 2004, the population in 2001 was officially recorded at 3,054,941. According to official data, 35 people died as a result of the tsunami and over 92,000 people were affected. The statistics of the district medical and health office (2005) show there were officially 48,931 persons with disabilities registered (27,437 males and 21,494 females). Leonard Cheshire International staff, who visited the region in the immediate aftermath of the tsunami, observed that "[in] the relief work undertaken by the government and NGOs, persons with disabilities were sidelined and not properly represented".

But even before the tsunami, persons with disabilities in Prakasam District did not have an adequate support system and even after the enactment of the Indian government's Persons with Disabilities Act 1995, full inclusion had not happened.

They did not have basic documents such as identity cards, income certificates and ration cards. In addition, the district did not have facilities to provide any of

Box 4.3 War-wounded youth in Liberia and Sierra Leone miss out

During the 1990s, Liberia and Sierra Leone suffered years of violent conflict which resulted in injuries and impairments for large numbers of people. Some of these were deliberately inflicted on people – for example, forced amputations; others were a consequence of fighting, such as war injuries sustained by combatants, including child soldiers. Yet more were a result of years of devastation to previously efficient public health programmes, including immunization campaigns.

In the aftermath of war, how have these persons with disabilities been treated by their respective governments? In many countries, those wounded as a result of fighting are often seen as war heroes. This has not been the case in West Africa. However, in both Sierra Leone and Liberia, those who became impaired as a result of a lack of medical care have received less support than the war-wounded.

In Liberia, many young people with visible impairments are assumed to be former combatants who 'deserved what they got'. Whatever the cause of their injuries or impairments, very few of the disarmament, demobilization and reintegration (DDR) programmes implemented by the UN and other international organizations in Liberia have made any provision for the large numbers of disabled youth, many of whom are former combatants. Consequently, many disabled youth are stigmatized and neglected – left no option but to beg on the streets of Monrovia, Liberia's capital.

In 2005, the Liberian government drafted a national youth policy in which disability was highlighted as an area of special concern, in line with national legislation. However, there were no specific interventions planned for the large numbers of young disabled ex-combatants remaining in Monrovia.

In nearby Sierra Leone, war-wounded and amputees elicit a more sympathetic response – even though the country lacks national disability legislation. In the years after the conflict, many INGOs provided the war-wounded and amputees with housing, skills training and prostheses. However, many of these settlements were built some distance from urban areas, therefore reducing opportunities for integration, schooling, shopping and employment, with subsequent problems of sustainability. In addition, despite promises by the Sierra Leone Truth and Reconciliation Commission, there has been limited reparation for victims. Many people who originally received support have resorted to begging on the streets of the Sierra Leonean capital, Freetown.

In both countries, the large numbers of unemployed and alienated youth are seen as potentially destabilizing forces within society. Discriminatory policies and practices towards young persons with disabilities will not make the situation any less fragile.

It need not be this way. In the Great Lakes region of Africa, including Angola, Burundi and Uganda, the World Bank has initiated a multi-country demobilization and reintegration programme (MDRP) which encompasses specific projects for persons with disabilities, including ex-combatants. The programme seeks to improve understanding of the links between demobilization and reintegration and cross-cutting issues such as disability and gender. ∎

International Federation of Red Cross and Red Crescent Societies

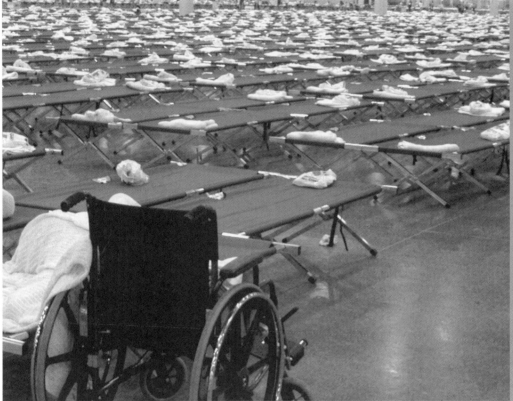

The Astrodome in Houston, Texas, provided emergency shelter for thousands of New Orleans residents. Hurricane Katrina left a trail of devastation and many disabled people in a vulnerable situation.

Daniel Cima/
American Red Cross

the support that can facilitate inclusion, such as prosthetic appliances and hearing aids.

In Chennai, the state capital of Tamil Nadu, persons with disabilities who were fortunate enough to be registered with local government agencies did receive some relief following the tsunami, mainly food, clothing and medical support. However, those who were not registered, for example if they had no fixed address, were not given any state support.

But the issue of registration is – like definitions – problematic. Many persons with disabilities are not willing to identify themselves as disabled for fear of becoming labelled and marginalized on this basis.

After the Indian Ocean tsunami, there were many examples of persons with disabilities being unable to escape the waves and drowning. In Sambodhi Residential Home in Galle, Sri Lanka, only 41 of its 102 residents survived; many of the rest were unable to leave their beds or failed to comprehend in time the need to escape. In many countries affected by violent conflict, families that are forced to flee may leave behind children and other family members who are not as mobile. In Sierra Leone, many children with disabilities were abandoned by their families during the conflict.

While shocking, such cases come as no surprise to many in the disability movement. What they demonstrate is that it is not just policies that need changing, but also deep-rooted attitudes and prejudices.

Cultural and attitudinal barriers, such as fear and misunderstanding, can be deeply entrenched and difficult to shift. In some instances, a child with a disability is seen as punishment or retribution (for example, for something the mother did during pregnancy). Children with disabilities are also at risk of abuse and withdrawal of care. This may be within their own families, where they are perceived to be an additional burden, but it can also come from other members of the community. Education, greater gender equality and good antenatal care can help dispel such myths. Women with disabilities are in effect doubly excluded from the mainstream, by disability and gender.

Meeting needs

When it comes to meeting the specific needs of people's disabilities before, during and after disasters, there is a growing amount of guidance and experience to draw on. Most of the documented experiences and research are from developed countries, especially the United States; but despite the vast differences in resources between low-income and high-income countries, the principles and basic approaches are universal.

In theory, disaster risk reduction aims to be inclusive, helping all people at risk and involving a wide range of institutional and community stakeholders. The challenges of inclusion and partnership need to be addressed well before the disaster or emergency occurs – as the executive director of the Center for Independence of the Disabled, New York, said after 9/11: "The time to build relationships is not in the middle of a crisis." One of the most important outcomes of such exercises should be awareness of the diversity of impairments and people's needs, and hence a recognition that there is no one-size-fits-all approach to supporting them. Adopting a broad and flexible attitude to disability ensures that nobody is left out.

The following paragraphs indicate some specific practical challenges and how they might be overcome.

Physical impairments of various kinds may make standard, domestic disaster risk reduction measures more difficult – such as putting up hurricane shutters, anchoring items inside or outside the home to stop them from falling down in an earthquake or turning into dangerous projectiles in high winds. The tasks of cleaning up and repairing homes after a disaster are, similarly, more challenging.

Improvements to the physical environment give greater protection and make evacuation easier. Homes, workplaces, escape routes and emergency facilities can be designed or redesigned with the needs of persons with disabilities in mind. In the home, for example, furniture and other possessions can be arranged and secured in such a way that they will not obstruct movement in an emergency. In public buildings and workplaces, the evacuation can be facilitated through the provision of ramps, handrails or pathway marking systems and other special signing, as well as the widening of passageways and staircases. Buildings and sites should be developed and improved according to the principle of universal design: an approach to the design of all products and environments to be as usable as possible by as many people as possible, regardless of age, ability or situation.

Public information systems giving information on hazards and risk, warnings of approaching events and advice during and after an emergency on what action to take, often do not present this information in appropriate media or formats for those with sensorial or intellectual impairments. As a result, when disaster strikes, persons with disabilities may not know what to do, where to go, or who to turn to for help. Advice may also be inappropriate, such as telling wheelchair users to take cover under tables in an earthquake.

Methods for communicating risk and early warnings should, therefore, be appropriate to the nature of the impairment. Examples are printed material in large type or Braille for partially-sighted or blind people, sign language or captions on television broadcasts for the deaf or hard of hearing, and face-to-face discussions with people who have learning difficulties or other health problems that may affect their understanding of messages. 'Phone trees' can be used to get messages out to large numbers of targeted individuals, as well as enabling them to alert emergency professionals to their situation.

Those with impaired mobility find it difficult or impossible to take protective action and get out of harm's way quickly. They may be unable to navigate debris inside damaged buildings. In larger buildings, when lifts and escalators stop working, they may be unable to use stairs. Evacuation procedures, designed to move large numbers of people away from a threat as rapidly as possible, may set persons with disabilities aside – in the planning and, even physically during an event – because they are seen as an impediment. When forced from their homes, persons with disabilities may find that emergency facilities (e.g. first-aid stations, emergency shelters, food and water distribution centres) and temporary housing are inaccessible.

Preparedness and response drills therefore need to be practised by persons with disabilities and those who are responsible for assisting them. This saved the lives of a number of people during the attack on the World Trade Center in New York on 11 September 2001. They included the blind and visually-impaired staff of the Associated Blind Organization, based on the ninth floor, which had developed an evacuation plan and drill for its staff with the help of the New York City Fire Department. Regular practice also helps to identify problems or issues needing further attention. However, persons with disabilities are often excluded from evacuation drills. John Glenn, a business continuity consultant, has observed workplace managers being notified before a drill "so that people with problems can ride the elevators down before the alarm sounds and the elevators stop moving".

In the chaos and confusion in the aftermath of a conflict or disaster, people with pre-existing impairments may lose family members or carers, be moved to temporary housing or shelter, and lose mobility and other aids, thus increasing their vulnerability. Some will not have been able to flee with their families, and may have been separated or left behind. They may have difficulty accessing information, food, water and sanitation sources. Conflict- or disaster-related injuries put additional strain on health care resources in already severely overstretched countries. Consequently, persons with disabilities are often a low priority in service provision – furthering isolation, social exclusion and marginalization.

Disabled and unable to get to the relief distribution points, this resident of Louisiana relied on daily visits from the American Red Cross in the aftermath of Hurricane Katrina.

Gene Dailey/
American Red Cross

International Federation
of Red Cross and Red Crescent Societies

Emergency service workers often fail to understand the specific situation and needs of persons with disabilities. This is particularly evident in the management of emergency shelters. In some instances, persons with disabilities have been turned away from shelters because of volunteers' lack of confidence regarding the shelter's ability to meet their needs. In the January 1994 Northridge earthquake in California, a man with a hearing problem was denied admission to an emergency shelter because its staff could not understand sign language, and people with cerebral palsy were ignored because shelter volunteers thought they were on drugs or alcohol. Other persons with disabilities were turned away from shelters and told to go to hospitals by staff members who assumed that they were sick or injured. After the Kobe earthquake in Japan, people with intellectual disabilities who did manage to get into shelters faced discrimination from the shelters' other occupants and found themselves pushed to the back of food queues. During a cyclone evacuation in Bangladesh, a family brought their child with a disability with them to the cyclone shelter but, because of the negative and hostile attitudes of others in the shelter, they decided to take a chance and return home rather than remain there.

There is evidence that in some of the temporary shelters and camps set up after the Indian Ocean tsunami, some persons with disabilities were not given their medication, for example their anti-epilepsy medication. This resulted in a marked deterioration of their condition.

Disability-awareness training is an essential element in all areas of disaster risk reduction activity. Emergency personnel must know how best to communicate with persons with disabilities, how to assist them and how to use relevant equipment. They should always regard a person with a disability as the expert on his or her disability, and ask them for advice when trying to help them. Few, however, may possess such expertise. For example, shelter staff and volunteers are often trained in first aid or other areas critical to the delivery of emergency services, but many are unfamiliar with the needs of persons with disabilities.

Emergency shelters should be accessible to persons with disabilities, and designed or organized with their needs in mind. For example, this might include the provision of crutches, portable ramps, wheelchairs, medical supplies and equipment, cold storage for essential medication, and facilities for guide dogs, as well as ensuring access to family members and caregivers. Some may ignore advice to leave their homes if they believe that shelters cannot support them.

In all of this, it must be remembered that they are not a homogenous group: as well as capabilities, diversity and differences vary according to a number of other factors, including gender, age, income, caste, tribe, and location. This has a bearing on how disability is mainstreamed into policy and practice.

Agency and activism of persons with disabilities

In theory, disaster risk reduction aims to be inclusive, helping all people at risk but, as has been demonstrated, in practice disaster planners and managers give low priority to persons with disabilities. They are rarely consulted at any level or any stage of the disaster cycle – like most disaster-affected people, from preparedness to recovery – yet they are among those most affected, and least likely to receive assistance.

The notion that all persons with disabilities are unable to help themselves and must be aided or directed by others is widespread, even among agencies that work with

Box 4.4 Skills of blind people can prove lifesaving

Colonel Kenneth A. Silberman is a blind, trained community emergency response team member in the United States. This is his story:

In the fall of 2005, I saw an article in the local newspaper, talking about an upcoming meeting to organize a community emergency response team (CERT). The article said that everyone was welcome and that there were no age or physical requirements. So I went, because I was interested in learning disaster skills that would help me and my neighbours. We were told that the purpose of a CERT team is to give citizens the basic training necessary to provide emergency services in the first 72 hours of a disaster when professional responders and high-tech equipment will be en route but unavailable. I signed up.

The 20-hour course was held at the Maryland Fire and Rescue Institute. It was taught by retired and active emergency medical services (EMS) personnel and covered basic training in disaster preparedness, fire safety, disaster medical operations, light search-and-rescue operations, CERT organization, disaster psychology and terrorism, and concluded with a disaster simulation.

The instructors were nervous about having me on the course but did let me participate. I was able to download the textbook from the FEMA [Federal Emergency Management Agency] web site in accessible Microsoft Word files. I had classmates and home readers help me with other handouts when they were not redundant to the book and not accessible.

The hands-on exercises also went well. Because we were trained to complement each others' skills as teammates, I simply used my white cane or used sighted assistance as appropriate. Conversely, my sighted colleagues relied on me in poor-visibility situations. Blindness skills proved invaluable in the search-and-rescue phase of the training, when we had to traverse a pitch-black, multi-storey maze and apartment looking for victims. There was a lot of panic due to disorientation. However, it was business as usual for me. So, I ended up leading the operation. The instructors and students accepted me completely after that.

As for the equipment, the students had to work with the basics. The first-aid kits consisted of just bandages, compresses and the like.

International Federation of Red Cross and Red Crescent Societies

So there was no instrumentation to read. Real blood would be sticky and warm and would be discernible through gloves. The fire extinguishers were simply point and shoot. I put out the test-stand fire by pointing at the forward base of the heat and sweeping the jet back and forth while moving it toward the back of the fire. In a real fire, the extinguisher will either work or not. The gauge is really for maintenance. Shutting off utilities was easy. Circuit-breakers, gas and water valves were easily felt.

During the advanced Metro Rail [underground] training, my cane skills saved the day again. I had no trouble and used sighted assistance when near the power rail. Blindness skills were critical during a fire simulation in a rail carriage. I was able to cut right through the smoke, grab the emergency kit from under the seat, and direct people to the door at the end of the car. The transit police were very supportive after that.

As a result of all of this training, I was elected as the deputy coordinator of the Greenbelt-CERT in November 2006. I hope that my experience will expand the discussion of disabilities and disaster preparedness to go beyond caring for disabled persons, to making them service providers.

This will prevent responders from diverting their attention from victims to persons with disabilities who are quite capable of taking care of themselves. Secondly, a pool of talented and capable disabled folks are likely to be either not utilized or underutilized. In a real disaster, all hands will be needed on deck. ■

them. At present, many of those organizations that do try to provide special services for them tend to plan from the top down: *for* persons with disabilities, but not *with* them. Yet they are in the best position to assess their needs and plan how to meet them during and after emergencies.

Many persons with disabilities have skills, experience and other capacities that can assist them in a disaster and be utilized by others engaged in disaster risk reduction or emergency response. For example, in a study for the U.S. Geological Survey following the 1989 Loma Prieta earthquake in California, researchers Mansour Rahimi and Glenn Azevedo found that persons with disabilities had a psychological advantage which made them less likely to become injured or to panic during and after the earthquake, "since they negotiate with altered and sometimes difficult physical and environmental limitations on a daily basis" (see Box 4.4).

Local DPOs can be a useful source of information and advice on the location and needs of persons with disabilities. In this way, persons with disabilities and their organizations can also play an active part in preparation, planning, recovery and reconstruction efforts.

Steps can be taken to work with persons with disabilities and to engage them in discussion and training regarding the specific disaster risks the community faces, as well as how to deal with them, how to improve the security of their homes and workplaces, how to warn them of impending events, how to find a safe place in the event of severe hazards, and how to obtain help if required.

There are numerous examples of how this can be done. The Indian Ocean tsunami did become a catalyst for agencies and planners to rethink their methods, and has put issues such as universal design and accessible reconstruction higher on the agenda. Many examples of peer support emerged in the aftermath of the tsunami. There were many cases of local DPOs in India and Sri Lanka responding to the disaster with few or no resources and little or no funding. When asked why, they simply responded they had to. Disabled Peoples' International (DPI) established a relief fund and regional assemblies assisted persons with disabilities in Aceh, Indonesia.

During and after disaster or conflict situations, many come together out of necessity to form their own DPOs or similar self-help groups. The challenge is to work with these local organizations as equal partners in the reconstruction process, and to build their capacity, particularly during the transitional period. It is vital for organizations to work with DPOs in order to deal with issues relevant to them at a community level, as well as to engage persons with disabilities themselves in the work. DPOs must be included in the wider development/reconstruction agenda (and vice versa). Finally, inclusion of everyone in communities destroyed by disasters or conflict can increase social capital and strengthen social bonds, which can have a positive impact on poverty reduction and sustainable peacebuilding efforts, while further promoting development aims.

Persons with disabilities and their organizations must become involved in the training of staff in disaster management organizations. They can join in as part of community organizations or as volunteers. Increasingly, disaster organizations are encouraging the formation of personal support groups, self-help networks and 'buddy' schemes, whereby groups of people agree to assist an individual with a disability before and during emergencies. The groups typically comprise people known to the person with a disability and trusted by them: they may be family members, friends, neighbours or work colleagues. They are aware of the person's needs, work with them to plan for potential disasters and, where necessary, assist them during crises. Guidelines typically recommend that such groups consist of at least three people in each place where the person with disabilities regularly spends a significant proportion of his or her time each week, to increase the likelihood of someone being available in an emergency.

In Sweden, the Deaf Crisis Group is a group of individuals, both deaf and hearing, who have received training in psychiatric and psychological aspects of disaster management. They cooperate with a number of national partners, including the

Swedish Rescue Services Agency and the National Swedish Board of Health and Welfare.

This more collaborative approach should be taken further. Initiatives to reduce risk must be developed in partnership with persons with disabilities, their support networks and their organizations. For example, discussions with users with disabilities could improve the layout, facilities and organization of emergency shelters.

The Northridge earthquake in Los Angeles in 1994 stimulated a more participatory approach to disaster/disability planning. A group was formed calling itself Disabled People and Disaster Planning. It met between 1996 and 1997 and came up with several recommendations for dealing with problems identified during and after the earthquake. It covered earthquake preparedness, the management of emergency shelters, the training of rescue workers, ways of assisting wheelchair users and communicating information to persons with disabilities, making emergency shelters and services more accessible after a disaster, and sources of online information. In Turkey, after the 1999 earthquakes, a non-governmental organization set up a programme to support deaf people. A core group of deaf people were trained as disaster awareness instructors, with the aim that they should then travel the country training others. By 2002, some 2,000 deaf people had been trained.

Disability rights and legislation

Activism of this kind, which is essential for identifying the needs of persons with disabilities and overcoming problems, can be greatly assisted by appropriate legal backing. This would bring disaster reduction in line with other, rights-based approaches to disability and development. Persons with disabilities are increasingly demanding that they are not simply treated as problems to be solved by planners, but as part of society entitled to equal opportunities and rights (see Box 4.5).

In many countries, legislation prohibiting discrimination on the grounds of disability could be applied to disaster risk reduction and response. For example, in the United States, federal legislation prohibits discrimination in disaster response and recovery on grounds of disability by any federal agency or federally-funded programme, and requires government agencies, including local government, to make their disaster risk reduction and response programmes accessible to persons with disabilities. The city of Chicago requires evacuation plans for persons with disabilities in any commercial or residential building over 80 feet high.

However, financial and administrative capacity, as well as political will, is needed to enforce compliance with such laws and regulations. Ratification of the UN

Box 4.5 Rays of hope in Bam

A new chapter was opened in Iran in removing exclusion and restoring rights for persons with disabilities through the adoption of the concept of inclusive learning. This idea was taken from the World Conference on Special Needs Education in Salamanca in 1994, at which representatives from 92 countries, including Iran, and 25 international organizations emphasized the need to maintain standard regulations on equal opportunities for persons with disabilities. In accordance with the spirit of the Salamanca Declaration, the Iranian government has advocated for the accommodation of all children in schools regardless of their intellectual, physical, social, emotional, linguistic and other conditions.

In Iran, the application of an inclusive learning approach is a process of addressing and responding to the diversity of needs of all students by increasing their participation in learning and in changing social attitudes. At present, all schools are in principle open to all children regardless of their physical and mental condition. However, there still remain schools aimed solely at children with mental disabilities. The existence of the latter is to allow for the process of acceptance and change in social attitudes towards inclusive learning, in particular on the part of parents, given that the ultimate decision on the choice of schools for children with mental disabilities rests with parents.

The necessity to accommodate a diversity of needs and requirements was taken fully into account when the International Federation of Red Cross and Red Crescent Societies decided to get involved in the construction of schools in Bam following the devastating earthquake that struck the city on 26 December 2003. The earthquake caused significant damage to the city; the destruction of 85 per cent of the buildings in Bam included 131 schools in the city and surrounding villages. This destruction made the rebuilding of the city's educational infrastructure a priority.

The International Federation's initial plan to construct nine standard schools was modified to include the construction of three schools aimed at children with mental disabilities, five standard schools and one model school complex for inclusive learning. The Arg-e-Bam Model School Complex (BMSC) is the product of the inclusive learning process in Iran. The BMSC was established in cooperation with the International Federation, the Iranian Ministry of Education and the UNESCO Tehran Cluster Office (UTCO), and the partners to the project committed themselves to establishing an Inclusive Learning Friendly Environment (ILFE). The Model School Complexincludes psychological support and health care, facilities for physical education and sport, technical and vocational education, cultural workshops, an amphitheatre, green spaces, and playgrounds. The school aims to embrace those excluded by the education system and to bring them back into an inclusive educational environment. The school can accommodate 400 students in 17 classrooms at pre-primary, primary and lower secondary levels.

The ILFE approach is based on fundamental elements, including an integrated educational approach to all children irrespective of their background, abilities or learning needs, or those affected directly or indirectly by any disaster or disability. There is a strong emphasis on collaboration, participation and

International Federation
of Red Cross and Red Crescent Societies

cooperation among students, teachers, parents and the community. Non-discrimination is an essential component of the ILFE approach. In concrete terms, the inclusive, learning-friendly environment in BMSC entails:

- including all children: girls and boys, those from different backgrounds, abilities, needs and those affected by disaster or disability, and so on.
- being culturally sensitive, celebrating differences, and stimulating learning for ALL children
- involving families, teachers and communities in children's learning
- being gender-fair and non-discriminatory
- promoting opportunities for teachers to learn, and benefit from that learning
- making learning relevant to children's daily lives, and ensuring children take responsibility for their learning
- promoting healthy lifestyles and life skills
- promoting participation, cooperation and collaboration
- keeping safe: protecting ALL children from harm, violence and abuse

The BMSC, which was officially inaugurated on 30 April 2007, has been designed and furnished to meet all the requirements to become a model school for an Inclusive Learning Friendly Environment. This will be a place where the children have the right to learn to their fullest potential, within a safe and welcoming environment. It places the children at the centre of learning and encourages their active participation in learning.

The Iranian education ministry and UTCO are currently working on training teachers and developing the curriculum for inclusive learning. Dr Abdin Salih, the UNESCO representative in Iran, is confident that the BMSC will bring about a breakthrough in promoting the inclusive learning concept in Iran and neighbouring countries. "The International Federation included the Arg-e-Bam Model School Complex in its construction programme of nine schools in Bam, which should be considered as a major contribution to the reconstruction of the Bam educational system," he said. "BMSC will serve as a model school in Iran and the Asia-Pacific region in creating an inclusive, learning-friendly environment by taking a new approach to teaching. The construction of BMSC has been a good example of successful cooperation between the International Federation and UNESCO." ∎

convention at national and international levels should be seen as a priority, as this can be used to uphold national disability legislation.

US disability policy consultant June Kailes argues that persons with disabilities "must be assertive to ensure that our safety needs are included in all emergency planning". They cannot rely on laws, policy-makers, administrations and emergency services to ensure adequate protection and support during disasters. Two important lessons learnt by non-governmental organizations in the United States working with and on behalf of persons with disabilities are: firstly, that they cannot rely on official disaster management agencies to provide all the necessary services; secondly, that disability NGOs and disabled people's organizations need to work together more, with each other as well as with official agencies.

Conclusions and recommendations

There are a number of practical recommendations that will not only do much to overcome the challenges relating to disability in all kinds of disaster contexts, but will also stimulate the kinds of attitudinal and institutional shifts that are ultimately needed to ensure their full inclusion in society and development.

Persons with disabilities need to be actively engaged at all levels (national and international) of disaster and emergency planning, disaster risk reduction, and recovery and reconstruction projects.

DPO capacity in disaster-prone countries needs to be strengthened, and included at all levels of planning, prevention and disaster risk reduction, while protection measures in the immediate aftermath of such crises need to be inclusive of, and accessible to, persons with disabilities.

In addition, support needs to be provided for DPOs in the dissemination of information about the UN convention, and in monitoring and assessing its implementation.

The drafting of IASC guidelines on inclusion would aid the implementation of policies and practices highlighted in this chapter, as well as acting as a lobbying and awareness-raising tool.

At the same time, a commitment should be made to mainstream disability across all humanitarian organizations, in line with Article 32 of the UN convention. Mainstreaming disability requires a multisectoral approach. This means that all areas of humanitarian and emergency intervention – from water and sanitation through to education – should be accessible to all.

Agencies involved in disaster preparedness and response, including UN agencies, NGOs, and the International Federation of Red Cross and Red Crescent Societies, should incorporate training and support using a rights-based approach at field level. This will facilitate better needs assessments at the early stages of planning. DPOs should also be involved in the planning and conducting of such needs assessments.

Principle contributors to this chapter and Box 4.1 and 4.3 were Maria Kett, assistant director of the Leonard Cheshire Centre of Conflict Recovery, University College, London; John Twigg, an independent consultant and Honourary Senior Research Fellow at the Benfield UCL Hazard Research Centre, London. Box 4.2 was contributed by Dr Nafeesur Rahman, director of the National Forum of Organizations Working with the Disabled, Bangladesh. Box 4.4 was contributed by Colonel Kenneth A. Silberman, a blind, trained community emergency response team member in the United States. Box 4.5 was contributed by Mehrnaz Komeyjani, Researcher of the Disabled Schools Organization and Member of the Board of Professors of Tehran Azad University and by Chang Hun Choe, Representative of the International Federation of Red Cross and Red Crescent Societies in Iran.

Note

This chapter uses the terminology referred to in the UN Convention on the Rights of Persons with Disabilities.

Sources and further information

American Red Cross. *Disaster Preparedness for People with Disabilities.* Washington DC: American Red Cross, 1997. Available at www.redcross.org/services/disaster/beprepared/disability.pdf

CSID. *Unveiling Darkness: the Situation Analysis on Disaster and Disability Issues in the Coastal Belt of Bangladesh.* Dhaka: Centre for Services and Information on Disability, 2002. Available at www.csidnetwork.org/research/research01. pdf

Harris, A. and Enfield, S. *Disability, Equality and Human Rights: A Training Manual for Development and Humanitarian Organisations.* Oxford: Oxfam GB in association with Action on Disability and Development, 2003.

Inter-Agency Standing Committee. *Protecting Persons Affected by Natural Disasters: IASC Operational Guidelines on Human Rights and Natural Disasters.* Washington DC: Brookings-Bern Project on Internal Displacement, 2006. Available at www.humanitarianinfo.org/iasc/content/news/newsdetails.asp?newsid=43&publish=0

Inter-Agency Standing Committee. *IASC Guidelines on Mental Health and Psychosocial Support in Emergency Settings.* Geneva: IASC, 2007. Available at www.humanitarianinfo.org/iasc/content/products/docs/IASC%20MHPSS%20guidelines%20Feb%2025%202007.pdf

International Disability Rights Monitor. *Disability and Early Tsunami Relief Efforts in India, Indonesia and Thailand.* Chicago: International Disability Network/Center for International Rehabilitation, 2005. Available at www.ideanet.org/cir/uploads/File/TsunamiReport.pdf

Kailes, J.I. *Emergency Evacuation Preparedness: Taking Responsibiliy for Your Safety, A Guide for People with Disabilities and Other Activity Limitations.* Pomona: Center for Disability Issues and the Health Professions, 2002. Available at www.cdihp.org/evacuation/emergency_evacuation.pdf

Kett, M. 'Conflict Recovery' in Barron, T. and Amerena, P. (eds.), *Disability and Inclusive Development.* London: Leonard Cheshire International, 2007, pp. 155–186.

Kett, M., Stubbs S. and Yeo, R. *Disability in Conflict and Emergency Situations: Focus on Tsunami-affected Areas.* Woking: International Disability and Development Consortium, 2005. Available at www.iddc.org.uk/dis_dev/key_issues/Final_report.doc

National Council on Disability. *Saving Lives: Including People with Disabilities in Emergency Planning.* Washington DC: National Council on Disability, 2005. Available at www.ncd.gov/newsroom/publications/2005/pdf/saving_lives.pdf

National Organization on Disability. *Guide on the special needs of people with disabilities for emergency managers, planners and responders.* Washington DC: National Organization on Disability, 2005. Available at www.nod.org/resources/PDFs/epiguide2005.pdf

National Organization on Disability. *Report on Special Needs Assessment for Katrina Evacuees (SNAKE) Project.* Washington DC: National Organization on Disability, 2006. Available at www.nod.org/Resources/PDFs/katrina_snake_report.pdf

Parr. A. 'Disasters and disabled persons: an examination of the safety needs of a neglected minority' in *Disasters*, 11(2) pp. 148–159, 1987.

Parr, A. 'Disasters and Human Rights of Persons with Disabilities: A Case for an Ethical Disaster Mitigation Policy' in *Australian Journal of Emergency Management*, 12(4) pp. 2–5, 1997–1998.

The Review of Disability Studies 2(3), 2006 (special issue on Disaster and Disability).

Sullivan, H. and Häkkinen, M. *Disaster Preparedness for Vulnerable Populations: Determining Effective Strategies for Communicating Risk, Warning, and Response.* Paper presented at the Third Annual Magrann Research Conference, Rutgers University, 2006. Available at http://geography.rutgers.edu/events/magrann_conference/2006/_papers/sullivan.pdf

Tierney, K.J., Petak, W.J. and Hahn, H. *Disabled Persons and Earthquake Hazards.* Boulder: University of Colorado Institute of Behavioural Science, Programme on Environment and Behaviour, Monograph No. 46, 1988.

Wisner, B. 'Disability and Disaster: Victimhood and Agency in Earthquake Risk Reduction' in Rodrigue C. and Rovai E. (eds.), *Earthquakes.* London: Routledge, in press. Draft chapter (2002). Available at www.radixonline.org/disability2.html

World Bank. *Report of the Online Forum on Disabled and Other Vulnerable People in Natural Disasters.* Washington DC: World Bank Disability and Development Team, 2006. Available at http://siteresources.worldbank.org/DISABILITY/Resources/News---Events/463933–1166477763817/EdisNatDisas.doc

Yeo, R. and Moore, K. 'Including Disabled People in Poverty Reduction Work: "Nothing About Us, Without Us"' in *World Development*, 31(3) pp. 571–590, 2003.

International Federation
of Red Cross and Red Crescent Societies

Web sites

Benfield UCL Hazard Research Centre
www.benfieldhrc.org/disaster_studies/disability&disasters/d&d_index.htm
Disability Resources, Disaster Preparedness for People with Disabilities
www.disabilityresources.org/DISASTER.html
Handicap International **www.handicap-international.org/**
International Disability and Development Consortium **www.iddc.org.uk**
Leonard Cheshire International **www.lcint.webbler.co.uk**
UN Convention on the Rights of Persons with Disabilities
www.un.org/disabilities/convention/facts.shtml
World Bank, Disability **www.worldbank.org/disability**
World Programme of Action Concerning Disabled Persons
www.un.org/esa/socdev/enable/diswpa01.htm

CHAPTER 4

CHAPTER 5

The urgency of equality: ending discrimination against women and its consequences in emergency situations

In the past decade, many instances of violations of women's human rights in emergency situations have been documented by the media, public institutions, non-governmental organizations (NGOs), human rights bodies and humanitarian aid agencies. In most cases, it has been found that the manifestations of violence that women and girls face in emergency situations are severe, and that these violations follow gender discrimination patterns that are widespread. This is why, in recent years, there seems to be a general consensus on the need to strengthen efforts to prevent and address adequately gender-based violence in emergency situations. To name but a few, some of the intergovernmental bodies and agencies that have looked at this issue include the World Bank, the International Labour Organization (ILO), the United Nations Commission on the Status of Women (CSW) and the Pan American Health Organization (PAHO). As a result, a significant number of valuable policy documents, guidelines and resources focusing on the need to undertake emergency efforts from a gender perspective are now available. At the same time, while these advances must be recognized, it is also timely to reflect on the need to develop a consistent understanding of discrimination against women in the context of conflict, natural disasters and other humanitarian emergencies.

Discrimination against women in disaster settings is a serious and life-threatening human rights issue requiring special attention in all phases of humanitarian intervention. Much can be gained by incorporating a better analysis of discrimination against women in efforts being undertaken on the ground. For this to be possible, it is necessary to consider the ways in which discrimination against women is being canvassed, reconceptualized and articulated in accordance with international human rights standards. It is also important to explore better means of implementing the recommendations that have been made to ensure the respect, protection, promotion and fulfilment of women's human rights in emergency situations.

While this chapter does not attempt to provide an exhaustive analysis of discrimination against women, it aims to explore some of the most pressing issues that need to be discussed within the context of humanitarian relief efforts. In order to be

Photo opposite page:
Israt Jahan is a student and volunteer trainer for the community disaster preparedness committee at the Khajura cyclone centre in Kalapara, Bangladesh.

© Shehab Uddin/Drik/
British Red Cross

able to present some key elements for the adequate analysis of gender-based discrimination in emergency situations, the chapter focuses on violence against women in natural disasters. Despite the fact that this is not a new problem, many of these issues gained increased attention in the aftermath of the Indian Ocean tsunami and Hurricane Katrina. Even though it is possible to draw parallels between discrimination against women in natural disasters, armed conflict and displacement, they are not the same. In comparison, the gendered consequences of natural disasters have received much less attention, while action lags behind the work being done in conflict settings.

The importance of understanding concepts as reality

International human rights standards can be used as a means to develop conceptual clarity around the steps that need to be taken in order to achieve gender equality and to eliminate discrimination against women and girls. From the outset, it is important to recall that according to Article 1 of the Universal Declaration of Human Rights, human rights are inherent to every human being because we are all "born free and equal in dignity and rights". In this respect, and in accordance with some of the most important human rights principles, all forms of disadvantage and inequality are social constructions that need to be progressively exposed, opposed, addressed and eliminated. The idea that follows on from this is that the elimination of discrimination against women is one of the major stepping stones to the actual realization of human rights for all. Sadly, since discrimination against women is still prevalent, gender equality could be referred to as a promise that, to varying degrees, states have not been able to keep.

Given that every marginalized and disadvantaged group of individuals that is affected in an emergency situation includes women and girls, gender equality needs to be seen as a cross-cutting issue. The *Sphere Humanitarian Charter and Minimum Standards in Disaster Response* builds on this point by adding that: "Humanitarian aims of proportionality and impartiality mean that attention must be paid to achieving fairness between women and men and ensuring equality of outcome." This is an important point because equal outcomes for men and women should be the basis of gender equality. This model of equality is commonly referred to as 'substantive equality' and is usually considered a starting point for understanding discrimination against women.

The United Nations Convention on the Elimination of All Forms of Discrimination against Women (CEDAW) provides a framework for the analysis of substantive equality and non-discrimination from a gender perspective. One of the advantages of using the convention is that it is an international treaty that creates legally binding obligations for the 185 states that have agreed to be bound by it. In addition, the convention is a tool that can be used in the process of developing a framework to address discrimination against women in the context of natural disasters. As already established by the CEDAW Committee in its General Recommendation Number 25:

> …the Convention requires that women be given an equal start and that they be empowered by an enabling environment to achieve equality of results. It is not enough to guarantee women treatment that is identical to that of men. Rather, biological as well as socially constructed differences between women and men must be taken into account. Under certain circumstances, non-identical treatment of women and men will be required in order to address such differences. Pursuit of the goal of substantive equality also calls for an effective strategy aimed at overcoming under-representation of women and a redistribution of resources and power between men and women.

While, in theory, it is accepted that the principle of gender equality needs to inform efforts undertaken in emergency situations, in practice there are challenges that need to be overcome. In this respect, the principle of substantive equality contained in the convention needs to be methodically applied in the context of natural disasters in order to ensure equal results and outcomes for men and women. Since gender equality is achieved through the elimination of all forms of discrimination against women, the next section explores these dimensions in greater detail.

Discrimination against women: why is it urgent to eliminate it?

Discrimination against women often correlates to the subordinate role assigned to women in society. Most international human rights bodies have established that gender assumptions and expectations made on the basis of the idea of the inferiority of women often impair the recognition, enjoyment and exercise of women's rights. It is, therefore, important to understand how women's human rights violations are caused by inequality, disadvantage and marginalization resulting from discrimination on the grounds of sex and gender. Since CEDAW is the only international human rights treaty that defines and specifically addresses discrimination against women, when trying to clarify the meaning of the concept it is important to refer to Article 1 (see Figure 5.1). It reads:

> For the purposes of the present Convention, the term "discrimination against women" shall mean any distinction, exclusion or restriction made on the basis of sex which has the effect or purpose of impairing or nullifying the recognition, enjoyment or exercise by women, irrespective of their marital status, on a basis of equality of men and women, of human rights and

fundamental freedoms in the political, economic, social, cultural, civil or any other field.

It is also useful to recognize that discrimination against women has been progressively interpreted through the general recommendations and concluding observations by the CEDAW Committee and by other international human rights treaty bodies. Nevertheless, in all instances, some of the most important aspects to bear in mind when analysing discrimination against women are:

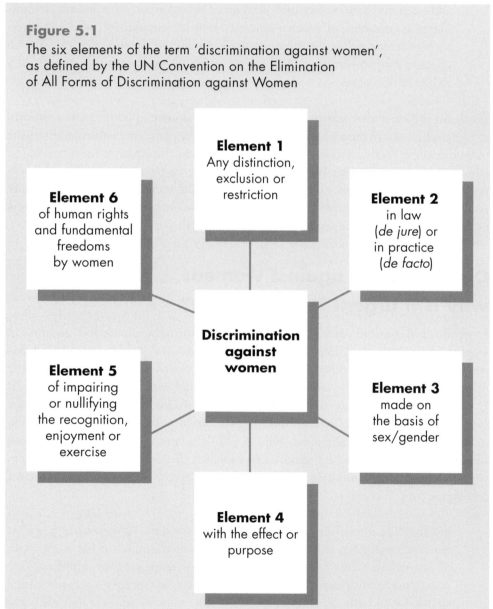

Figure 5.1
The six elements of the term 'discrimination against women', as defined by the UN Convention on the Elimination of All Forms of Discrimination against Women

Element 1
Any distinction, exclusion or restriction

Element 2
in law (*de jure*) or in practice (*de facto*)

Element 6
of human rights and fundamental freedoms by women

Discrimination against women

Element 3
made on the basis of sex/gender

Element 5
of impairing or nullifying the recognition, enjoyment or exercise

Element 4
with the effect or purpose

International Federation
of Red Cross and Red Crescent Societies

- Discrimination against women is an outcome and, as such, it does not matter whether it is direct or indirect.
  a. According to General Comment Number 16 of the United Nations Committee on Economic, Social and Cultural Rights (CESCR), direct discrimination occurs "when a difference in treatment relies directly and explicitly on distinctions based exclusively on sex and characteristics of men or of women, which cannot be justified objectively". While in most cases direct discrimination against women is intentional, it can often trigger additional negative effects that were unforeseen and which, therefore, are unintended. That is why it is important to consider the ongoing effects of policies, laws and programmes that aim to impair or nullify the enjoyment of women's rights. Discrimination triggers human rights violations that are both intended and unintended.
  b. General Comment Number 16 states that indirect discrimination occurs "when a law, policy or programme does not appear to be discriminatory… but has a discriminatory effect when implemented". For example, in country X, a public housing programme aimed at helping those affected by a flood requires all applicants to have completed primary school. Since in country X girls were not allowed to go to school until recently, none of the women affected by the flood is eligible to apply. While the housing programme does not directly exclude women from applying, it clearly affects them negatively.
  c. Finally, progressive steps towards the elimination of discrimination against women and the achievement of the practical (de facto) and legal (de jure) aspects of gender equality must be addressed holistically.
- Discrimination against women is a human rights violation that does not distinguish between acts that are committed in the private or in the public spheres. Consequently, the definition of discrimination applies to acts or decisions by the state (public officials, government representatives, etc.) as well as non-state actors (humanitarian aid agencies, NGOs, religious organizations, families, etc.).
- In emergency situations, rescue, relief and recovery initiatives should be undertaken in ways that avoid distinctions, exclusions and restrictions that may result in discrimination against women. Gender equality is an absolute obligation of state and non-state actors and, as such, it should be considered a priority. In all stages of humanitarian relief, the elimination of discrimination should be considered urgent and necessary.
- It is also important to note that, in accordance with international human rights treaties, it is ultimately the obligation of the state to respect, protect and fulfil women's human rights. This means that, ideally, the state is responsible for overseeing plans to ensure that violence against women and other manifestations of discrimination are prevented and addressed before, during and after a natural disaster.

Intersectionality: acknowledging the ongoing effects of multiple forms of discrimination

According to the report of the UN expert group meeting on *Environmental management and the mitigation of natural disasters: a gender perspective*, which took place in Ankara in 2001, women's responses to routine or catastrophic disaster reflect "their status, role and position in society". Thus, women and girls that belong to marginalized sectors or groups in society become more vulnerable to discrimination in emergency situations. For this reason, a better analysis of discrimination against women can be helpful in the process of identifying groups of women that are particularly vulnerable to discrimination and that are at risk of violence in emergency situations.

As already outlined by feminist scholars and activists, there are groups of women that face multiple barriers to the enjoyment of their human rights and to the achievement of substantive equality. These barriers are a result of the intersection of gender discrimination and discrimination based on other grounds such as race, ethnicity, age, sexual orientation, economic status, and disability. Consequently, intersectional discrimination multiplies vulnerabilities and increases the risks that some women face in natural disasters. Overall, intersectional discrimination compounds the negative effects of inequality and disadvantage. At a practical level, the UN expert group meeting acknowledged that there are many casualties among women during disasters because the kind of early warnings issued do not take into account their literacy, mobility, minority status, etc. In other words, vital information on early warnings shared on television does not often reach women that are already disadvantaged because they live in a remote area and only speak a minority language. A better understanding of intersectional discrimination may help to avoid these problems in the future (see Box 5.1).

At another level, economic, civil, cultural, political and social fields are often the main sites of discrimination against women. In this respect, the principles of interdependence and the indivisibility of human rights should also inform the framework for developing components of relief work. When discrimination against women is not properly addressed, the ongoing effects of violations ultimately trump the enjoyment and exercise of women's rights in every field. As already expressed by the expert group meeting, the lack of comprehensive strategies encompassing all the sites of discrimination against women in the context of natural disaster can exacerbate gender inequality and negatively affect discriminated groups of women:

> The economic and social rights are violated in disaster processes if mitigation, relief, and reconstruction policies do not benefit women and men equally. The right to adequate health care is violated when relief efforts do not meet the needs of specific physical and mental health needs of women throughout the life cycle, in particular when trauma has occurred. The right to security of

International Federation
of Red Cross and Red Crescent Societies

Box 5.1 HIV or silent disaster: the response of the International Federation in Cameroon

HIV is fast becoming the most serious disaster facing the world and Africa is the worst-affected continent, with thousands of people dying every day. If nothing is done, Africa will lose most of its sons and daughters, and this will seriously jeopardize its development.

Several organizations have joined forces with governments to respond to HIV and, as part of this alliance, the Cameroon Red Cross Society, with the support of the International Federation's Central Africa Sub-Regional Office, has set up the *Filles Libres* project. This pilot project, which derives its name from the term for young female sex workers, *filles libres*, provides psychosocial and medical support to about 2,000 sex workers. One of the most important aspects of the project is the provision of therapeutic support to 250 *filles libres* in Cameroon's capital, Yaoundé. The project, which is currently being implemented in Douala, the economic capital, will soon be extended to other towns across the country.

The *Filles Libres* project is also supported by the *Association des Filles Dynamiques* in Douala, a local association composed of *filles libres* which has been facilitating regular contact with over 1,000 young women. Its members, who have been trained in peer education by the Cameroon Red Cross Society, organize educational talks and conduct sensitization campaigns and interpersonal communication. The National Society also runs theatre groups in Yaoundé and Douala, whose role is to reinforce educational talks.

Women in Cameroon suffer serious health and psychological problems as a result of gender-based violence. Women suffering from violence are afraid to talk about their experience because of society's reaction. Even when they do talk, excuses are found to justify what men did to them. This fear prevents them from negotiating their own sexuality; they cannot even impose the use of condoms on their sexual partners, their aim being to get through the day without being brutalized.

Women are regularly subjected to forced sexual intercourse which exposes them to the risk of HIV. The Cameroon Red Cross Society has been encouraging victims of gender-based violence to refer immediately to the nearest health centre, even when they are not willing to denounce the perpetrator of the violence. This could help prevent sexually transmitted diseases (STIs) and HIV infection, as well as unwanted pregnancies.

The Henry Dunant Health and Social Welfare Centre is a product of the *Filles Libres* project. The centre, which is open to the public, welcomes targeted young women and guarantees them confidentiality, offering special rates for tests and treatment. With the opening of the centre, *filles libres* can now be screened for STIs, including HIV, without fear of being exposed by health workers in the event that they test positive.

People in Cameroon are afraid of AIDS and there is much ignorance about the subject, despite various information, education and communication campaigns. The knowledge or suspicion that someone is HIV-positive often provokes feelings of panic and hostility towards that person, who is made to feel ashamed and isolated. People believe this attitude will prevent them from having any contact with an HIV-positive person, which, according to them, means getting infected.

Because of discrimination, people living with HIV (PLHIV) are stigmatized and are virtually treated as outcasts due to their status. By targeting *filles libres* within the framework of this project, the Cameroon Red Cross Society is encouraging people to view this group as victims who need assistance.

Choosing sex workers as a target group was a courageous decision, as the most commonly known target groups included truck drivers, soldiers and youths. Why, then, did the Cameroon Red Cross Society decide to focus on sex workers? This was mainly because of their high level of vulnerability. By working with *filles libres* and PLHIV, the Cameroon Red Cross Society is sending a strong message to other actors in the fight against the AIDS pandemic. The society believes it takes more than just words to respond effectively to HIV: there is a need for action to include all targeted groups in the fight in order to achieve a greater impact.

Reinsertion is another important feature of the project in the sense that one of the main causes of sex work is poverty. During the ongoing pilot phase of the project in Yaoundé and Douala, some *filles libres* were trained in female entrepreneurship, while others have already benefited from the funding of income-generating activities. The aim is to offer *filles libres* an alternative to sex work, namely, another livelihood so they have the option to stop sex work. At the same time, the HIV-prevention programme empowers sex workers to protect their lives and that of their clients, making them front-line, HIV-prevention educators.

There is still a long way to go, but the project has already created a climate of hope which is progressively dispelling fears and eliminating discriminatory attitudes. In other towns where the project will be copied, existing public and private medical centres will be identified to ensure medical and psychosocial support to *filles libres*. The building of the Henry Dunant centre can be considered a success, but the greatest achievement of the project lies in its ownership by the *filles libres* themselves, as they are currently involved in all the activities of the project. ∎

persons is violated when women and girls are victims of sexual and other forms of violence while in relief camps or temporary housing. Civil and political rights are denied if women cannot act autonomously and participate fully at all decision-making levels in matters regarding mitigation and recovery.

Ultimate manifestations of discrimination: violence against women and other women's human rights violations resulting from natural disasters

For gender inequality and discrimination against women to be addressed in emergency situations, it is necessary to challenge the myth that violence against women is inevitable. This section aims to illustrate how discrimination against women has the effect of leaving some groups of women vulnerable to human rights violations and at risk of sexual violence in emergency situations. In order to illustrate the extent of discrimination against women in emergency situations, various examples of violence against women in natural disaster settings are briefly described. From the

✚C International Federation of Red Cross and Red Crescent Societies

outset, however, it is also necessary to emphasize that while disasters such as the Indian Ocean tsunami are natural phenomena, its effects are not. In addition, this section touches on the gaps that exist as a result of a lack of a consistent approach to address gender-based discrimination in the context of humanitarian and relief efforts.

Risks faced by women in emergency situations

In most circumstances, humanitarian actors do not have access to the affected populations in the crisis phase of a natural disaster. Even if relief and rescue efforts are mobilized quickly, gaining physical access may take some time. It is during this acute crisis phase, when communities are scrambling to survive or seeking refuge in temporary, and often unplanned, shelters, that women and girls may be most vulnerable and at risk of violence. For example, in her article on sexualized violence and the tsunami, Claudia Felten-Biermann refers to reports by *medica mondiale*, the Asia Pacific Forum on Women, Law and Development (APWLD) and others which established that there were many instances of women being raped by rescuers and strangers who took advantage of the lawlessness and chaos immediately following the disaster. Interestingly, the Oxfam briefing note on gender and the tsunami also mentioned that years of conflict in the north-east of Sri Lanka and in Aceh "left a legacy of human rights abuses and a history of sexual and other violence against women" which exacerbated risks of violence in overcrowded camps.

At the peak of a crisis resulting from a natural disaster, law and order breaks down, families are separated, community and social supports and formal and informal means of protection fall apart. At the same time, the level of distress, insecurity and desperation among individuals often triggers the social consequences of natural disaster, which are frequently reflected by waves of violence. For these reasons, during the relief phase women and girls directly affected by these disasters are at greater risk of being subjected to violence.

There is general agreement among experts that women and girls are at higher risk of sexual violence, sexual exploitation and abuse, trafficking and domestic violence in disasters. As mentioned earlier, these manifestations of discrimination against women result in grave and systematic violations of women's human rights. Furthermore, as a result of intersectional discrimination, poor, single, elderly women, adolescent girls, girl children and women with disabilities are often at greatest risk because they have fewer personal, family, economic and educational resources from which to draw protection, assistance and support.

Another concern is that data on gender-based violence and discrimination against women is not routinely compiled and made public (the notable exception to this is the work of the Gender and Disaster Network). Research by the International Medical Corps (IMC) into post-Katrina health and security issues is the first such study and provides valuable new information for understanding violence against women in the aftermath of disasters (see Box 5.2).

Research also suggests that different groups of women are likely to experience natural disasters and cope with the consequences in diverse ways. For example, women that are part of the formal workforce and earn a steady income are more likely to find ways of borrowing money to buy or rent housing, etc. It should also be stressed that the accumulated losses of recurrent small- to medium-scale disasters often make it harder for women affected by discrimination to advance towards equality. Since such losses are often significant, these situations should be addressed from a rights-based approach that takes into account the continuing effects of discrimination and that incorporates a sustainable development model.

A woman and children at the Lologo transit camp for refugees and internally displaced people in Juba, southern Sudan. Women and children in camps may face discrimination, abuse and even violence from fellow residents.

© Tomas Bertelsen/ Danish Red Cross

International Federation
of Red Cross and Red Crescent Societies

Box 5.2 Violence against women soars in post-Katrina trailer parks

The 2005 hurricane season devastated the US Gulf Coast and forced over 3.2 million people from their homes. Of these internally displaced people (IDPs), some 99,000 relocated to temporary trailer camps in Louisiana and Mississippi, according to the Federal Emergency Management Agency (FEMA).

In order to inform recovery efforts, the International Medical Corps (IMC), a US-based NGO, conducted a survey in 2006 (using systematic random sampling) which is representative of all those still living in trailer camps.

The survey found alarmingly high rates of gender-based violence following the disaster compared with baseline rates provided by the US Department of Justice. Some 5.9 rapes were documented per day per 100,000 women following displacement. This equates to 527 rapes among the 32,841 women displaced to trailer parks. This rape rate is 53.6 times higher than the highest baseline state rate (0.11 per day per 100,000 women in Mississippi in 2004).

The above data refer to 'non-perpetrator specific' rape. Equally disturbing were the high rates of violence perpetrated by intimate partners or spouses. Intimate partner rape was 16 times higher than the US yearly rate. In the 274 days following the disaster, the rate of women experiencing beatings by a spouse was 3.2 per cent – more than triple the US yearly rate.

High rates of respondents in this study claimed they knew someone who had experienced intimate partner violence, which suggests that intimate partner violence in this population was under-reported, despite the extraordinarily elevated rates.

Many factors increase the risk of gender-based violence during disasters, including educational level, financial autonomy, the level of empowerment, social support, alcohol and drug abuse, employment status and cohabitation or marital status.

The story of Hannah (not her real name) makes this clear. She reported beginning a relationship with a man in a shelter following the storm. After only a month of dating, they got married. The following month, Hannah found out her new husband was still married to another woman, making their new marriage void.

Despite Hannah's desire to leave, she was trapped financially: they had received a travel trailer as a couple and all their ongoing benefits were being provided in his name. With no family in the area, she was completely reliant on him for food and shelter – even while trying to reach the government for separate assistance. During this time, Hannah's new husband forced her to have sex on several occasions. She was only able to escape the situation when she was provided with a new trailer – located directly across the road from her 'husband'.

Hannah's situation exemplifies many of the root causes that increase gender-based violence following disaster. The sudden destruction of lifestyles, livelihoods and community ties left survivors physically, emotionally and financially vulnerable. Stressed relationships became violent. A lack of security meant perpetrators could strike with impunity.

Data from the survey substantiate these causes:

- Suicides were five times the states' baseline rate – attempted suicides were 79 times the baseline rate.
- Fourteen per cent of respondents had increased substance abuse since displacement.

- Forty-nine per cent of respondents did not feel safe walking around their trailer park at night.

In Gulf Coast IDP camps, efforts to curb gender-based violence are limited to inadequate security and understaffed social service providers. Only half of all IDP camps had any kind of security. Even so, security does nothing to prevent intimate partner violence, which is frequently perpetrated in the privacy of the home.

Gender-based violence can be prevented, but it requires initiatives across many sectors.

Collaboration between organizations engaged in law enforcement, legal aid, health care, public health, education, social services and economic development are needed to ensure integrated prevention and response.

Sexual violence in humanitarian emergencies is a human rights issue, primarily affecting women and girls, with serious health consequences. Programming to meet their needs should follow well-developed, international models of rights-based care. ■

It is also important to mention that the Hyogo Framework for Action adopted by the 2005 World Conference on Disaster Reduction specifically addresses the gender perspective of disaster management. However, it is essential to highlight that one of the main priorities agreed is to "reduce the underlying risk factors" for vulnerable groups. In this respect, the elimination of discrimination against women should be an integral part of all strategies undertaken in the present and in the future.

Barriers faced by women in emergency situations

As discussed in the previous sections, it is important to acknowledge that some women will be more vulnerable to discrimination in emergency situations and at risk of sexual violence. While it is accepted that gender-based violence prevents many women from benefiting equally from relief, rescue and recovery efforts, at a more practical level a more sophisticated understanding of intersectional discrimination is lacking. One of the benefits of understanding intersectional discrimination is that it is likely to help identify groups of women most at risk of bearing the brunt of discrimination in emergency situations.

Certain conditions and situations that trigger discrimination on multiple grounds are exacerbated in natural disasters and lead to more extreme manifestations of violence against women. Nevertheless, efforts to predefine target groups for relief and rescue should take into account the fact that there are, as described in the UNHCR *Executive committee conclusion on women and girls at risk*, a range of factors that may put women and girls at risk of further violations of their rights. At another level, the report continues, "identification and analysis of the presence and severity of these different factors help determine which women and girls are at heightened risk and enable targeted responses to be devised and implemented".

International Federation
of Red Cross and Red Crescent Societies

To illustrate this point, information on those made homeless by Hurricane Mitch in Honduras shows that 51 per cent were women. In addition, these women were on mainly low incomes, while 16 per cent of women in shelters declared they were pregnant. Similarly, following the Indian Ocean tsunami, some authors such as Claudia Felten-Biermann and some NGOs have stressed that there is evidence to show that, overall, the disaster had a greater negative effect on women. For example, according to some reports, many young girls and women in Sri Lanka, Aceh and India were forced to marry 'tsunami widowers' because their families were no longer able to provide for them. Other reports, for instance the Oxfam briefing, note that in some areas the ratio between female and male deaths was three to one and that the loss of property, mobility, work and family members has aggravated the situation of many women who were already considered to be below the poverty line.

Since it is clear that most of these women were experiencing varying levels of discrimination and did not enjoy all their human rights before the natural disaster, women that were subjected to violence in the emergency are more likely to continue to be negatively affected by the ongoing effects of these violations. In addition, violence against women and other forms of discrimination may result in 'extended risk' for some women. Yet these barriers to equality and the advancement of women are not always acknowledged in emergency situations. Power imbalance, the abuse of power by some and the exclusion of women in planning and implementing programmes and services contribute to ongoing manifestations of discrimination (see Box 5.3). Overcrowded camps and shelters and inadequate humanitarian relief also contribute to extending the risks of sexual violence for women and children.

Documenting and researching gender-based violence is extremely sensitive and can be dangerous, even life-threatening, to interviewees and participants (generally these are community members, including survivors of violence against women), communities and those involved in collecting the information. The ethical and safety issues are difficult to manage in emergency settings, particularly in the early phases. At the same time, it is also important to note that the principles of equality and non-discrimination are not always included as part of an overarching framework for understanding and documenting violence against women in emergency situations.

Despite these challenges, experiences described in *Gender and Natural Disasters*, a PAHO factsheet, show that women's capacity to respond to disasters can fast-track equality by having the effect of changing society's perceptions about women's capabilities. For example, in the aftermath of Hurricane Mitch, women in Guatemala and Honduras took an active role in "building houses, digging wells and ditches, hauling water and building shelters". Similarly, when reflecting on the lessons learnt from earthquakes in Turkey, a participant at the UN expert group meeting mentioned earlier stated that "disaster creates socially acceptable and legitimate reasons for women to get into the public arena". In addition, a paper by Lynn Orstad refers to

CHAPTER 5

Box 5.3 The role of power

Discrimination is more than just distinction or differentiation; it is action based on prejudice resulting in the unfair treatment of others. At the core of this discriminatory action lies the misuse of power. Discrimination can occur, continue and devastate when power is abused.

Power dynamics in disaster settings are very complex. Existing power relationships between women and men, adults and children, the young and the elderly, persons with disabilities and those without, and different political, religious and ethnic groups, all become intensified during disasters. Power equations, like those between displaced populations and the native community, develop. People who had power may lose it or those with little power may see it increased: resentment over power can develop, fester, and lead to violence.

Humanitarian workers have heightened power in disasters; they have money, resources, information, networks, emblems and authority. They come into contact with people in difficult and desperate situations, who are feeling powerless, whose lives have been ripped apart. Aid workers and organizations make decisions about who is vulnerable, who needs protection, who receives aid and about the actual process of working with individuals and communities. The risk of discrimination is high.

The success of disaster operations and the prevention of discrimination may depend on the way in which power is exercised. An awareness of the power dynamic is crucial to understanding how it can be used effectively, or misused, in interactions with vulnerable people.

Types of power
There are several types of power, including:

- **Relationship power**. A person with greater relationship power has power because of their determined standing within the social system. For example, adult-child, aid worker-beneficiary.
- **Organizational power**. Different positions within organizations bestow specific authority, rights and privileges as determined by job descriptions.
- **Position power**. A person with position power has the capacity to influence and obtain respect, resources and support from others.
- **Expert power** is based on the perception of a person's expertise, skills and knowledge.
- **Information power** is based on a person's possession of or access to valuable information.
- **Connection power** is determined by a person's influential connections and relationships within or outside an organization.
- **Network power** is derived from membership of formal or informal networks.
- **Personality power** is based on gender, ethnic identity, age, physical appearance and personal presence.
- **Resource power**. A person with resource power has the ability to access human, financial, technical and/or educational resources.
- **Reward power** is based on a person's ability to give or to withhold rewards, benefits and services.

Power questions
Every humanitarian aid worker has power. With power comes a responsibility to use the power to advance the safety, dignity and sta-

tus of vulnerable people. The questions we must ask ourselves are:

- Where does my power come from?
- How do I use my power in a responsible way?
- What are the power dynamics within the disaster setting?
- What kind of power do vulnerable people, like children, have in the disaster setting?
- How might my power be misused?
- In what situations am I at risk of misusing my power?
- How do I respond when I know that power is being misused?
- How do I maintain a power balance with beneficiaries?

Understanding power is critical to preventing discrimination and violence. Power will either be used positively or negatively; it does not stand neutral. ■

studies showing that women perform well in disasters when they are collectively organized and even better when they have received prior training to adequately respond to situations that may emerge on the ground (for example, an increase in domestic violence in the aftermath of a natural disaster).

Gaps identified by those working with women in emergency situations

Some of the gaps relating to efforts aimed at assisting women in emergency situations identified by relief workers, researchers and other experts working on the ground include:

- **Inadequate women's reproductive health services**. While basic health needs are often taken into account in emergency situations, it is essential for obstetric care and specialized care services to be made available to pregnant women and women that have been affected by violence.
- **Inadequate design and location of shelters**. Reports and studies focusing on instances of violence against women in shelters set up in the aftermath of Hurricane Katrina and the Indian Ocean tsunami (particularly in Sri Lanka and Aceh) stress the need to consider the personal security and protection of women and girls when setting up such shelters. Special measures should be adopted in shelters that are overcrowded, where communal sleeping and living spaces are shared by all. As a starting point, the guidelines for the protection of refugee and internally displaced women already promoted by UNHCR should be considered in emergencies resulting from natural disasters.
- **Invisibility of women's experiences in natural disasters**. Although it is widely accepted that women face violence and other forms of discrimination in emergency situations, statistics and data gathered during and after natural disasters rarely reflect these problems. For instance, when trying to analyse the interventions taken in response to Hurricane Mitch, a study conducted by the

Economic Commission for Latin America and the Caribbean (ECLAC) found that "there are not many statistics on the differentiated effects on the basis of gender". The report recalls how "the majority of the agencies that were interviewed indicated that they do not consider gender explicitly and that they do not disaggregate their data according to sex or analyse their results from a gender perspective".

Sadly, these problems are also common all over the world and that is why, even today, data collection, disaggregation and analysis from a gender perspective need to improve. Furthermore, the lack of appropriate data also veils the scale and extent of discrimination against women. This, in turn, makes it very difficult to address intersectional discrimination at a practical level because the degree of inclusion of women depends on the groups of women considered to be part of the target groups. Without an understanding of discrimination in the context of data-gathering and analysis, the specific needs of women and girls in situations of emergency and in the context of natural disaster will not be adequately addressed in the long term (see Box 5.4).

In an effort to address some of these problems, UNHCR began piloting a new and improved system for confidential data collection and analysis of gender-based violence in refugee settings in 2006 which could eventually be used in natural disasters. UNHCR and its partners in other UN agencies and international non-governmental organizations (INGOs) are currently exploring how best to use and streamline such a system, while at the same time ensuring ethical and safe practices.

Another problem is that the links between gender equality and non-discrimination are rarely included as part of the framework and methodologies for analysis in emergency situations. As a result, gaps in efforts aimed at improving the situation of women could be addressed through better coordination and cooperation among all players involved in emergency relief efforts. All entities and individuals intervening in emergency situations resulting from natural disasters should be committed to eliminating discrimination against women and addressing violence against them.

Recommendations for a unified approach: breaking the cycle of discrimination and ending violence against women in emergency situations

In 2005, the Inter-Agency Standing Committee (IASC) published its *Guidelines for Gender-based Violence Interventions in Humanitarian Settings*. These guidelines are designed for use in the early stages of any emergency, including disasters. The purpose of the guidelines is to enable humanitarian actors and communities to rapidly plan, establish and coordinate a set of minimum, multi-sectoral interventions to prevent

International Federation
of Red Cross and Red Crescent Societies

and respond to sexual violence during the early phase of an emergency, and to expand interventions as the situation becomes more stable. The interventions in the guidelines are a set of good practices from conflict and disaster settings worldwide. The guidelines put forth a rights-based approach, emphasizing issues of gender, the needs of women and girls in emergencies and their involvement in designing and implementing programmes and services. In order to strengthen this initiative, the IASC recently published the *Gender Handbook in Humanitarian Action*. The handbook, which complements the guidelines mentioned above, provides a range of concrete strategies for promoting gender equality.

In this connection, other efforts to develop frameworks to address the situation of women in emergency situations include the UNHCR *Executive committee conclusion on women and girls at risk*, and the recommendations of the UN expert group meeting on *Environmental management and the mitigation of natural disasters: a gender perspective*. However, although these documents are very comprehensive, this section sets out recommendations that specifically address the need to develop conceptual clarity and consistent approaches to deal with the issue of discrimination against women in emergency situations.

Substantive equality needs to become a central element in the prevention of gender-based violence and, for that to be possible, all forms of discrimination against women need to be recognized. While relief and rescue initiatives often consider immediate effects – without adequately including the discrimination dimension – the urgency for gender equality is often reduced in the process of reconstruction. It is also important to mention that the analysis and recommendations in this section are meant to supplement the work already undertaken by practitioners, experts, aid organizations and other institutions.

The following recommendations are organized according to the phases of humanitarian and development work undertaken in situations of emergency resulting from natural disasters.

CHAPTER 5

Box 5.4 In the margins

Children – those under 18 years of age – represent the single largest demographic group in most disasters. Because of their size, age, knowledge, reasoning and level of dependency, they are the most vulnerable. Despite international legal protection under the United Nations Convention on the Rights of the Child, which also covers non-discrimination, children experience discrimination and violence before, during and after disasters.

Before a disaster, children are all too often exploited and abused. Young children and boys are at greatest risk of physical violence, while sexual violence most often affects those who have reached puberty – especially girls. Children are bought, sold, trafficked, exploited, abandoned, neglected, forced into the sex trade and armed conflict, tortured, maimed, abused and misused. They suffer discrimination in its most violent forms.

Discrimination that takes places before a disaster is magnified during and after the disaster. Children's safety is compromised not just by the disaster but by the adults, agencies and communities that gather to help, to await rescue or to observe. In the chaotic environment of a disaster, where family and community support systems are under stress, existing discrimination against children is intensified.

Children who are separated from caregivers or orphaned, or seen as 'different' due to gender, disability, religion, health status, community status, language or ethnicity, can face even greater levels of discrimination. Disasters peel away the layers of protection and leave vulnerabilities even more exposed.

Layers of discrimination

Discrimination against children operates on many levels: by individuals and systematically by institutions, communities and societies.

1. Individual level

During a disaster, the main risk to children comes from people in positions of power: in families, schools, displacement camps, transition centres, places of refuge. In most cases, the people who hurt children are the very people that children know and trust.

Violence against children in disasters can also be inflicted by strangers, many of whom rush into a community after a disaster strikes. This violence often takes the form of sexual exploitation, abduction and human trafficking.

In recent years, aid workers from numerous humanitarian agencies have been accused of sexual exploitation and abuse of children. They have misused their power and have harmed the most vulnerable.

2. Systematic level

Systematic discrimination can be overt or covert:

- **No standards**. According to the UN's *World Report on Violence against Children*, just 2 per cent of the world's children are legally protected from violence – sexual, physical, and emotional – in all settings. In disasters, there are no common standards across humanitarian agencies to protect children from harm such as sexual abuse and exploitation.

- **Not a priority**. Before a disaster, most humanitarian agencies do not prioritize or integrate child protection into operations, policies or training programmes. During disasters, assessments addressing children's unique needs are often superficial and conducted without the appropriate expertise or tools. Staff and volunteers are often not effectively screened. Many aid workers are ignorant of children's rights and needs.

- **No participation**. Children normally have a minimal, if any, social or political voice. In a disaster response, despite the available tools, few humanitarian agencies make the effort or commitment to ensure that assessments and the design of programmes include sincere child participation. This results in interventions and programmes – even those specific to children – that do not include children's voices.

- **Girls versus boys**. Girls and boys are equally vulnerable, but in different ways, to many threats including violence before a disaster ever occurs. During disasters, both genders need resources, support and protection. Boys cannot be excluded in order to protect girls. Similarly, girls cannot be excluded in order to protect boys.

- **Media images**. In a disaster, it is common to see images of children, often vulnerable, often unwell, used by humanitarian agencies to generate compassion and funds. While the images can create the desired effect with donors, children's protection and special needs are rarely incorporated within budget lines and programmes, resources are not prioritized, and there is a lack of clear strategies to support and protect children. Children are too often used to generate support, but they do not always enjoy the benefits.

What children's vulnerability requires

Children's vulnerability requires a comprehensive approach by all humanitarian agencies – not just those with specific mandates to focus on children. All humanitarian agencies have a responsibility to ensure the safety of children in disasters.

Recommendations

1. Prohibit all violence against children. This includes pursuing clear policies to stop violence in all settings during disasters, such as corporal punishment, emotional abuse, neglect, sexual abuse and sexual exploitation.
2. Prioritize prevention of discrimination and violence against children. This means clear budget lines for prevention programmes and services.
3. Enhance the capacity of all humanitarian personnel through education on children's rights, unique vulnerabilities and reporting procedures.
4. Ensure the participation of children. Involve children in all disaster preparedness, response and recovery programmes, services and operations that have an impact on them.
5. Create accessible, safe and child-friendly reporting systems and services. This includes safe, well-publicized, confidential and accessible mechanisms for children, their caregivers and others to prevent and to report violence against children.
6. Ensure accountability and end impunity. This means holding humanitarian workers and organizations accountable for safe environments.
7. Meet children's unique needs. Ensure that girls and boys who are especially vulnerable – such as those with disabilities, those who have been separated from caregivers, orphaned or stigmatized – all receive programming that incorporates their unique needs.
8. Develop and implement tracking systems. These can help identify the number of children affected by a disaster response, the most vulnerable children, and data collection on reports of violence.
9. Improve collaboration between humanitarian agencies. This includes developing clear systems and standards to prevent and respond to all forms of violence against children at all stages of a disaster – preparedness, response and recovery.

Despite the rhetoric and good intentions, children's unique needs in disasters continue to be marginalized. Children are not getting the support and protection they need. This marginalization *is* discrimination, discrimination that has painful consequences. Children must be moved away from the margins and back to the centre of disaster response. It is their moral and legal right. ■

Phase 1: preparing for natural disasters

Effective prevention of discrimination against women must begin during disaster preparedness and continue through recovery and beyond. In order to develop plans of action for emergencies, it is first necessary to consider the overall situation of women in a particular country or region. Before discussing and preparing general plans of action for emergency situations, it may be useful for key players and institutions to conduct a review of the following:

- national and state-level plans of action for women
- country reports prepared by states parties to CEDAW every four years
- country-specific recommendations by CEDAW
- reports by international organizations, NGOs and human rights institutions on discrimination against women in that particular country or area

Understanding the factors that make particular groups of women vulnerable to discrimination and put them at risk of violence in 'normal' circumstances will improve the effectiveness of actions to address these situations in times of emergency. For this reason, communication strategies for delivering information on disaster preparedness should also take into account women's basic literacy levels and other social factors that may make it difficult for women to enjoy timely and adequate access to information.

Phase 2: rescue

Once the natural disaster reaches its peak, it is necessary to identify groups of women at risk and vulnerable to grave and systematic violations of women's rights. It is essential to ensure that the identification of target groups in rescue efforts does not have the unintended effect of enhancing vulnerabilities or contributing to extend the risks of violence for women and girls facing intersectional discrimination. Furthermore, relief workers should have the capacity to rescue and assist women and girls who may have been victims of violence during the crisis stage of the natural disaster. It is also important to note that plans for rescue efforts should be undertaken in association with police and military forces, with the aim of providing safety and protection to women at extended risk of violence and other grave violations. In this context, there should be codes of conduct for all those participating in rescue efforts in order to ensure that rescuers – including police and military forces – do not become perpetrators of violence against women.

Phase 3: relief

All relief efforts should take into account the protection needs of women and thereby develop adequate responses to gender-based discrimination. From the earliest stages of relief, efforts should, as a minimum, include:

International Federation of Red Cross and Red Crescent Societies

- The active involvement of women in planning, designing and implementing programmes, facilities and services. This includes equal participation of women in decision-making and leadership.
- The adequate presence of security (for example, the police) to properly maintain the rule of law and order. At the same time, monitoring processes and rules should be in place to ensure that security staff do not perpetrate violence against women.
- An awareness of gender discrimination and risks of violence against women when designing the layout of shelters, camps and settlements, including the location of and access to services and facilities.
- Access to psychological care and support from health providers or community-based providers, such as women in the community.
- Adequate means of documenting gender-based discrimination, its manifestations and its effects.
- The adoption of measures to assist women (with legal aid) in denouncing and taking action against perpetrators of violence against women in emergency situations.
- Adherence, by all actors involved in providing direct assistance or support to women that have experienced violence and other grave forms of discrimination, to a set of guiding principles in all work with survivors. These include:
  a. Safety – at all times, the safety and security of the survivor must be the highest priority.
  b. Confidentiality – maintain confidentiality; do not reveal any information about the survivor or her situation without her informed consent.
  c. Respect – respect the dignity, autonomy and ability of the survivor. Do not ask irrelevant questions; do not subject her to multiple interviews; do not tell her what to do.
  d. Non-discrimination – assist all survivors of violence against women equally, without regard for race, ethnicity, nationality, marital status or any other factor.

Phase 4: recovery

In the recovery phase, it is important to ensure that women's immediate and long-term needs are met. For this reason, it is necessary to ensure women are benefiting equally (that is, there are equal outcomes) from programmes and services aimed at helping those most affected to cope with the effects of disaster. In many cases, it will be necessary to develop models for temporary special measures – also known as affirmative action – which must be adopted by governments as well as by all key players and bodies involved in responses to natural disasters.

In accordance with CEDAW Article 4.1, the adoption by states parties of temporary special measures "aimed at accelerating de facto equality between men and women shall not be considered discrimination as defined in the present Convention… [and] shall be discontinued when the objectives of equality of opportunity and treatment have been achieved". In this respect, CEDAW General Recommendation Number 25 on temporary special measures could be used to inform strategies and steps adopted as a response to natural disasters and other emergency situations. It is at this phase that access to justice becomes more relevant to survivors of violence against women during natural disasters. After immediate care and support is provided and safety is guaranteed, women will benefit from the mechanisms of redress and remedies available to them. For this reason, a legal response to perpetrators of violence against women should be expected. At the very least, incidents of violence against women and other criminal offences affecting women that are reported to the authorities should be investigated. From a gender equality perspective, impunity for perpetrators of violence against women in emergency situations is unacceptable and non-negotiable.

Phase 5: redevelopment – sustainable outcomes in relation to the advancement of women

The reconstruction stage after natural disasters makes it evident that the processes of sustainable development and disaster prevention are interrelated. According to the report of the expert group meeting on *Environmental management and the mitigation of natural disasters: a gender perspective*, quoting Sri Lankan gender and disaster specialist Madhavi Ariyabandu, "sustainable development is not reachable and complete unless disaster prevention is an essential element in it, and disaster prevention is not something which can be discussed removed from development". At the same time, there is no doubt that gender equality and non-discrimination are cross-cutting principles that should be central to these efforts. While it is accepted that "in reaching gender equality, the methods of analysis and tools of application can be the same", there is a need to undertake a comparative analysis of existing tools, guidelines and methodologies being used in the field.

The gender equality and non-discrimination outcomes of emergency responses and programmes need to be durable and ongoing. For this to be possible, a wide number of players need to be involved. In a statement made by CEDAW in response to the Indian Ocean tsunami, the committee stated:

> Proactive steps must be taken to ensure that women and girls living in the affected communities, as well as local women's groups, women community leaders and government officials are full, equal and effective participants in all relief, rehabilitation and reconstruction efforts, including in distribution of assistance of all kind.

Consequently, all state and non-state actors collaborating to respond adequately to emergencies should be committed to the elimination of all forms of discrimination against women. One example of good practice in this regard is a training programme undertaken by the International Federation earlier this year that aimed to enhance the capacity of field staff working in earthquake-affected areas in Pakistan. The topics covered were participatory development and gender awareness-raising processes, which are seen as integral components of every project.

As already outlined in *Comparative advantage in disaster response*, a study undertaken by the US-based Hauser Center for Nonprofit Organizations, recent natural disasters have shown "that the world of responders has grown beyond international aid agencies". Interestingly, this study maps the way government involvement has significantly increased and describes the way armed forces, private companies and individuals are responding to these situations. One of the most important findings of the study is that "different types of actors…bring strengths and weaknesses that both are inherent to their organizational type and that can be exacerbated, or perhaps even reversed, depending upon the specific context of the disaster".

In the future, an in-depth study on the strategic and comparative advantages of various initiatives that have already been undertaken by a range of actors to minimize discrimination against women in times of emergency and, more specifically, to try to address violence against women, should be considered.

It is also important to note that the patriarchal attitudes entrenched in particular organizations and institutions often affect their approach to discrimination against women and their responses to violence against women. In the long term, these gender biases are also forms of discrimination against women that should be exposed and addressed when evaluating responses in times of emergency. Once again, the importance of understanding discrimination is that it provides a framework for addressing inequality and moving forward.

A cross-cutting requirement: building capacity in discrimination against women

All players taking action in emergency situations should understand discrimination against women and the overarching principles of CEDAW. After all, it is the only international human rights treaty dealing specifically with discrimination against women. As outlined in this chapter, it is important to bear in mind that violence against women is a manifestation of discrimination and to recognize that there is room for improvement in terms of the analysis of gender discrimination in emergency situations.

Given that CEDAW is a stepping stone to understanding discrimination, capacity-building in gender equality and women's human rights is needed at every level. For this reason, it is essential to sensitize and educate relief staff and officials on gender-based discrimination and its consequences. The importance of human rights education and the incorporation of women's rights into codes of conduct cannot, therefore, be overlooked.

Adding new dimensions to international standards on discrimination against women in emergency situations

As humanitarian organizations, institutions and NGOs continue to gather data and analyse the situation of women in emergency situations, it is important to continue to undertake advocacy efforts in order to ensure that the dimensions of gender-based discrimination are reflected and included in evolving international standards. It is important for the key players in relief efforts to keep on adding to existing analytical tools, standards and frameworks on discrimination against women in emergency situations that are in place globally. When informed and based on local experiences and lessons learnt, international human rights standards become more relevant and meaningful.

To illustrate this point, as already stressed by the CEDAW Committee and women's NGOs, it is important to undertake advocacy for the adoption of a UN Security Council, action-oriented resolution on the gender perspectives of disaster relief and humanitarian assistance. This resolution could supplement Security Council Resolution 1325, Women, Peace and Security, which was passed in 2000. It could potentially fill some of the gaps that exist in relation to the analysis of discrimination against women in emergency situations.

Conclusion

As already discussed, many instances of violence against women in the context of natural disasters and other kinds of emergency situations can be prevented. For this to be possible, consistent approaches and methodologies need to be developed to be able to incorporate an analysis of discrimination against women in emergency situations. Policies, programmes and services aimed at protecting women and girl children at risk of violence in times of emergency should be part of a comprehensive and ongoing plan of action for the elimination of all forms of discrimination.

It is also important to continue to discuss the ways in which emergency situations can potentially open windows of opportunity to further women's human rights and to strengthen gender equality. At the same time, while a better understanding of discrimination against women in emergency situations is likely to offer many possibilities for change, it also poses practical challenges. For this reason, efforts to

International Federation
of Red Cross and Red Crescent Societies

adequately document, analyse and evaluate responses that have already been tested in various contexts are likely to strengthen the process of drawing lessons for the future.

This chapter was contributed by María Herminia Graterol Garrido, a women's human rights lawyer and visiting research associate at the Australian Human Rights Centre, University of New South Wales, Sydney, who also contributed Figure 5.1; Beth Vann, an independent consultant specializing in gender-based violence in humanitarian emergencies. Box 5.1 was contributed by Jean-Jacques Kouoh, head of the Communications and External Relations Department of the International Federation's Central Africa Sub-Regional Office. Box 5.2 was contributed jointly by Lynn Lawry and Mike Anastario, respectively Director of Research and Research Associate at the US-based Center for Disaster and Humanitarian Assistance Medicine, and Ryan Larrance, Senior Research Associate at the International Medical Corps, a global, humanitarian, non-profit organization. Box 5.3 was contributed by Judi Fairholm, National Technical Director of RespectED, a Canadian Red Cross programme that aims to prevent child/youth abuse, neglect, harassment and interpersonal violence. Box 5.4 was contributed jointly by Judi Fairholm and Gurvinder Singh, child protection delegate for the Canadian Red Cross in Sri Lanka.

Sources and further information

Akcar, Sengul. Grassroots Women's Collectives – *Roles in post-disaster effort: potential for sustainable partnership and good governance (Lessons learned from the Marmara Earthquake in Turkey)*. Expert paper presented at the UN Expert Group Meeting on Environmental Management and the Mitigation of Natural Disasters: a Gender Perspective, Ankara, Turkey, November 2001. UN Doc: EGM/NATDIS/2001/EP.11.

Asia Pacific Forum on Women, Law and Development (APWLD). *Guidelines for Gender Sensitive Disaster Management: Practical Steps to Ensure Women's Needs are Met and Women's Human Rights are Respected and Protected during Disasters.* Chiang Mai, Thailand: APWLD, 2006. Available at www.apwld.org/pdf/Gender_Sensitive.pdf

Bradshaw, Sarah. *Socio-economic impacts of natural disasters: a gender analysis*, ECLAC Serie Manuales – No. 32. Santiago, Chile: United Nations Publications, 2004. Available at www.eclac.org/mujer/reuniones/conferencia_regional/manual.pdf

Chew, Lin and Ramdas, Kavita. *Caught in the Storm: The Impact of Natural Disasters on Women.* Global Fund for Women, 2005. Available at www.globalfundforwomen.org/cms/images/stories/downloads/disaster-report.pdf

Dearing, Tiziana. 'Katrina, One Year Later: What Have we Learned?' in *Philanthropy News Digest*, August 2006. Available at http://foundationcenter.org/pnd/commentary/co_item.jhtml;jsessionid=TRG4QRHDPOVMXTQRSI4CGW15AAAACI2F?id=156000013

Dearing, Tiziana and Merz, Barbara. *Comparative Advantage in Disaster Response.* The Hauser Center for Nonprofit Organizations Working Paper No. 38. Harvard University, Cambridge, United States, 2007. Available at www.ksg.harvard.edu/ hauser/ PDF_XLS/workingpapers/workingpaper_38.pdf

Felten-Biermann, Claudia. 'Gender and Natural Disaster: Sexualized Violence and the Tsunami' in *Development*, journal of the Society for International Development, Volume 49, Issue 3, pp. 82-86. Palgrave Macmillan, 2006.

Inter-Agency Standing Committee (IASC). *Gender Handbook in Humanitarian Action: Women, Girls, Boys and Men: Different Needs – Equal Opportunities.* IASC, Geneva, 2006. Available at www.humanitarianinfo.org/iasc/gender

IASC. *Guidelines for Gender-based Violence Interventions in Humanitarian Settings: Focusing on Prevention of and Response to Sexual Violence in Emergencies.* IASC, Geneva, 2005. Available at www. humanitarianinfo.org/iasc/gender

International Federation. Report of training on social mobilization, participation, project cycle and gender awareness-raising, Pakistan, 26 May-2 June 2007.

International Women's Rights Action Watch Asia Pacific (IWRAW Asia Pacific). *Addressing Intersectional Discrimination with Temporary Special Measures.* IWRAW Asia Pacific Occasional Papers Series No. 8. IWRAW Asia Pacific, Kuala Lumpur, 2006. Available at http://iwraw-ap.org/aboutus/pdf/OPSVIII.pdf

Larrance, R., Anastario, M. and Lawry, L. 'Health Status Among Internally Displaced Persons in Louisiana and Mississippi Travel Trailer Parks: A Global Perspective' in *Annals of Emergency Medicine*, Volume 49, Issue 5, pp. 590-601, 2007.

New York City Alliance Against Sexual Assault. *Katrina, Natural Disasters and Sexual Violence.* Factsheet. Available at www.nycagainstrape.org/media/factsheets/ fsht_111.pdf

Orstad, Lynn. *Tools for Change: Emergency Management for Women.* Expert paper presented at the UN Expert Group Meeting on Environmental Management and the Mitigation of Natural Disasters: a Gender Perspective, Ankara, Turkey, November 2001. UN Doc: EGM/NATDIS/2001/EP.2.

Oxfam International. *The tsunami's impact on women.* Oxfam briefing note. Oxfam International, March 2005. Available at www.oxfam.org.uk/what_we_do/issues/ conflict_disasters/downloads/bn_tsunami_women.pdf

Pan American Health Organization (PAHO). *Gender and Natural Disasters.* Factsheet. Available at www.paho.org/English/AD/GE/genderdisasters.PDF

Pittaway, Eileen and Bartolomei, Linda. *Refugee Women at Risk: Assessment Tool and Response Mechanism.* The Centre for Refugee Research, University of New South Wales and the Australian National Committee on Refugee Women (ANCORW). Available at www.crr.unsw.edu.au/documents/Women%20at%20Risk%20 Assessment%20tool%20and%20process%20Final.pdf

The Sphere Project. *Humanitarian Charter and Minimum Standards in Disaster Response*. The Sphere Project, Geneva, 2004. Available at www.sphereproject.org/handbook

United Nations. Convention on the Elimination of All Forms of Discrimination against Women (CEDAW). Available at www.un.org/womenwatch/daw/cedaw

United Nations. Convention on the Elimination of All Forms of Discrimination against Women – General recommendations. Available at www.un.org/womenwatch/daw/ cedaw/recommendations

United Nations Division for the Advancement of Women (DAW), Inter-Agency Secretariat of the International Strategy for Disaster Reduction (UN/ISDR). *Environmental Management and the Mitigation of Natural Disasters: a Gender Perspective*. Report of the Expert Group Meeting, Ankara, Turkey, 6-9 November 2001. Available at www.un.org/womenwatch/daw/csw/env_manage/documents/EGM-Turkey-final-report.pdf

United Nations. Economic and Social Council, Committee on Economic, Social and Cultural Rights (CESCR) – General Comment Number 16. Available at www.unhchr.ch/tbs/doc.nsf/898586b1dc7b4043c1256a450044f331/7c6dc1dee6268e32c125708f0050dbf6/$FILE/G0543539.pdf

United Nations Inter-Agency Secretariat of the International Strategy for Disaster Reduction (UN/ISDR). 'Priorities for action 2005-2015' in *Hyogo Framework For Action 2005-2015: Building the Resilience of Nations and Communities to Disasters*. Extract from the final report of the World Conference on Disaster Reduction, Kobe, Hyogo, Japan, 18-22 January 2005. Available at www.unisdr.org/wcdr/intergover/official-doc/L-docs/Hyogo-framework-for-action-english.pdf

United Nations. Optional Protocol to the Convention on the Elimination of All Forms of Discrimination against Women. Available at www.un.org/womenwatch/daw/cedaw/protocol

United Nations. Statement by the Committee on the Elimination of Discrimination against Women, in regard to the Tsunami disaster in South East Asia, 26 December 2004. Available at www.un.org/womenwatch/daw/cedaw/c-recent-stats/ Tsunami.statement%20with%20design.pdf

United Nations. *World Report on Violence against Children*. United Nations Secretary-General's Study on Violence against Children, 2006. Available at www.violencestudy.org/r229

United Nations High Commissioner for Refugees (UNHCR). *Executive Committee Conclusion on Women and Girls at Risk*. UNHCR, Geneva, 2006. Available at www.unhcr.org/excom/EXCOM/45339d922.html

UNHCR. *Sexual and Gender-Based Violence against Refugees, Returnees and Internally Displaced Persons: Guidelines for Prevention and Response*. UNHCR, Geneva, 2003.

CHAPTER 5

World Health Organization (WHO). *Gender Considerations in Disaster Assessment.* WHO, Geneva, 2005. Available at www.who.int/gender/other_health/en/gwhdisasterassessment.pdf

Vann, Beth. *Gender-Based Violence: Emerging Issues in Programs Serving Displaced Populations.* Reproductive Health for Refugees Consortium, Arlington, Virginia, United States, 2002. Available at www.rhrc.org/pdf/gbv_vann.pdf

Vann, B., Beatty, M. and Ehrlich, L. 'Supporting displaced communities to address gender-based violence' in *Forced Migration Review*, Issue 19, pp. 28-29, 2004. Available at www.fmreview.org/FMRpdfs/FMR19/FMR19full.pdf

Yonder, A., Akcar, S. and Gopalan, P. *Women's Participation in Disaster Relief and Recovery.* SEEDS pamphlet series – No. 22. The Population Council, New York, 2005. Available at www.popcouncil.org/pdfs/seeds/Seeds22.pdf

International Federation
of Red Cross and Red Crescent Societies

Web sites

Asia Pacific Forum on Women, Law and Development **www.apwld.org**

Commission on the Status of Women **www.un.org/womenwatch/daw/csw**

Committee on the Elimination of Discrimination against Women
www.ohchr.org/english/bodies/cedaw/index.htm

Gender and Disaster Network **www.gdnonline.org**

Global Fund for Women **www.globalfundforwomen.org**

International Medical Corps **www.imcworldwide.org**

International Women's Rights Action Watch Asia Pacific **www.iwraw-ap.org**

Office of the United Nations High Commissioner for Human Rights
www.ohchr.org

UN Special Rapporteur on Violence against Women
www.ohchr.org/english/issues/women/rapporteur

Reproductive Health Response in Conflict Consortium (information on gender-
based violence) **www.rhrc.org/resources/index.cfm?sector=gbv**

WomenWatch **www.un.org/womenwatch**

World Health Organization (Department of Gender, Women and Health)
www.who.int/gender/en

World Health Organization Regional Office for South-East Asia (Department of
Gender, Women and Health – Gender and disaster)
www.searo.who.int/EN/Section13/section390_8282.htm

International Federation
of Red Cross and Red Crescent Societies

Dealing with discrimination in disaster recovery

Rationed exclusion

Lakshmi Sumathi is the mother of two children in the village of Panchalpuram in coastal Tamil Nadu, India. As with almost all of the other 55 village families, the 2004 Indian Ocean tsunami destroyed her home and most of her possessions. In an attempt to target support at the neediest, the Cuddalore district collector from the government of Tamil Nadu created a system of tsunami cards that included the name, age and address of holders. The cards served as proof of entitlement that allowed local and external humanitarian organizations to provide recovery support to the cardholders. Donors and relief distributors would consult the tsunami card and provide relief that was not listed on the card. Though this effort was apparently designed to better coordinate recovery assistance, the cards were "provided to supporters of the village leaders first", as Lakshmi explained. As a result, Lakshmi and other villagers became frustrated, feeling that the support intended to help them recover had been mishandled.

Assistance based on need alone?

Non-discrimination is a central concept in several humanitarian system-wide agreements. The second principle of the *Code of Conduct for the International Red Cross and Red Crescent Movement and NGOs in Disaster Relief* (the code of conduct) states that "aid is given regardless of the race, creed, or nationality of the recipients and without adverse distinction of any kind. Aid priorities are calculated on the basis of need alone". The Sphere Project states that "humanitarian agencies have the responsibility to provide assistance in a manner that is consistent with human rights, including the right to participation, non-discrimination and information". Additionally, the Principles and Good Practice of Humanitarian Donorship, as endorsed in 2003 by 17 donor governments and intergovernmental organizations, states that "humanitarian action should be guided by... impartiality... without discrimination between or within affected populations". Yet, too many humanitarian responses result in accusations by the media of discrimination, with project evaluations reporting on those who were left out of the relief effort.

This chapter provides examples of how to incorporate strategies for reducing discrimination into the disaster recovery process as a particular phase of the disaster management cycle, as this is the area in which the All India Disaster Mitigation Institute (AIDMI) has greatest experience. It begins by demonstrating the absence of detailed practical assistance available for stakeholders involved in humanitarian

Photo opposite page: Women in the village of Ikaatini, Kenya, meet to discuss water facilities. As women are often responsible for collecting water, it is important that they are involved in deciding where the collection points are located.

Daniel Cima/ American Red Cross

response. Then it provides advice on detecting discrimination and integrating anti-discrimination into disaster recovery management. Based on recent experience in both large- and small-scale disasters, this chapter suggests four key strategies for reducing the negative impacts of discrimination. These include encouraging multi-stakeholder input, developing organizational anti-discrimination capacity, creating grievance-handling processes and supporting local capability to recover. Suggestions are given on how these can be integrated into the basic project cycle management phases of recovery; assessment, implementation, and monitoring and evaluation.

For this purpose, our focus moves from humanitarian agency headquarters and policy documents to the views and opinions of the field workers and the affected communities to gain a more operational perspective on what many of them have called dilemmas of discrimination. If various global agreements and system-wide standards are to achieve any added impact on the ground, then a better and deeper understanding of how discrimination is played out at an operational level – and what those field workers and affected community members suggest could be done – is important (see Box 6.1).

Box 6.1 Community-based targeting

Much external aid is guided by the principle of targeting those most in need. Whether aid is getting to the right people is often the first question asked about humanitarian action, especially in situations where there is conflict and aid may be stolen. We know that the most exploited groups are worst hit by disasters, so does it not make sense to try to discriminate positively in favour of these groups? Accumulated evidence shows that, in some post-disaster circumstances, governments and aid agencies do a reasonable job of providing aid to these groups, but could do much better. Yet is 'positive discrimination' always a good idea, and what do we really know about targeting and discrimination? The following considers these questions in relation to food aid.

Sharing versus targeting

Many societies, communities and households are organized around shared decision-making and shared resources. Cultural norms about sharing are bound to be influenced by the targeting of resources by outsiders after a disaster.

Targeting is by its nature discriminatory. Evidence from recent evaluations shows that the targeting of food aid to the most vulnerable is largely ineffective. Once food aid reaches the community, community leaders and members prefer to distribute it according to local cultural and social norms, and not only to the most vulnerable.

Targeting may damage livelihoods

We know that most post-disaster relief is provided by affected populations, through individual and community livelihood strategies. We also know that external agencies struggle to understand these strategies and build aid around them. The implications of this mismatch between local and external practice

International Federation of Red Cross and Red Crescent Societies

are not well understood. What happens to food aid once it is distributed within a community, or even within a household? Redistribution of resources is an important livelihood strategy after disasters. We should not romanticize the culture of sharing or the benefits it brings to the marginalized, but we need to learn more about it.

Disrupting this culture of sharing may have a long-term negative impact on livelihoods. As such, the targeting of food aid may undermine rather than build on indigenous coping mechanisms and abilities to adapt to crisis. As a review conducted for Save the Children, *Community-Managed Targeting and Distribution of Food Aid*, notes: "The concern that excluding the traditionally better-off from the distribution may undermine long-term, intra-community support mechanisms has considerable merit, and should be investigated further."

Community-based targeting: is it a solution?

Agencies are increasingly turning to community-based targeting (CBT) after disasters for a number of reasons: to promote participation and a fair system of distribution, to build interventions of local norms and culture, but also to justify cuts in food aid. CBT systems grew from programmes piloted by Oxfam in Uganda during the late 1980s. CBT was perceived as a way of incorporating developmental principles into relief. Today, CBT includes community-elected relief committees for food distribution and information on entitlements.

Most of the experience of CBT comes from eastern and southern Africa, Bangladesh and Myanmar. A growing body of evidence suggests that, given the right circumstances, CBT can positively discriminate towards the most vulnerable in a way that is acceptable to communities. For example, a 2005 World Food Programme review of targeting found that: "In the four case studies where CBTD [community-based targeting and distribution] were implemented [Ethiopia, Kenya, Malawi, and Myanmar], distribution problems involving powerful groups 'siphoning off food aid' were largely avoided. The inclusion and exclusion errors which did occur under CBTD programming were generally as a result of community consensus around perception of need in conjunction with scarcity of resources."

The study identified five key findings:

1. The level of resources provided should be appropriate to the context. CBT has failed if it is used to justify targeting criteria because of a decline in food aid.
2. Even with CBT, some degree of redistribution will usually take place, but it will be significantly less than with targeting.
3. So far, CBT has not worked during complex emergencies or in situations where there is intense political pressure on community leaders to favour certain groups.
4. CBT may work better during and after natural disasters where a relatively high proportion of the population is targeted.
5. Social targeting criteria may be easier to use in CBT than economic ones, which are more contentious. ∎

Paucity of detailed discrimination debate

The code of conduct and the Sphere Project have given strong mandates to assistance organizations and helped to establish system-wide standards for improving humanitarian action. In recent years, there has been additional work done to create benchmarks for standards of accountability to beneficiaries. Benchmark 5 of the Humanitarian Accountability Partnership (HAP) 2007, which was launched to promote accountability to disaster survivors, states:

> "The agency shall establish and implement complaints-handling procedures that are effective, accessible and safe for intended beneficiaries, disaster-affected communities, agency staff, humanitarian partners and other specified bodies."

To go beyond statements and actually to reduce discrimination in the field, during project operations, the providers of humanitarian recovery support could benefit from a greater awareness of what actually takes place in recovery operations, as well as more tools that guide their programmes on how to reduce discrimination. New tools such as *The Good Enough Guide* offer basic guidelines on how to be accountable to local people and how to measure impact based on experiences drawn from East Africa. Many other global initiatives focus on *what* should be done, but do not go any further to illustrate *how*.

Examples of inadequate attention to the *how* of discrimination in humanitarian response include the variety of tools or mechanisms that have been developed in recent years to support quality relief and early recovery. These tools represent major assets in reducing the risk to disasters and supporting sustainable recovery, but they do not offer enough guidance when a practitioner tries to use them to reduce discrimination in a humanitarian support project. Patterns and trends on different types of discrimination that result from humanitarian action – as well as who does it, and in what way – have yet to be identified and mapped out across humanitarian stakeholders, such as local institutions, governments, the United Nations and non-governmental organizations (NGOs).

Dilemmas for practitioners

We have to make choices based on hard realities that may result in discrimination. Sometimes, this takes the form of targeting poor or traditionally neglected individuals and families. Short-term differentiation – also known as affirmative action – is designed to correct long-term discrimination. For the purpose of this chapter, discrimination is taken to refer to improper differentiation. Fairness is a crucial point; in humanitarian action, fairness distinguishes differentiation from discrimination. Knowing that work is done in good faith, humanitarian personnel can benefit from considering who might or could have suffered because of their actions. Perhaps the key lies in being aware of what we do rather than just being aware of tools, systems and indicators.

Individuals are often torn between the need to meet different needs while responding. A lead member of the logistics team of an international medical NGO working on the Thailand-Myanmar border with locally displaced tribal groups states: "We cannot stop responding because there is discrimination on the ground. We go ahead and then turn back to ensure that the initial, unintentional discrimination is corrected. For example, we provide for all those who ask for food in the first five distributions and, in the sixth, focus on those who seem to have received more than they should and search for those who are left out." But how long is soon enough? What happens to those who are discriminated against, and can such cases of neglect always be corrected? According to Khurshid Alam, a leading needs assessment consultant from Bangladesh: "Once discrimination occurs, it has its own chain of actions and reactions... almost always these are not correctable." Once boatless fishing labourers are left out of relief distributions or 'cash for work' (CFW) programmes for one or two months, it is very difficult to locate them on the coast as they move on in search of other opportunities. Similarly, once a family is excluded from a distribution list for temporary shelter assistance after an earthquake, it becomes much harder for them to secure permanent shelter.

Helping disaster-affected people tackle long-standing inequity can result in a clash of principles. According to Tony Vaux, an international consultant with experience in disasters and development: "The outsider has a responsibility to infuse the [recovery support] process with a focus on the poorest." The clash of principles, he says, may come as this focusing on the needs of the poor "may not necessarily be the way a community works".

These dilemmas are also found within the affected communities. Speaking in 2002, members of riot-affected communities in relief camps, which were set up after the 2001 Gujarat earthquake, asked: "Why protest? Let some resources start coming to our village...What is new about this relief discrimination, we are always discriminated against, and this is one more time."

Access problems can often lead to whole communities being denied humanitarian assistance. The humanitarian community rarely makes sufficient effort to reach people that are very difficult to access. Cyclone Gafilo, which zigzagged across Madagascar in 2004, caused great destruction in the north-east of the country and heavy flooding across the island. Aid efforts focused mainly on the coastal towns in the north-east and south-west. A small team from the Malagasy Red Cross Society, together with a relief delegate from the International Federation of Red Cross and Red Crescent Societies, took a week to reach communities in the interior, travelling by truck over rough roads. "I will never forget the condition of whole villages when they came out to meet us, naked and living in abject poverty, whose situation was made so much worse by the floods," says Dian Mamadou, International Federation relief delegate. It was not until much later that the devastation of the vanilla crops was known and the inadequacy of recovery highlighted.

Detecting discrimination

Detecting and addressing discrimination is much easier when more time is spent with communities in project areas. This simple principle, as described by emergency and recovery project managers, is too often either overlooked or blatantly ignored by intervening organizations. In a report to the UK's Department for International Development (DFID) entitled *Social Vulnerability, Sustainable Livelihoods and Disasters*, Terry Cannon *et al* note that "agency staff's respect for local capacities [is a] far more important determinant of the developmental impact of relief projects than any other staff qualifications (including previous disaster relief experience)". Detecting discrimination can be reduced to filling in endless forms and writing reports. Often, a day-long, open and frank discussion on how the humanitarian response will support every affected individual's right to recover properly and how this should be promoted is more useful.

There are constraints to detecting discrimination: the need to cover many affected areas and the inability to spend significant time understanding the situation in each area are likely to lead to project managers being unable to recognize and address discrimination.

Agency mandates for employing local staff from affected areas do ensure a capacity to understand local issues. Well-established systems of transparency, such as maintaining detailed beneficiary records, are effective, organizational-level anti-discrimination measures.

The humanitarian system can make further progress towards detecting discrimination in communities and humanitarian responses. What will work is an organizational culture among large humanitarian organizations to encourage field staff to take their own initiative to achieve improved inclusion, by enabling free thinking and field-level decision-making. In reality, there are limits to humanitarian intervention: there is so much that is invisible to humanitarian agencies that are not part of the community.

Integrating anti-discrimination measures into disaster recovery management

Anti-discrimination strategies

Disasters and response bring opportunities for learning. Recent humanitarian system-wide efforts have made progress towards expanding understanding, gaining commitment, and improving the practice of humanitarian actors. These have included the UN Office of the Special Envoy for Tsunami Recovery and the Tsunami Evaluation Coalition (TEC). Among the recommendations made – such as supporting local capacities to recover, supporting human rights and NGO professionalism and the role of needs assessments – actions have emerged from community-level experience and research on how discrimination may be reduced.

This chapter identifies four strategies that may be utilized by humanitarian actors to help prevent discrimination in recovery:
1. encouraging multi-stakeholder input
2. developing organizational anti-discrimination capacity
3. creating grievance-handling processes
4. supporting local capability to recover

A discussion of each is followed by details on how these can be implemented in the project phases of needs assessment and targeting, implementation, and monitoring and evaluation.

1. Encouraging multi-stakeholder input
Participation by affected communities in recovery efforts is critical to reduce the negative effects of discrimination. Recovery efforts should incorporate the views of community representatives, local officials, women, and poor communities. One option for establishing multi-stakeholder input is through the organization of a community recovery committee (CRC) to manage relief and recovery activities (see Box 6.2). A CRC benefits disaster-affected individuals in two ways. Firstly, it helps to ensure that communities lead their own recovery. Secondly, by ensuring that a diverse group of individuals has a role and voice in the committee, the recovery effort is more likely to meet the needs of a greater variety of constituents, including those historically discriminated against such as the poor and low-caste families. Additionally, strong humanitarian partnerships help balance individual interests and discrimination and improve recovery because no single individual is sufficiently capable of responding to any crisis.

Focusing relief and recovery on women, as a key group of stakeholders, can ensure that investment is more likely to be spent on long-term family needs. Joint support to women and men in a household has been very successful in shelter support. For example, registering structures jointly (between husband and wife) prevents women from being excluded if the husband dies. This good practice was noted in the 2001 Gujarat earthquake, the 2004 Indian Ocean tsunami and the 2005 South Asia earthquake.

2. Developing organizational anti-discrimination capacity
Often, humanitarian organizations that want to overcome discrimination focus on an anti-discrimination policy or checklist. This is a good and useful step, especially if they use locally-resourced people, but they could go further by reviewing their own organizational culture of discrimination.

Box 6.2 Better Programming Initiative: an International Federation tool to reduce discrimination in aid programmes. The Honduran Red Cross example

In October 1998, Hurricane Mitch devastated much of Central America. The unprecedented international response to the disaster provided affected countries with the opportunity to go beyond relief and rehabilitation – it provided the chance to undertake real sustainable development. In Honduras, the government and the Honduran Red Cross, supported by sister Red Cross societies and the Spanish government, began a major construction project in the Amarateca valley. The aim of the project was to provide 541 families from Tegucigalpa – whose houses were literally erased from the map by landslides – with safer, quality housing and a water and sanitation system. It also aimed to link the physical reconstruction with longer-term regeneration, which would integrate social, economic, environmental and cultural elements. However, problems soon started to arise as community participation in the local committees decreased sharply and intra-familial and youth violence increased.

The Honduran Red Cross responded by organizing a workshop with the community. Using the Better Programming Initiative (BPI), they examined the reasons for the drop in the community's commitment and involvement in the implementation of the projects.

What is BPI?

BPI is an impact assessment tool adapted by the International Federation from the Local Capacities for Peace Project (LCPP) and is based on the 'do-no-harm' approach. BPI analyses the positive and negative impact of aid and humanitarian programmes on communities. It helps to better understand how the assistance that the aid organization is proposing to deliver affects community power and social relations. By using BPI, the International Federation is able to implement programmes that not only avoid reinforcing existing inequality and discrimination, but can also help local people strengthen their capacities, thereby encouraging longer-term, sustainable recovery.

How does BPI work?

BPI is a tool that can be used at any stage of the project planning cycle. It facilitates systematic context analysis to ensure that programming decisions are made with a thorough investigation of the interaction between the context and the intervention.

The BPI methodology applies five analytical steps:

1. **Context analysis:** identify and rank the dividers and connectors that characterize the context.
2. **Aid programme description:** describe planned actions in detail: why, where, what, when, with whom, by whom and, most importantly, how is aid being offered?
3. **Impact identification:** will aid reinforce or weaken existing dividers and connectors? Aid may have impact through material consequences – who receives what – and symbolic consequences – who is legitimized and who is not.
4. **Options:** for each impact identified in step 3, brainstorm programming options that will decrease negative impact and reinforce positive impact.
5. **Repeat the analysis:** contexts change rapidly, as do constraints and opportunities for aid programming. Analysis should be undertaken as frequently as the project cycle permits.

International Federation of Red Cross and Red Crescent Societies

The context analysis in Amarateca revealed some key dividers: breakdown of family units, power struggles among community leaders, violent youth groups (*maras*), a dependency on external aid, economic inequalities and a new community formed by arrivals from neighbouring areas. There were, however, some key connectors: common public services, the shared experience of poverty and Hurricane Mitch, religion, hope for a better quality of life and the commitment to reduce violence.

Lessons learnt from BPI implementation
The BPI analysis in Amarateca showed that significant inequalities had been allowed to develop among beneficiaries. Projects did not reach all members of the community, the selection of local committee members was inappropriate and there was a lack of coordination between some organizations – the quality of houses varied and they were allocated on the basis of varying criteria. Representatives from key community groups, such as youth groups, were not part of local committees. Whether done inadvertently or intentionally, excluding community members increases suspicion and local tensions. It is clear that a lack of knowledge and understanding of the local context can lead to discrimination in humanitarian work. Thorough context analysis that is reviewed during the project cycle is essential.

For humanitarian organizations, there are a number of lessons to be learnt. Accepting beneficiary selection from third parties or assigning excessive importance to one source of information is likely to result in accusations of discrimination and partiality. Genuinely vulnerable groups may be overlooked.

Furthermore, the perception of an aid organization is influenced by its structure and composition. If an organization's local staff base is not representative of all the groups in affected communities, its impartiality and reputation will be weakened.

Information for community members about aid allocation and the rationale behind it should not be overlooked. A lack of information fosters resentment and may leave some members of the community feeling excluded and irrelevant.

Conclusion
Thanks to the BPI tool, the International Federation can better understand the impact of the interaction between its work and the context in which it operates. The use of BPI helped the Honduran Red Cross to understand that when a recovery project involves moving a community to a different location, pre-existing social and economic issues need to be considered. The Honduran Red Cross invited beneficiaries, including youth groups and teachers who were previously excluded, to revisit the programme together and to propose new activities, mainly managed by young people from the community, which helped reduce social tensions and violence. ■

Dr Bhanu, a field manager responding to the floods that hit India and Bangladesh in July 2006, claims: "Large organizations such as ours invite a consultant, often from outside the affected area or community or even from Geneva, to hold training on how to address discrimination in humanitarian work."

Such training initiatives may address some discriminatory attitudes and practices but, as they focus on field staff, they may not address organization-wide attitudes and practices. The field teams, who are often the only ones to receive such training, are quickly disillusioned. "Soon, the quality and quantity of anti-discrimination measures drop and mechanical activities continue. Creative energy to make a real difference is lost," concludes Ms Nafisa, a coordinator for an NGO working in Pakistan on the 2005 earthquake operation.

Becoming more inclusive means going beyond methodologies and projects. Lasting impact should not be sacrificed for the short-term win of a successful project.

3. Creating grievance-handling processes

Some success has been seen with the establishment of grievance procedures for disaster-affected communities. In Indian-administered Kashmir, following the 2005 earthquake, a *lok adalat* (people's court) was established for affected areas. The court did not consist of a physical building but a group of people who moved from village to village. People could go to the court and register their complaints about the relief process. The court considered few cases of intentional discrimination based on lines of caste or social or economic status. Most complaints were about inadvertent discrimination by NGOs and governments between equally needy neighbours, weaknesses in relief systems and unfair treatment. A court such as the *lok adalat* serves as a proactive effort to register injustices by offering a rapid and convenient grievance procedure.

When establishing a formal grievance system, relief organizations should consider proactively seeking out groups that may have concerns with the recovery process. The poorest and most disadvantaged groups may be the least likely to come forward to complain.

Village members in the Indian districts of Villupuram and Nagapattinam created methods for maintaining transparency, with written lists displayed on public buildings, such as on a school or temple wall, detailing all external assistance received by each household. This helped citizens to see what the *panchayat* (locality) received in their name and from which organization.

4. Supporting local capability to recover

The TEC found that some groups, such as fishermen after the 2004 Indian Ocean tsunami, were better organized than others and also more successful at accessing aid than other less organized groups, such as coastal farmers. This reflects their collective power and their ability to work together effectively in focusing agency actions on their needs.

Increasing the voice of disadvantaged community claim-holders is especially important. When it is not possible to arrange multi-stakeholder governance systems, parallel systems should be set up to ensure that neglected groups do not fall further behind. For example, separate meetings organized solely for women may encourage them to talk openly and to discuss their needs. Member-based organizations may provide services only to those within their organizations. These actions, while discriminating against those outside their membership, are seen as legitimate as the members are the organization's investors.

Constraints and limitations

Strategies to make relief and recovery interventions work better sometimes fail or have unintended impacts. Some of these result in discrimination that increases risk for those who are to be assisted. Targeting service provision may exacerbate community and political tensions. This may happen when programme support targets low-caste individuals and fails to help other poor families.

Agencies may be overly focused on particular strategies and unable to consider that important groups may be excluded. For example, support for sustainable livelihoods is widely considered good practice. However, a sharp focus on replacing livelihood assets means that some of the most vulnerable individuals, such as manual labourers, are not assisted simply because they lacked assets in the first place.

Constraints that often accompany development and recovery assistance – for example, the pursuit of established project results within budget limitations, time and donor pressure and the need for visibility – often do not allow humanitarian agencies the flexibility they require to make just decisions on the ground. The 2004 Indian Ocean earthquake and tsunami affected two areas that simultaneously suffered from civil conflict. In Sri Lanka, some areas affected by conflict had been home to displaced people for decades. When the tsunami came, so did funding to support tsunami-affected groups – sometimes to the exclusion of conflict-affected groups. As one farmer living on the border of Ampara and Batticaloa districts in Sri Lanka said: "It is hard to tell if we are recovering from the impact of tsunami or from the impact of ongoing conflict. To me, what matters is recovery." Unfortunately, the inflexibility of back donors, who are not sensitive to the actual situation on the ground, means that funds are earmarked for specific disaster types – not for communities.

Anti-discrimination in the project management cycle

Project cycle management may be organized into several general steps: needs assessment and targeting, implementation, and monitoring and evaluation. In disaster management, pressure to act and save lives may distort this. The following discussion is in line with this process, explaining how the four strategies listed above can be integrated in order to reduce discrimination.

Needs assessment and targeting

The humanitarian teams leading the field-level actions need to have experience and an understanding of humanitarian discrimination and its challenges. "They need to know who is being included in the relief process, but also who is not, and be restless about the fact that almost all humanitarian actions end up discriminating against one or the other group," says Kartik Manoj, a field worker with an international non-governmental organization (INGO) in southern India.

If humanitarian response has to build on local capacities, it will need to start by differentiating between local people who will not tolerate discrimination and those who perpetuate it. When the assessment team consists of outsiders, they should establish relations with or include and employ local community members to lead the recovery effort. "As local people, we reach out to groups better and faster, but may also turn a blind eye to exclusion without often realizing it ourselves," reflected Revathi, a local social worker employed by an INGO. She described how she had to struggle to promote small and Dalit farmers, whose land became saline after the tsunami and who were discriminated against by many INGOs because they had decided only to support fishermen.

In some instances, the inclusion of community members is achieved through the establishment of a community recovery committee, or through existing rural or village development societies. In such cases, the community leads the process. The CRCs are very useful for those who are included, but represent a "wall of stone" for those who are excluded, as described by members of such a committee from Kutch, Gujarat, following the 2001 earthquake. Individuals of this committee should be trained in conducting inclusive and equitable needs assessments. Increasingly, such CRCs are formed but they are not always given the time to start up and the resources to carry out their tasks. In addition, they lack the skills required to communicate their findings in the formal relief and humanitarian system (see Box 6.3).

There are several advantages to a trained local recovery committee conducting the assessment: very often they know who is poor in their own community and what is needed, and they possess the requisite language skills. "They also know the methods to collect information rapidly and without much cost," noted NGO team leader Sukhdev Patel. The committee should include a diverse group, in terms of ethnicity, background and gender, as well as several individuals from the affected community, as this will increase pressures for equity in decision-making. Nevertheless, a diverse group does not ensure the inclusion of a diversity of victims as the needs assessment, reporting, field visit methods, and tools may not be diversity sensitive. Incorporating a diversity of views into community assessments is sometimes difficult. One approach to address this is for the CRC to conduct assessments and distributions jointly with other community organizations, government officers, or external relief agencies.

Box 6.3 Community surveys

The community survey method was developed by the All India Disaster Mitigation Institute (AIDMI) based on the experience they gained since 1998 conducting reviews. The community survey method was further expanded to document community views following the 2001 earthquake in Gujarat, India. Its development has led to a wider use of surveys, notably after the Indian Ocean tsunami of 2004. The method was specifically designed to consult, capture and analyse community feedback on disaster relief and recovery. It can be a useful tool for anti-discrimination practice by improving accountability towards beneficiaries and by providing feedback to relief organizations on community experiences.

The method is straightforward. Researchers facilitate community discussions with the assistance of three adaptable, participatory exercises: a matching game, a ranking exercise and a timeline exercise. The community focus group discussions are complemented with individual interviews to allow cross-checking. A set of tables, record sheets and matrix sheets were designed to assist the research team in gathering information. Focusing on the allocation of relief, community involvement and changes in community capacity has allowed researchers to gain insights into discrimination in the relief process.

Following the Gujarat earthquake, there was an evaluation of the Disasters Emergency Committee's (DEC) expenditure. According to Sarah Routley, who took part in the evaluation, the Gujarat survey found that "[t]here were many examples where the processes used by agencies led to discrimination according to gender, location, caste, wealth/poverty, and visibility... Women, lower caste groups and those representing smaller numbers of people stated they were left out of decision-making... and hence were also omitted from relief distributions often because the process used excluded them from participating".

Tony Vaux, a consultant with international experience in disasters and development, has been a team leader of evaluations utilizing this methodology. He notes: "Community surveys are an important tool for identifying and monitoring discrimination... It is generally best to leave decisions about distributions to local communities while building in checks to ensure that the community is not captured by an elite." Community surveys are one of these checks and serve as an example of how multi-stakeholder input in the project cycle can help humanitarian agencies – as well as donors, the media and others – detect and rectify both intended and unintended discrimination. ■

For the intervening organization, there should be a well-established rationale, criteria and processes for intervention (see Box 6.4). There should also be guidelines for field teams – with whom the organization should work – encouraging local people to manage their recovery through community committees. It should also give them a structure to do so. The poorest groups may be overlooked because they live in physical isolation from their own village; therefore, discovering who may be discriminated against is difficult. An oversight mechanism should exist among field managers to ensure that discrimination against poor and marginalized groups is minimized in the work of the CRC. They may also provide technical input to the CRC when necessary.

Cross-checking the assessments of the CRCs is usually straightforward. Humanitarian agencies offering support can quickly verify CRC assessments.

Avoiding discrimination is a key component of more effective programming: the Health and Peacebuilding Filter and its associated Companion Guide presents a set of questions that any project might ask of itself and its partners. The filter adopts a 'do-no-harm' approach and seeks to ensure that any project or programme does not inadvertently make matters worse in already sensitive settings.

Project and programme designers are invited to respond to four statements, identifying whether or not the project effectively addresses these:

1. The project seeks to promote tolerance and reduce discrimination.
2. The project contributes to addressing inequalities within the community.
3. The project makes effective provision for inclusion of specific vulnerable groups.
4. The project ensures that access is not limited by economic or other barriers.

1. The project seeks to promote tolerance and reduce discrimination

Discrimination is the unfair treatment of individuals or communities on the basis of attributes such as race, colour, gender, language, religion, politics, national or social origin, wealth or some other influence on status.

In order to promote tolerance and avoid discrimination, agencies may consider the following:

- What are the existing tensions and forms of discrimination in the community? To what extent is group discrimination present? Are there any systematic forms of discrimination that lead to differential access to food, water, education, shelter, employment opportunities or other income-generating activities? Are these reflected in differential access to services, resources, information and rights?
- Do the services discriminate between groups in relation to how services are offered or accessed? To what extent does the recruitment of staff, the delivery of services, or involvement of various community groups in project management suggest discriminatory approaches to different communities?
- Does the project identify and respond to those with greatest need in the area?

2. The project contributes to addressing inequalities within the community

Clearly, aside from not doing harm, the project could more explicitly assist in addressing inequalities that are present in the communities involved.

- Does the project identify the nature of inequalities in the community? What are the patterns? Have these patterns changed over time? Are they getting better or worse? What are they based on? What could be done to modify and address them and, more particularly, to reduce the gaps between the haves and have-nots?
- Consider the various inequalities in health or education or employment status, in access to services, and in access to those factors that influence these entitlements.
- Does the project or service attempt to address these, and in what way?

3. The project makes effective provision for inclusion of specific vulnerable groups

Particular attention should be paid to the most vulnerable communities and individuals – those with the least resources to protect and sustain themselves.

- These groups may not be proactive in seeking the services they need. Could they be assisted to demand the services to which they are entitled?
- What special measures, if any, has the project taken to ensure it effectively reaches these populations? What more could be done?
- Does the project or programme monitor access to services by vulnerable groups? Are data collected and disaggregated by age, sex and the area from which people come so as to determine whether all people have comparable access?

4. The project ensures that access is not limited by economic or other barriers

Access to services may be limited by economic and financial concerns, geographical factors such as distance and social factors. Examples of these barriers may include: charges for services, the cost of transport to get to services, distance and time to get to a particular place, insensitivity to culture experienced within services, and discrimination against particular groups.

- Are the project services available to all groups, at broadly equivalent cost and in the same way to everyone regardless of ethnicity, gender, economic status and other attributes?
- Are there any hidden costs associated with accessing project services such as transport or insecurity? Does the project attempt to address these difficulties in order to enhance access?
- Are any systems and mechanisms in place to ensure that those least well-off are still able to access services? Have efforts been focused on the most vulnerable individuals and groups? Are some communities offered exemptions from charges? On what basis are these decisions made and who operates these systems?
- Is the activity promoted throughout the community? Are people who are not literate at all, or only literate in a particular language, able to fully access information about the services available? Are services promoted and offered to all language groups? Does the project promote dignity and respect for beneficiaries, community members and all social subgroups, especially the most vulnerable groups?

These key questions can help any project or programme assess what it is doing to reduce discrimination and promote more equitable access to services. This material, compiled from the Health and Peacebuilding Filter, can be further adapted for local use. These questions can also be used as a means of provoking discussion, debate and better practice. ■

Project proposals based on initial assessments should include photos and data. Recently, there has been a trend in favour of discrimination that can be measured and counted, and against discrimination that is anecdotal. Stories of discrimination are not always enough to pursue compensation from government authorities or humanitarian agencies.

Organizations with experience in disaster recovery generally conduct their own needs assessments and design their own intervention plan before submission to a donor. Local agencies with an established reputation for equity and good performance are, however, not always able to demonstrate this through the proposal systems that are typically required by donors. In addition, pressure with respect to time and resources, as well as the complexities of coordination across and within support teams, sometimes preclude local organizations from developing proposals that suit large donors' submission guidelines. As a result, there is funding discrimination in favour of those who write proposals quickly but may have a weaker local presence.

Implementation

The Mombasa branch of the Kenya Red Cross Society only registers women as heads of households in communities where there are multiple families with only one father or husband. This prevents the marginalization of less influential wives and their children. Creating CRCs is likely to increase the participation of local individuals in project design and implementation which, in turn, builds local organizational and recovery capacities. For example, when community members themselves manage the

A construction project gets under way in Choluteca, Honduras. The programme will provide permanent housing for survivors of Hurricane Mitch.

Yoshi Shimizu/ International Federation

International Federation
of Red Cross and Red Crescent Societies

recovery effort, they may learn and use skills in project management and in other technical areas that they may not already possess.

The ownership of permanent shelters built with government or private assistance is an area of challenge and discrimination. An example of good practice is to register new structures in the name of both the male and female heads of the household. This helps secure the female position in the family and social structure. According to John Twigg, the author of *Technology, Post-disaster Housing Reconstruction and Livelihood Security,* "joint ownership made women feel more secure and proud, and it appeared to reduce the incidence of marital conflict and domestic violence as well as improving relationships between mothers-in-law and daughters-in-law".

At the centre of discrimination in implementation are two basic formal forces. Firstly, the institutional distinction between relief and risk reduction dictates that the majority of disaster management resources are directed towards, and consumed in, relief efforts. Recent global efforts to mainstream risk reduction have helped improve this. They have been successful, to an extent.

Secondly, the industry standard of credibility is more focused on financial credibility than credibility in the eyes of recovering communities. Even beneficiary surveys, popular since the Gujarat earthquake – such as the 2002 UK Disasters Emergency Committee evaluation and the 2002 *Community Survey: Gujarat Earthquake 2001* by AIDMI and the ProVention Consortium – are for head offices and donors. Efforts to share the results of these surveys more widely within the humanitarian response sector and with the communities themselves rarely come to fruition, as pressures from many sides limit the follow-up.

In order to reduce improper discrimination against local recovery efforts, tools and techniques are required to assess and monitor an agency's credibility within a community that could result in a 'community credibility rating'. Methods to award such ratings already exist, as was shown in the UK Disasters Emergency Committee's Gujarat earthquake evaluation; but they are often not used or encouraged. Resources should be prioritized to organizations that score high on such a rating. "But is it possible? Whose recovery is it? Is recovery a project of NGOs or INGOs? Or is recovery a right of affected communities towards human security?" asks a southern India-wide coastal network coordinator, Jacob Dharamaraj (see Box 6.5).

Monitoring and evaluation

Identifying and reducing humanitarian discrimination during monitoring and evaluation can be encouraged through clearly identified and open evaluation procedures. The ability of individual evaluators to distil and share lessons on discrimination for future use is critical.

Box 6.5 Local organizations managing recovery

Community recovery committees (CRCs) – made up of local people – emerge following disasters to lead efforts in relief and long-term recovery. CRCs are created in the aftermath of a disaster or they evolve from existing structures and take on new roles and responsibilities.

In Kenya, local non-governmental organizations (NGOs) and communities participate with the district government authorities in district disaster management groups (DDMGs). These DDMGs have been invested with decision-making powers, devolved from central government disaster management structures, to determine not only the needs on the ground and the resources required, but also to decide which humanitarian agency will take the lead for specific humanitarian activities. The fact that these DDMGs were able to coordinate local humanitarian agencies at the district

level, led the Kenya Red Cross Society and the International Federation of Red Cross and Red Crescent Societies to modify their normal approach to disaster assessment. They planned their responses to the 2004–2006 droughts on assessments at the district level, rather than organizing their own needs assessments.

When CRCs work in tandem with humanitarian agencies, there is significant scope for reducing action that may be inadvertently discriminatory. In response to severe flooding in Gujarat, India, during 2006, a committee in the town of Kheda worked with a support agency to determine which 15 families out of the 200 requesting assistance would receive shelter support. The CRC and support agency visited the locations of the families to assess who was most in need of assistance. ■

There is also concern among the humanitarian evaluation community that evaluators are selected based on whom they have evaluated for in the past and not for their understanding of the local context. How many local evaluators are hired by international organizations? Thus, the bias against observing discrimination and the local context in favour of observing institutional and project objectives continues. Moreover, "once discrimination is found, what actions are taken? How many agencies that we know are denied funds or operational responsibility for being able to be inclusive enough?" asked Palani Thurai, of Gandhigram University, Tamil Nadu, during the evaluation of a global federation of INGOs. Donors committed to eliminate discrimination should invest in such a 'joint anti-discrimination index' and make it public. However, this is easier said than done. Federative structures such as the UK Disasters Emergency Committee may take a lead in recognizing and rating the actions of its members to promote anti-discrimination.

New and innovative systems for conducting evaluations that address inclusion are neglected in favour of old methods. As previously stated, evaluations are typically project- or organization-dominated. This reflects neither the multidisciplinary effects

International Federation
of Red Cross and Red Crescent Societies

that disasters and humanitarian responses have on local systems nor the multidisciplinary nature of discrimination. The trend towards joint evaluations is an important development that should be supported to improve further accountability and application. AIDMI is proposing joint and mixed evaluations, with mixed coverage, mixed methods, and mixed teams for evaluation. Evaluations have suffered from a lack of creativity and imagination in their methods, presentation and use. Will we ever see multimedia evaluations? Discrimination, when reported through multimedia, is better communicated. Evaluations conducted with respect to needs, rights and wider impacts, not project objectives, will help identify situations where discrimination has taken place (see Box 6.6).

Agencies will be better able to identify and address discrimination by organizing a diverse group of individuals to conduct *their* evaluations. The group should include individuals from both the agency and the disaster-affected community.

In order to support an environment that is conducive to reducing discrimination in evaluation, the following are recommended:

- Evaluations should not be conducted based on needs that were assessed in the past, nor should they use a top-down approach.
- Communities and local agencies should be supported to evaluate donor ability to learn from projects conducted in the name of the community.
- Community ratings are needed of NGO and donor performance.

Conclusion

Resolutions, commitments, codes and principles have helped and continue to help guide the humanitarian system towards relief and recovery strategies that are more effective. These are both too many and not enough. They are too many in the sense that humanitarian actors are overwhelmed by a variety of issues and priorities that they should mainstream into their efforts; from anti-discrimination to gender balance and risk reduction. Yet, they are not enough in that a new organizational culture is needed among major humanitarian actors to encourage field staff to take their own initiatives towards achieving improved inclusion.

In humanitarian crises, local and external recovery teams are pressured into making decisions rapidly and with less than adequate information. Some degree of discrimination will result at each level and in each phase. Recovery specialists should be aware that inclusion requires constant vigilance throughout the project cycle.

Above all, understanding and respect for the complex cultural context of the relief and recovery interventions and the use of the various strategies and mechanisms to detect, minimize and address discrimination will greatly improve the effectiveness and equity of recovery assistance.

CHAPTER 6

Box 6.6 Challenging discrimination: measuring the impact of what we do in emergencies

Save the Children UK has developed an impact, monitoring and assessment framework that aims to provide accountability to the people with and for whom we work – especially children. While itially designed to assess impact in ongoing development work, the system is proving to be equally applicable in emergencies and humanitarian interventions. Global Impact Monitoring (GIM) was developed in 2001 to improve the way the organization measures and summarizes the impact of its work.

In addition, as Save the Children moved increasingly towards a child rights-based approach to programming, it needed a system for monitoring and assessing impact that would reflect this approach.

The key elements of GIM are:

- a focus on impact
- a common framework, which affords comparison across country and regional programmes within a particular theme of work
- a country-level process that identifies positive and negative changes in people's lives in conjunction with external and internal stakeholders, and a focus on what works and what does not under different circumstances

After being piloted from 2001 to 2003, it was rolled out across the whole organization in 2004. GIM measures changes that have occurred as a result of interventions along five dimensions of change. These dimensions are:

1. changes in the lives of children and young people
2. changes in policies and practices that affect children's rights
3. changes in children's and young people's participation and active citizenship
4. changes in equity and non-discrimination of children and young people

5. changes in civil society's and communities' capacity to support children's rights

The GIM process requires programmes to first identify the specific changes they want to achieve, ensuring they encapsulate all five dimensions of change; then develop monitoring systems to gather data, both qualitative and quantitative, about whether these changes have occurred and their impact. This should be built into ongoing monitoring and periodic review and reflection processes. Country programmes choose methods of data collection that are most appropriate to the given context, but all programmes must involve stakeholders – including children and young people – as part of this process and make their voices paramount when judging success. Involving stakeholders and looking beyond predetermined indicators has the added advantage of highlighting any unintended and negative impacts.

In 2006, a Global Impact Monitoring exercise was conducted for the Tsunami Response Programme in Chennai, India. It became clear from the GIM stakeholder meetings that long-standing issues of discrimination that existed pre-tsunami made some communities more vulnerable post-tsunami. These findings led Save the Children to commission a larger report, *A Study on Non-Discrimination in the Tsunami Rehabilitation Programme in India*. The report indicated that children already subjected to some form of discrimination were possibly not only more affected by the tsunami but also, in some cases, excluded from relief and rehabilitation support. Information available suggests that there were more deaths among girls and children with disabilities than boys. Mobility and ability to swim appear to be two key factors in explaining the statistics.

International Federation of Red Cross and Red Crescent Societies

During the relief stage, entrenched patterns of discrimination were not addressed and were possibly reinforced. Dalit children received leftover clothing in relief camps and, as one Dalit girl said: "We are still living in a hut. Look at our neighbours from that village over there. Some of them have better houses than they had before."

Some post-tsunami policies had a detrimental effect on specific groups. The state government offered 20,000 rupees for marriages that had to be abandoned because of the tsunami. This led to a rise in the marriage of adolescent girls, in some cases to men who were old enough to be their fathers. Adolescent boys were another vulnerable group. The provision of new boats saw many forced into unpaid and hazardous work as boat labourers. These examples reflect just a fraction of the findings from the report, with tribal groups, female-headed households and settlers also being affected.

As a result, Save the Children made a series of recommendations for itself, other agencies, and district and state governments. The recommendations include the need for a greater focus on pre-existing social hierarchies and better awareness of discrimination in disaster preparedness activities – to ensure that those children who are marginalized, such as those with disabilities, are able to participate and be accounted for in disaster planning. It is also recommended that relief and rehabilitation interventions should map pre-existing patterns of discrimination and, if necessary, ensure a focus on those groups who have been previously excluded. ■

Recommended good practices to minimize discrimination in disaster recovery

1. Agencies that have a well-established rationale, criteria and processes for intervention and issue guidelines for field teams – with whom the agencies should work – are more likely to foster productive relations with communities and local partners.

2. Community recovery committees – a diverse group including different ethnicities, backgrounds and genders that are well trained, with adequate resources and able to communicate with the formal humanitarian system – can greatly assist equitable assistance. An oversight mechanism to ensure that discrimination against poor and neglected groups is minimized in the committees is needed and their assessments should be cross-checked.

3. Grievance processes that allow people to file their complaints and rapidly receive rulings regarding weaknesses in the relief system, discrimination and unfair treatment.

4. Providing access for communities to important information and services, such as multilingual pamphlets detailing entitlements, can increase community capabilities to coordinate with government and aid agencies and help them lead the recovery of their communities.

5. In situations where there is 'positive discrimination' for certain groups who have been traditionally left out of development and humanitarian assistance, or for

specific assistance priorities (infrastructure, livelihoods etc.), then higher levels of participation of community members will allow them to understand the rationale for such discrimination.

6. Registering new structures built in the aftermath of a disaster in the name of both male and female heads of household may help secure the female position in the family and social structures.

7. Displaying lists of external assistance received by each household on public institutions (schools, religious and community buildings) establishes local transparency systems.

8. Donor awareness of the importance of comprehensive needs assessments is necessary to reduce the potential for discrimination.

9. Identifying and reducing humanitarian discrimination during monitoring and evaluation can be encouraged through clearly identified and open evaluation procedures, and through joint and mixed evaluations. The use of mixed methods – including multimedia and open and frank discussions, and mixed teams involving evaluators with an understanding of the local context – is useful. Certain tools such as social equity audits and 'missing voices' interviews can also help.

Note

Some of the names in this chapter have been changed to protect those who have contributed to the work of AIDMI.

Principal contributors to this chapter were Mihir Bhatt, Honorary Director of the All India Disaster Mitigation Institute, a community-based action research, planning and advocacy organization, who also contributed Box 6.3 and Box 6.5; Steve Penny, a disaster and security management consultant, who is currently working in the area of disaster risk reduction, security management and inter-agency collaboration. We would also like to acknowledge the contribution of Mehul Pandya and Tommy Reynolds, respectively coordinator of the Regional Risk Transfer Initiative, AIDMI, and consultant, AIDMI. Box 6.1 was contributed by Tony Beck, a researcher and author who investigates the ways in which poor women and men cope with natural disasters. Box 6.2 was contributed by Iñigo Barrena, an independent consultant specializing in disaster risk reduction and recovery. Box 6.4 was contributed by Anthony Zwi, Professor of Public Health and Community Medicine at the Faculty of Medicine, The University of New South Wales, Sydney, Australia. Box 6.6 was contributed by Tina Hyder, Global Diversity Adviser at Save the Children UK.

Sources and further information

AIDMI. *Community Survey: Gujarat Earthquake 2001*. AIDMI and ProVention Consortium, 2002.

AIDMI. 'Joint Evaluations and Disaster Risk Reduction' in *southasiadisasters.net*, issue number 14. Ahmedabad, India: AIDMI, 2006.

ALNAP. *Humanitarian Action: Improving Performance through Improved Learning*. London: ODI, 2002.

Anderson, Mary B. *Do no harm: How aid can support peace – or war*. Lynne Rienner publishers, 1999.

Benson, C., Twigg, J. and Rossetto, T. *Tools for Mainstreaming Disaster Risk Reduction: Guidance Notes for Development Organisations*. Geneva: International Federation/ProVention Consortium, 2007. Available at www.proventionconsortium.org/themes/default/pdfs/tools_for_mainstreaming_DRR.pdf

Bhatt, M.R. *Integration of DRR in UNDP's Tsunami Recovery Programme in Sri Lanka*. Unpublished evaluation report, 2006.

Cannon, T., Twigg, J. and Rowell, J. *Social Vulnerability, Sustainable Livelihoods and Disasters: Report to DFID, Conflict and Humanitarian Assistance Department (CHAD) and Sustainable Livelihoods Support Office*. London: DFID, 2003. Available at www.benfieldhrc.org/disaster_studies/projects/soc_vuln_sust_live.pdf

Christoplos, Ian. *Links between relief, rehabilitation and development in the tsunami response*. London: Tsunami Evaluation Coalition, 2006. Available at www.tsunami-evaluation.org/NR/rdonlyres/01E8DB26-7306-4B30-B6D3-F6272D0ECF3A/0/lrrd_final_report.pdf

DFID. *Sustainable livelihoods guidance sheets*. London: DFID, 2001. Available at www.livelihoods.org/info/info_guidancesheets.html

DFID. *Post-Disaster Recovery Guidelines of the United Nations Development Programme*. London: 2001.

Emergency Capacity Building Project. *Impact Measurement and Accountability in Emergencies: The Good Enough Guide*. Oxfam Publishing, 2007.

Flint, M. and Goyder, H. *Funding the tsunami response*. London: Tsunami Evaluation Coalition, 2006. Available at www.tsunami-evaluation.org/NR/rdonlyres/BBA2659F-967C-4CAB-A08F-BEF67606C83F/0/funding_final_report.pdf

Grewal, M. K. *Approaches to Equity in Post-Tsunami Assistance. Sri Lanka: A Case Study*. New York: Office of the UN Special Envoy for Tsunami Recovery, 2006. Available at www.tsunami-evaluation.org/NR/rdonlyres/06B7033C-446F-407F-BF58-7D4A71425BFF/0/ApproachestoEquity.pdf

Humanitarian Initiatives with AIDMI. *Independent Evaluation: The DEC Response to the Earthquake in Gujarat*. London: DEC, 2001.

International Federation. *Aid: supporting or undermining recovery? Lessons from the Better Programming Initiative.* Geneva: International Federation, 2003.

La Trobe, S. and Davis, I. *Mainstreaming disaster risk reduction: a tool for development organisations.* Teddington, UK: Tearfund, 2005.

Mathys, Ellen. *Community-Managed Targeting and Distribution of Food Aid: A review of the experience of Save the Children UK in sub-Saharan Africa.* London: Save the Children, 2004. Available at www.savethechildren.org.uk/scuk_cache/scuk/cache/cmsattach/2008_CMTD_for_web.pdf

Murthy, Ranjani K. and Sagayam, Josephine. *A Study on Non-Discrimination in the Tsunami Rehabilitation Programme in India.* Chennai, India and Kathmandu, Nepal: Save the Children Tsunami Rehabilitation Programme and Save the Children Sweden Regional Office for South Central Asia, 2006.

Reynolds, T., Sinha, D. and Oza, S. *Assessing Tsunami Relief: A Community Survey in India.* Ahmedabad, India: AIDMI, 2006.

Routley, Sarah. 'Public Opinion Research Findings' in *Independent Evaluation of Expenditure of DEC India Earthquake Appeals Funds.* Humanitarian Initiatives, Disaster Mitigation Institute, Mango, 2001.

Scheper, E., Parakrama, A. and Patel, S. *Impact of the tsunami response on local and national capacities.* Annex 7: Sri Lanka claim-holder survey – summary. London: Tsunami Evaluation Coalition, 2006.

Twigg, John. *Technology, Post-disaster Housing Reconstruction and Livelihood Security.* Benfield HRC Disaster Studies Working Paper No. 15. London: Practical Action/Benfield HRC, 2006/2002. Available at www.benfieldhrc.org/disaster_studies/working_papers/pdfs/workingpaper15.pdf

World Food Programme (WFP). *Full Report of the Thematic Review of Targeting in WFP Relief Operations.* Rome: WFP, 2005. Available at documents.wfp.org/stellent/groups/public/documents/reports/wfp086129.pdf

Zwi, Anthony *et al. The Health and Peacebuilding Filter.* Sydney, Australia: The University of New South Wales, 2006. Available at www.med.unsw.edu.au/SPHCMWeb.nsf/resources/AUSCAN_Filter.pdf/$file/AUSCAN_Filter.pdf

Zwi, Anthony *et al. The Health and Peacebuilding Filter companion manual.* Sydney, Australia: The University of New South Wales, 2006. Available at www.med.unsw.edu.au/SPHCMWeb.nsf/resources/AUSCAN_Comp_Manual.pdf/$file/AUSCAN_Comp_Manual.pdf

International Federation
of Red Cross and Red Crescent Societies

Web sites

Active Learning Network for Accountability and Performance in Humanitarian Action (ALNAP) **www.alnap.org**

All India Disaster Mitigation Institute (AIDMI) **www.southasiadisasters.net**

Department for International Development (DFID) **www.dfid.gov.uk**

Disasters Emergency Committee **www.dec.org.uk**

Good Humanitarian Donorship **www.goodhumanitariandonorship.org**

Humanitarian Accountability Partnership (HAP) International **www.hapinternational.org**

ProVention Consortium **www.proventionconsortium.org**

The Sphere Project **www.sphereproject.org**

Tsunami Evaluation Coalition (TEC) **www.tsunami-evaluation.org**

UN Office of the Special Envoy for Tsunami Recovery **www.tsunamispecialenvoy.org/about**

International Federation
of Red Cross and Red Crescent Societies

World Disasters Report

Annex

ANNEX

International Federation
of Red Cross and Red Crescent Societies

Disaster data

In 2006, 427 natural disasters were reported worldwide – around the same level as in 2005 – according to the Centre for Research on the Epidemiology of Disasters (CRED). The number of people reported to be affected by these disasters (142 million) dropped 10 per cent, while the number of people reported as killed (23,833) plunged by nearly 75 per cent, compared to the previous year.

By contrast, the number of technological disasters in 2006 (297) dropped 20 per cent compared to 2005, with the death toll (9,900) decreasing by 15 per cent. However, the number of people reported as affected grew from 100,000 to 172,000.

The combined death toll from natural and technological disasters (33,733) during 2006 was the lowest of the decade, far below the 120,000 decade average. Natural disasters accounted for 70 per cent of the fatalities. The deadliest disaster last year was an earthquake in Yogyakarta, Indonesia, on 27 May 2006 that resulted in the deaths of 5,778 people.

Natural disasters were responsible for the overwhelming majority of people reported to be affected by all disasters, but the total number was almost 50 per cent less than the decade average of 268 million per year.

During 2006, 27 disasters (nine windstorms, nine droughts, eight floods and one earthquake) affected more than 1 million people each. Twenty of these disasters occurred in Asia, while the seven remaining disasters were all droughts that occurred in Africa. None of these events was on the scale of the floods in Asia in 2004, which affected over 100 million people in Bangladesh, India and China.

The cost of damage inflicted by natural disasters last year was estimated at nearly US$ 34.5 billion – the second lowest figure of the decade and less than half the decade average of US$ 78.7 billion per year. Of the costs reported, windstorms accounted for almost half of the total and floods for almost a quarter.

Comparing data for the past decade (1997–2006) with data for the previous decade (1987–1996), the number of reported disasters grew from 4,241 to 6,806 – an increase of 60 per cent. Over the same period, the number of reported deaths doubled, from more than 600,000 to over 1.2 million; and the average number of people reported affected per year rose by 17 per cent, from approximately 230 million to 270 million. Meanwhile, the total cost of reported damage increased by 12 per cent, from US$ 717 billion to US$ 802 billion (2006 prices). Better reporting of smaller disasters partially explains these increases. However, more severe disasters are also on the increase (**see Tables 1–13**).

Photo opposite page: August 2005: Houston Astrodome becomes a camp for survivors of Hurricane Katrina. Over the past decade, natural disasters have claimed 1.2 million lives – double the previous decade. An average of 270 million people were reported affected each year, while total disaster damage amounted to US$ 800 billion.

Daniel Cima/ American Red Cross

Official Development Assistance (ODA) from members of the Development Assistance Committee (DAC) of the Organisation for Economic Co-operation and Development (OECD) grew substantially to US$ 106.8 billion in 2005 (the latest year for which complete data are available). This represents a leap of over US$ 25 billion or 32 per cent in real terms, compared to 2004. Much of the increase in aid went as debt relief for Iraq and Nigeria, plus generous aid to tsunami-affected countries. Across all 22 DAC donors, ODA averaged 0.33 per cent of GNI in 2005 – well below the UN's target of 0.7 per cent, but an improvement on 2004's average of 0.26 per cent. In 2005, humanitarian aid from DAC donors rose to US$ 7.2 billion, boosted by tsunami assistance. This total does not include relief provided by multilateral institutions and non-governmental organizations, nor support for refugees in donor countries (**see Figures 1–5**).

EM-DAT: a specialized disaster database

Tables 1–13 on natural and technological disasters and their human impact over the past decade were drawn and documented from CRED's EM-DAT. Established in 1973 as a non-profit institution, CRED is based at the School of Public Health of the Catholic University of Louvain in Belgium and became a World Health Organization (WHO) collaborating centre in 1980. Although CRED's main focus is on public health, the centre also studies the socio-economic and long-term effects of large-scale disasters.

Since 1988, with the sponsorship of the United States Agency for International Development's Office of Foreign Disaster Assistance (OFDA), CRED has maintained EM-DAT, a worldwide database on disasters. It contains essential core data on the occurrence and effects of more than 15,000 disasters in the world from 1900 to the present. The database is compiled from various sources, including UN agencies, non-governmental organizations, insurance companies, research institutes and press agencies.

Priority is given to data from UN agencies, followed by OFDA, governments and the International Federation. This prioritization is not a reflection of the quality or value of the data but the recognition that most reporting sources do not cover all disasters or may have political limitations that could affect the figures. The entries are constantly reviewed for redundancies, inconsistencies and the completion of missing data. CRED consolidates and updates data on a daily basis. A further check is made at monthly intervals. Revisions are made annually at the end of the calendar year.

The database's main objectives are to assist humanitarian action at both national and international levels; to rationalize decision-making for disaster preparedness; and to provide an objective basis for vulnerability assessment and priority setting.

Data definitions and methodology

CRED defines a disaster as "a situation or event which overwhelms local capacity, necessitating a request to national or international level for external assistance (definition considered in EM-DAT); an unforeseen and often sudden event that causes great damage, destruction and human suffering".

For a disaster to be entered into the database, at least one of the following criteria must be fulfilled:
- ten or more people reported killed
- a hundred people or more reported affected
- declaration of a state of emergency
- call for international assistance

The number of people killed includes persons confirmed as dead and persons missing and presumed dead. People affected are those requiring immediate assistance during a period of emergency (i.e. requiring basic survival needs such as food, water, shelter, sanitation and immediate medical assistance). People reported injured or homeless are aggregated with those reported affected to produce a 'total number of people affected'.

The economic impact of a disaster usually consists of direct consequences on the local economy (e.g. damage to infrastructure, crops, housing) and indirect consequences (e.g. loss of revenues, unemployment, market destabilization). In EM-DAT, the registered figure corresponds to the damage value at the moment of the event and usually only to the direct damage, expressed in US$ (2006 prices).

EM-DAT distinguishes two generic categories for disasters (natural and technological), divided into 15 main categories, themselves covering more than 50 sub-categories. For the production of the tables, natural disasters are split into two specific groups:
1. **hydro-meteorological disasters**: avalanches/landslides, droughts/famines, extreme temperatures, floods, forest/scrub fires, windstorms and other disasters, such as insect infestations and wave surges
2. **geophysical disasters**: earthquakes, tsunamis and volcanic eruptions

The technological disasters comprise three groups:
1. **industrial accidents**: chemical spills, collapses of industrial infrastructure, explosions, fires, gas leaks, poisoning, radiation
2. **transport accidents**: by air, rail, road or water means of transport
3. **miscellaneous accidents**: collapses of domestic/non-industrial structures, explosions, fires

In Tables 1–13, 'disasters' refer to disasters with a natural and technological trigger only, and do not include wars, conflict-related famines, diseases or epidemics.

The classification of countries as 'high', 'medium' or 'low human development' is based on the 2006 Human Development Index (HDI) of the United Nations Development Programme. For a small number of countries not appearing in the HDI, the World Bank's classification of economies by the countries' level of income is used ('high', 'middle' and 'low').

In EM-DAT and in the Tables, data are considered at country level for many reasons: first, it is at this level that they are reported most of the time; and second, because of issues regarding possible aggregation and disaggregation of data. For droughts and food insecurity, which are often multi-year disasters, their long-term impact must be taken into account (see Box 1).

CRED has therefore adopted the following rules (bearing in mind that data on deaths and economic damage from drought are infrequently reported):

- Total number of deaths reported for a drought is divided by the number of years for which the drought persists. The resulting number is registered for each year of the drought's duration.
- The same calculation is done for reported economic damage.
- For the total number of people reported to be affected, CRED considers that the same number is affected each year that the disaster persists.

Some disasters begin at the end of a year and may last some weeks or months into the following year. In this case, CRED has adopted the following rules:

- For those reported to be affected, the total number is recorded for both the 'start' year and the 'end' year.
- For the numbers of people reported to be killed, CRED distinguishes between disasters which are sudden-onset (earthquakes, flash floods, landslides etc.) and slow-onset (wildfires, some floods, extreme temperatures etc.), as follows:
  a. sudden-onset: all those killed are registered according to the start year of the disaster.
  b. slow-onset: the total of all those killed is divided by two and a half and is attributed to each year of persistence.
- Reported economic damage is always attributed to the end year of the disaster. This is because damage is related to both the strength of a disaster and its duration.

By using these rules, some data bias correction is attempted. However, they are far from perfect and CRED will try to improve them, as well as the database as a whole, in the future.

International Federation
of Red Cross and Red Crescent Societies

Box 1 New methodology for droughts and famines

Until recently, drought/famine events were inconsistently recorded in EM-DAT. These inconsistencies arose from the slow-onset, spatially extensive, prolonged and complex nature of drought. They included inconsistent establishment of start and end dates, misattribution of drought-related losses and difficulties with handling multi-year and multi-country events.

CRED, in collaboration with the International Research Institute for Climate and Society (IRI), has undertaken a comprehensive review of over 800 drought disaster events and 76 famines from 1900–2004, recorded in EM-DAT against 1,500 original sources. They have established a standardized methodology for characterizing drought events and reclassifying famine events contained in EM-DAT, by addressing four principal problems:

1. lack of a standard method for establishing attribution of drought-related losses
2. inconsistencies in recording start and end dates
3. problems created by multi-year droughts
4. problems created by droughts affecting multiple countries

This methodology for recording and tracking drought disasters in EM-DAT has important implications, such as facilitating the verification of drought losses in EM-DAT and improving the precision with which loss data are recorded in future entries.

Results from the application of the above methodology to EM-DAT are as follows:

1. The number of drought disaster entries has been reduced to 392 drought events.
2. Levels of drought-related losses have consequently been affected (e.g. 20 per cent increase in reported deaths, 35 per cent increase in estimated economic losses).
3. Issues affecting the interpretation of results have been raised (e.g. lack of precise information on location, inconsistencies in comparing different sources of information, limitations of tools used etc.).

The methodology is not perfect by any means, but users now have access to clear criteria against which CRED classifies these events in EM-DAT. The EM-DAT team will continue to work on improving the classification system to make it as transparent and rational as possible for users. For more information on the methodology, see: www.em-dat.net/documents/Methodology WebPage.pdf ■

Caveats

Key problems with disaster data include the lack of standardized collection methodologies and definitions. The original information, collected from a variety of public sources, is not specifically gathered for statistical purposes. So, even when the compilation applies strict definitions for disaster events and parameters, the original suppliers of information may not. Moreover, data are not always complete for each disaster. The quality of completion may vary according to the type of disaster (for example, the number of people affected by transport accidents is rarely reported) or its country of occurrence.

Data on deaths are usually available because they are an immediate proxy for the severity of the disaster. However, the numbers put forward immediately after a disaster may sometimes be seriously revised, occasionally several months later. The death tolls from food insecurity in the Democratic People's Republic of Korea (1995–2002) and from the heatwave in Europe (2003) are good examples of such revisions. In both cases, data from new analyses on the impacts of these disasters led CRED to revaluate EM-DAT's numbers.

Data on the numbers of people affected by a disaster can provide some of the most potentially useful figures, for planning both disaster preparedness and response, but they are sometimes poorly reported. Moreover, the definition of people affected remains open to interpretation, political or otherwise. Even in the absence of manipulation, data may be extrapolated from old census information, with assumptions being made about percentages of an area's population affected.

Data can also be skewed because of the rationale behind data gathering. Reinsurance companies, for instance, systematically gather data on disaster occurrence in order to assess insurance risk, but with a priority in areas of the world where disaster insurance is widespread. Their data may therefore miss out poor, disaster-affected regions where insurance is unaffordable or unavailable.

For natural disasters over the past decade, data on deaths are missing for around one tenth of reported disasters; data on people affected are missing for around one fifth of disasters; and data on economic damage are missing for 85 per cent of disasters. The figures should therefore be regarded as indicative. Relative changes and trends are more useful to look at than absolute, isolated figures.

Dates can be a source of ambiguity. For example, a declared date for a famine is both necessary and meaningless – a famine does not occur and end on a single day. In such cases, the date the appropriate body declares the beginning and/or end of an official emergency has been used. Changes in national boundaries cause ambiguities in the data and may make long-term trend analysis more complicated.

Information systems have improved vastly in the past 25 years and statistical data are now more easily available, intensified by an increasing sensitivity to disaster occurrence and consequences. Nevertheless there are still discrepancies. An analysis of quality and accuracy of disaster data, performed by CRED in 2002, showed that occasionally, for the same disaster, differences of more than 20 per cent may exist between the quantitative data reported by the three major databases – EM-DAT (CRED), NatCat (Munich Re) and Sigma (Swiss Re).

Despite efforts to verify and review data, the quality of disaster databases can only be as good as the reporting system. This, combined with the different aims of the three major disaster databases (risk and economic risk analysis for reinsurance companies, development agenda for CRED) may explain differences between data provided for some disasters. However, in spite of these differences, the overall trends indicated by the three databases remain similar.

The lack of systematization and standardization of data collection is a major weakness when it comes to long-term planning. Fortunately, due to increased pressures for accountability from various sources, many donors and development agencies have started giving attention to data collection and its methodologies.

Part of the solution to this data problem lies in retrospective analysis. Data are most often publicly quoted and reported during a disaster event, but it is only long after the event, once the relief operation is over, that estimates of damage and death can be verified. Some data gatherers, like CRED, revisit the data; this accounts for retrospective annual disaster figures changing one, two and sometimes even three years after the event.

Improved data in EM-DAT

Last year, significant efforts were made to improve the EM-DAT information available to the public. These changes, made according to a systematic and strict methodology, affect the results in some tables and may modify some trends. The main areas of change are as follows:

- Economic loss/damage: Information gaps and the lack of a single, consistent methodology led CRED to revise its dataset on economic data and consolidate its methodology on economic data entry. The revision of data led to significant increases for the years 2002–2005.
- Technological disasters: An ongoing review of data registered over the past three years led to an increase in the reported number of disasters, deaths and people affected, especially for 2005.

United States Committee for Refugees and Immigrants

The United States Committee for Refugees and Immigrants (USCRI) is the successor to the merged non-governmental organizations Immigration and Refugee Services of America and United States Committee for Refugees. USCRI resettles refugees, reports on the situation of refugees and asylum seekers abroad and encourages the public, policy-makers and the international community to respond appropriately and effectively to the needs of uprooted populations.

USCRI travels to the scene of refugee emergencies and protracted situations to gather testimony from uprooted people, to assess their needs and to gauge governmental, civil and international response. The committee conducts public briefings to present its findings and recommendations, testifies before the United States Congress, communicates concerns directly to governments and provides first-hand assessments to the media. USCRI publishes the annual *World Refugee Survey*, the twice-yearly *Refugee Reports* and issue papers.

USCRI provided the data in Tables 14–16. The quality of the data in these tables is affected by the less-than-ideal conditions often associated with flight. Unsettled conditions, the biases of governments and opposition groups and the need to use population estimates to plan for providing humanitarian aid can each contribute to inaccurate estimates. The estimates reproduced in these tables are accurate as at May 2007.

Table 14 lists refugees and asylum seekers by country of origin, while Table 15 lists them by host country. Refugees are people who are outside their home country and who are unable or unwilling to return to that country because they fear persecution or armed conflict. But most refugees never receive a formal status determination. Asylum seekers are people who claim and, prima facie, appear to be refugees. While not all asylum seekers are refugees, they are in need of international protection, at least until it is clear that they are not refugees. USCRI also includes persons granted various subsidiary forms of protection if based on factors related to the refugee definition, as distinct from, for example, protection granted because of natural disaster.

Table 16 concerns internally displaced people (IDPs). Like refugees and asylum seekers, IDPs have fled their homes, but remain in their home country. No universally accepted definition of IDPs exists, nor is it clear when their situation ceases to be of concern. USCRI generally considers people who are uprooted within their country because of armed conflict or persecution – and who would thus be refugees if they were to cross an international border – to be internally displaced. Others employ broader definitions, however, sometimes including people uprooted by natural or human-made disasters or other causes not directly related to human rights. IDPs often live in war-torn areas and are neither registered nor counted in any systematic way. Estimates of the size of IDP populations are frequently prone to great margins of error.

Philippe Hoyois, senior research fellow with CRED, Regina Below, manager of CRED's EM-DAT disaster database and Debarati Guha-Sapir, director of CRED, prepared the sections on natural and technological disasters. For further information, please contact: Centre for Research on the Epidemiology of Disasters (CRED), School of Public Health, Catholic University of Louvain, 30.94, Clos Chapelle-aux-Champs, B-1200 Brussels, Belgium. Tel.: +32 2 764 3327 Fax: +32 2 764 3441 E-mail: cred@esp.ucl.ac.be Web: www.em-dat.net. Box 1 is based on an article submitted for publication: Below R., Grover-Kopec E. and Dilley M., Drought-related disasters: A global reassessment, *2006.*

The section on refugees, asylum seekers and IDPs was prepared by the US Committee for Refugees and Immigrants, 1717 Massachusetts Avenue NW, Suite 200, Washington DC 20036, United States (www.refugees.org). For questions regarding this section or data, please contact msmith@uscridc.org.

ANNEX

ANNEX

Figure 1
ODA net disbursements by DAC member countries
(US$ million, 2005 prices): 1996–2005

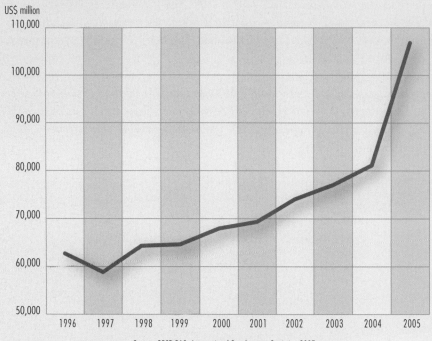

Source: OECD DAC: *International Development Statistics*, 2007

Official development assistance (ODA) from the 22 members of the Development Assistance Committee (DAC) of the Organisation for Economic Co-operation and Development (OECD) to developing countries leapt to a record US$ 106.8 billion in 2005 (the latest year for which complete data are available). This represents an increase of US$ 25.6 billion or 32 per cent compared with 2004, when taking account of both inflation and exchange rate movements.

The figures (at constant 2005 prices) reveal that in 2005 wealthy governments gave 81 per cent more aid in real terms than in 1997, the lowest point of ODA over the past decade.

The main factors which accounted for the increase in 2005 were:
- Debt relief for Iraq and Nigeria. In 2005, DAC members provided debt forgiveness grants of US$ 13.9 billion to Iraq and US$ 5.5 billion to Nigeria.
- Tsunami aid. DAC members provided US$ 2.2 billion in official assistance to countries affected by the devastating Indian Ocean tsunami in December 2004.

Humanitarian aid rose by 15.8 per cent. The largest recipients of net ODA in 2005 were: Iraq (US$ 21.4 billion), Nigeria (US$ 6 billion), Indonesia (US$ 2.2 billion), Afghanistan (US$ 2.2 billion), China (US$ 1.7 billion) and Sudan (US$ 1.5 billion).

These figures do not take into account non-DAC donors' development assistance, private flows, grants by non-governmental organizations, or disbursements to countries in transition.

International Federation
of Red Cross and Red Crescent Societies

Figure 2

ODA net disbursements by DAC member countries in 2005
(US$ million, 2005 prices)

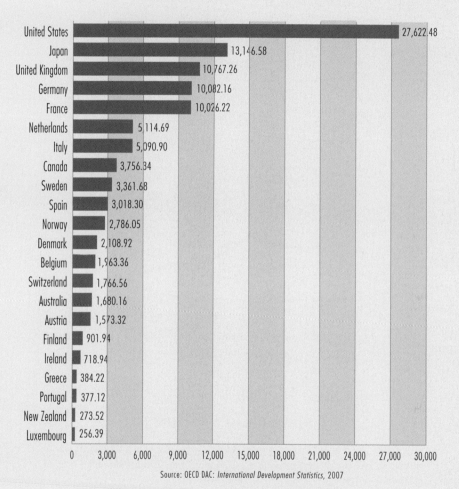

Source: OECD DAC: *International Development Statistics*, 2007

The five biggest donors of ODA in 2005 were the United States
(26 per cent of all ODA), Japan (12 per cent), the United Kingdom
(10 per cent), and Germany and France (both 9 per cent). Their combined
total of US$ 71.6 billion (2005 prices) represents two-thirds of all ODA.

If the contributions of the 15 countries forming the European Union (before its
enlargement) are aggregated, their ODA amounts to US$ 55.7 billion (2005
prices), representing 52 per cent of all ODA.

Figure 3

ODA: evolution of DAC member countries' contributions (US$ million, 2005 prices)

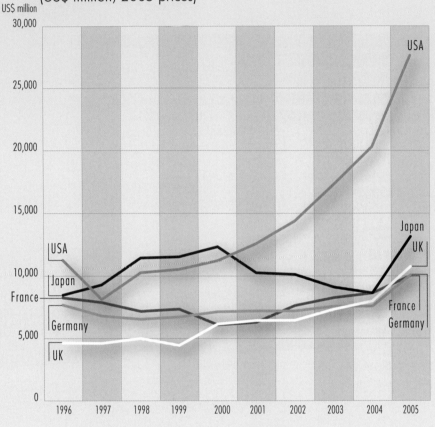

Source: OECD DAC: *International Development Statistics*, 2007

In 2005, each of the five biggest DAC donors set new records for the decade in disbursing aid to developing countries. Compared with 2004, their dollar and percentage increases in 2005 in real terms were:

• United States: up US$ 7.3 billion – 36 per cent
• Japan: up US$ 4.5 billion – 52 per cent
• United Kingdom: up US$ 2.8 billion – 35 per cent
• Germany: up US$ 2.5 billion – 33 per cent
• France: up US$ 1.4 billion – 16 per cent

Compared with their lowest levels of the decade, the amount of United States' development assistance more than tripled in 2005, while the amount of aid from the United Kingdom was more than double, in real terms.

Japan's more generous aid in 2005 reversed a downward trend which had seen its development assistance decline since 2000.

International Federation of Red Cross and Red Crescent Societies

Figure 4

ODA as percentage of DAC member countries' GNI, 2005

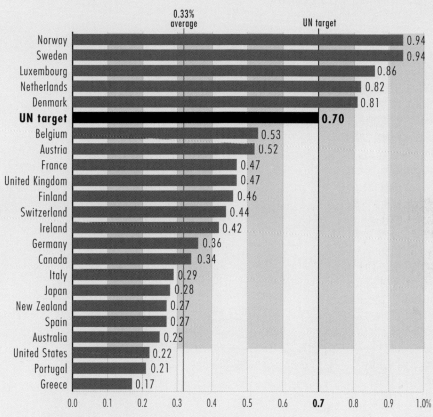

Source: OECD DAC: *International Development Statistics*, 2007

Expressed as a percentage of donor countries' gross national income (GNI), only five countries (Norway, Sweden, Luxembourg, the Netherlands and Denmark) exceeded the UN's 0.7 per cent target for ODA during 2005.

Compared with 2004, the proportion of aid as a percentage of GNI increased in 2005 for all countries except: Australia, Denmark, Greece and Portugal. Austria registered the biggest proportional increase, from 0.23 to 0.52 per cent of GNI. Portugal registered the biggest proportional decrease, from 0.63 to 0.21 per cent of GNI.

Across all 22 donors, aid averaged 0.33 per cent of GNI in 2005 – well below the UN's target, but an improvement on 2004's average of 0.26 per cent.

Figure 5

Emergency/distress relief from DAC member countries in 2005
(US$ million, 2005 prices)

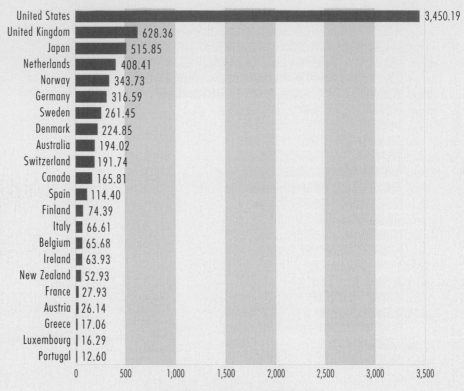

United States	3,450.19
United Kingdom	628.36
Japan	515.85
Netherlands	408.41
Norway	343.73
Germany	316.59
Sweden	261.45
Denmark	224.85
Australia	194.02
Switzerland	191.74
Canada	165.81
Spain	114.40
Finland	74.39
Italy	66.61
Belgium	65.68
Ireland	63.93
New Zealand	52.93
France	27.93
Austria	26.14
Greece	17.06
Luxembourg	16.29
Portugal	12.60

Source: OECD DAC: *International Development Statistics*, 2007

In 2005, humanitarian aid from DAC donors totalled US$ 7.2 billion
(2005 prices), a 36 per cent increase on 2004.

The United States accounted for nearly half of DAC humanitarian aid in
2005, followed by the United Kingdom (9 per cent), Japan (7 per cent)
and the Netherlands (6 per cent).

In 2006, the DAC replaced the term 'emergency/distress relief' with a new
definition of humanitarian aid. Reporting on support for refugees in donor
countries, which was previously included in the emergency/distress relief
total, is now excluded from humanitarian aid and recorded as a separate
item in DAC statistics.

The combined total for DAC member countries' humanitarian aid and
support for refugees in donor countries in 2005 was US$ 9.3 billion.

Table 1 Total number of reported disasters[1], by continent and by year (1997 to 2006)

	1997	1998	1999	2000	2001	2002	2003	2004	2005	2006	Total
Africa	57	80	146	201	183	195	170	163	169	198	1,562
Americas	103	115	137	152	129	155	123	138	139	105	1,296
Asia	200	216	242	304	288	303	287	319	358	306	2,823
Europe	62	69	79	128	94	112	92	98	122	97	953
Oceania	15	17	15	13	18	19	20	21	16	18	172
High human development[2]	141	143	153	204	165	184	153	161	181	160	1,645
Medium human development	251	289	377	456	404	471	420	470	482	414	4,034
Low human development	45	65	89	138	143	129	119	108	141	150	1,127
Total	**437**	**497**	**619**	**798**	**712**	**784**	**692**	**739**	**804**	**724**	**6,806**

Source: EM-DAT, CRED, University of Louvain, Belgium

[1] In Tables 1–13, 'disasters' refer to those with a natural or technological trigger only, and do not include wars, conflict-related famines, diseases or epidemics.
[2] See note on UNDP's Human Development Index country status in the section on disaster definitions in the introduction to this annex.

With 724 reported disasters, 2006 was the fifth worst year of the decade.

Asia remains the most frequently hit continent in 2006, accounting for 42 per cent of the year's disasters.

For Africa, 2006 was the second worst year of the decade.

In countries of low human development, disasters peaked in 2006.

Table 2 Total number of people reported killed, by continent and by year (1997 to 2006)

	1997	1998	1999	2000	2001	2002	2003	2004	2005	2006	Total
Africa	4,079	3,316	2,708	5,700	4,501	7,584	6,152	4,246	3,241	5,768	47,295
Americas	3,073	21,832	34,001	2,062	3,440	2,079	2,152	8,267	5,475	1,555	83,936
Asia	93,082	104,613	98,148	87,904	105,292	89,469	38,525	238,362	90,830	20,572	966,797
Europe	1,177	1,445	19,451	1,586	2,202	1,717	72,140	1,259	1,006	5,814	107,797
Oceania	358	2,229	116	205	9	91	64	35	46	24	3,177
High human development[1]	2,628	3,315	5,543	2,459	2,089	2,013	72,720	1,579	3,622	5,009	100,977
Medium human development	94,966	119,893	147,129	90,314	110,098	91,780	43,520	242,822	93,641	24,636	1,058,799
Low human development	4,175	10,227	1,752	4,684	3,257	7,147	2,793	7,768	3,335	4,088	49,226
Total	**101,769**	**133,435**	**154,424**	**97,457**	**115,444**	**100,940**	**119,033**	**252,169**	**100,598**	**33,733**	**1,209,002**

Source: EM-DAT, CRED, University of Louvain, Belgium

[1] See note on UNDP's Human Development Index country status in the section on disaster definitions in the introduction to this annex.

In 2006, the number of people reported killed was the lowest of the decade.

In 2006, 61 per cent of people killed by disasters lived in Asia, below the decade's average of 80 per cent. Africa's share of deaths from global disasters in 2006 was four times higher than the decade's average, while the share of deaths for low human development countries was three times higher than the decade's average.

The decade saw a number of major disasters: famine in the Democratic People's Republic of Korea from 1995 to 2002 (more than 600,000 deaths); the Indian Ocean tsunami, 2004 (226,408 deaths); the South Asia earthquake, 2005 (74,647 deaths); a heatwave in Europe, 2003 (more than 70,000 deaths); floods in Venezuela, 1999 (30,000 deaths); three earthquakes: one in Iran, 2003 (Bam: 26,796 deaths), one in India, 2001 (Gujarat: 20,005 deaths), one in Turkey, 1999 (Izmit: 17,127 deaths); and a hurricane in Central America, 1998 (Mitch: 18,791 deaths).

International Federation
of Red Cross and Red Crescent Societies

Table 3 Total number of people reported affected, by continent and by year (1997 to 2006) in thousands

	1997	1998	1999	2000	2001	2002	2003	2004	2005	2006	Total[2]
Africa	10,123	10,852	37,650	41,102	44,845	43,980	28,301	35,902	21,847	21,965	296,567
Americas	3,304	17,268	17,294	979	10,806	2,097	3,995	9,703	8,291	1,447	75,184
Asia	65,998	326,368	232,920	202,229	184,827	660,942	234,977	132,509	127,458	119,095	2,287,323
Europe	549	3,401	6,311	2,911	787	1,443	1,547	538	530	256	18,273
Oceania	530	822	145	7	31	46	38	119	28	38	1,804
High human development[1]	1,961	2,242	8,694	1,234	7,412	1,955	1,073	6,269	6,919	758	38,517
Medium human development	69,259	349,269	253,313	207,068	190,538	663,263	242,036	153,954	130,490	118,681	2,377,870
Low human development	9,285	7,200	32,313	38,927	43,347	43,290	25,749	18,548	20,744	23,363	262,766
Total	**80,505**	**358,711**	**294,320**	**247,228**	**241,296**	**708,508**	**268,858**	**178,771**	**158,154**	**142,801**	**2,679,151**

Source: EM-DAT, CRED, University of Louvain, Belgium

[1] See note on UNDP's Human Development Index country status in the section on disaster definitions in the introduction to this annex.

[2] Since slow-onset disasters can affect the same people for a number of years, it is best to use figures on total numbers affected to calculate annual averages over a decade rather than as absolute totals.

On the basis of available data, an average of almost 270 million people were reported to be affected annually by disasters from 1997–2006; 85 per cent of them in Asia.

In 2006, the number of people affected was almost half the decade's average. It was the lowest for the decade in Europe and in high human development countries.

Over the decade, 10 per cent of those affected lived in countries of low human development. In 2006, this proportion grew to 16 per cent.

Table 4 Total amount of disaster estimated damage, by continent and by year (1997 to 2006) in millions of US dollars (2006 prices)

	1997	1998	1999	2000	2001	2002	2003	2004	2005	2006	Total
Africa	42	264	710	1,008	704	176	6,064	1,580	30	229	10,807
Americas	9,204	23,872	26,293	5,042	13,698	8,385	18,311	49,041	178,093	5,398	337,337
Asia	32,332	53,955	40,917	24,561	13,945	10,330	19,519	68,459	25,306	25,133	314,457
Europe	12,375	7,300	40,904	9,760	1,783	32,652	15,559	1,947	6,308	2,428	131,016
Oceania	294	416	1,085	628	309	2,445	658	589	226	1,286	7,936
High human development[1]	21,206	23,390	68,586	24,279	16,408	42,324	41,626	93,203	182,062	9,890	522,972
Medium human development	33,023	60,233	41,304	16,122	14,025	11,608	18,264	28,358	27,900	24,582	275,420
Low human development	18	2,183	18	598	7	56	222	54	1	3	3,162
Total	**54,247**	**85,807**	**109,909**	**40,999**	**30,439**	**53,988**	**60,111**	**121,616**	**209,963**	**34,475**	**801,553**

Source: EM-DAT, CRED, University of Louvain, Belgium

[1] See note on UNDP's Human Development Index country status in the section on disaster definitions in the introduction to this annex.

As mentioned in the introduction, damage assessment is frequently unreliable. Even for the existing data, the methodologies are not standardized and the financial coverage can vary significantly. Depending on where the disaster occurs and who reports it, estimations may vary from zero to billions of US dollars.

Amount of damage reported for 2006 was the second lowest of the decade after 2001.

In 2006, ten disasters caused damage estimated at more than US$ 1 billion: two floods in India and the United States, two typhoons in China and one in Japan, one tornado in the United States, one tropical storm in Australia, one heatwave in China and one cold wave in Russia.

In 2006, the six costliest disasters occurred in Asia. This continent accounted for 73 per cent of damage, far above its 39 per cent average of the decade. By contrast, in the Americas, the amount of damage was low compared to the previous nine years.

High human development countries accounted for 29 per cent of damage in 2006, far below their average of 65 per cent for the decade.

Table 5 Total number of reported disasters, by type of phenomenon and by year (1997 to 2006)

	1997	1998	1999	2000	2001	2002	2003	2004	2005	2006	Total
Avalanches/Landslides	13	22	15	29	21	19	21	17	12	19	188
Droughts/Food insecurity	19	32	33	43	42	39	23	18	27	18	294
Earthquakes/Tsunamis	22	29	33	31	25	36	40	43	24	24	307
Extreme temperatures	3	12	8	31	23	15	22	19	29	32	204
Floods	79	87	112	155	158	173	160	133	194	235	1,486
Forest/scrub fires	15	16	22	30	14	23	14	8	13	10	165
Volcanic eruptions	4	4	5	5	6	7	2	5	9	12	59
Windstorms	58	73	86	102	97	112	77	125	125	77	942
Other natural disasters[1]	3	2	2	4	2	0	0	12	0	0	25
Subtotal hydro-meteorological disasters	*210*	*244*	*278*	*394*	*357*	*381*	*317*	*332*	*400*	*391*	*3,304*
Subtotal geophysical disasters	*26*	*33*	*38*	*36*	*31*	*43*	*42*	*48*	*33*	*36*	*366*
Total natural disasters	**236**	**277**	**316**	**430**	**388**	**424**	**359**	**380**	**433**	**427**	**3,670**
Industrial accidents	35	43	37	51	54	48	52	81	76	61	538
Miscellaneous accidents	30	29	52	58	49	52	44	62	66	32	474
Transport accidents	136	148	214	259	221	260	237	216	229	204	2,124
Total technological disasters	**201**	**220**	**303**	**368**	**324**	**360**	**333**	**359**	**371**	**297**	**3,136**
Total	**437**	**497**	**619**	**798**	**712**	**784**	**692**	**739**	**804**	**724**	**6,806**

Source: EM-DAT, CRED, University of Louvain, Belgium

[1] Insect infestations and waves/surges.

In 2006, the three most frequent types of reported disasters were floods (32 per cent), transport accidents (28 per cent), extreme temperatures and volcanic eruptions.

Over the past decade, 2006 saw the highest number of floods, extreme temperatures and windstorms (10 per cent).

By contrast, the number of droughts, wild fires and miscellaneous accidents was among the lowest of the decade.

ANNEX

Table 6 Total number of people reported killed, by type of phenomenon and by year (1997 to 2006)

	1997	1998	1999	2000	2001	2002	2003	2004	2005	2006	Total
Avalanches/Landslides	801	1,141	351	1,023	692	1,149	706	357	646	1,647	8,513
Droughts/Food insecurity	76,510	76,530	76,370	76,392	76,472	76,893	38	80	88	74	459,447
Earthquakes/Tsunamis	3,059	7,391	21,869	216	21,348	1,634	29,617	227,317	76,241	6,692	395,384
Extreme temperatures	619	3,211	771	916	1,653	3,369	73,164	556	790	5,214	90,263
Floods	6,971	9,534	34,369	6,040	4,662	4,122	3,717	6,957	5,808	5,862	88,042
Forest/scrub fires	32	119	70	47	33	6	47	14	45	16	429
Volcanic eruptions	53	n.a.	n.a.	n.a.	n.a.	200	n.a.	2	3	5	263
Windstorms	5,332	24,740	11,918	1,148	1,735	1,116	1,002	6,557	5,325	4,323	63,196
Other natural disasters[1]	400	2,182	3	1	n.a.	ndr	ndr	n.a.	ndr	ndr	2,586
Subtotal hydro-meteorological disasters	90,665	117,457	123,852	85,567	85,247	86,655	78,674	14,521	12,702	17,136	712,476
Subtotal geophysical disasters	3,112	7,391	21,869	216	21,348	1,834	29,617	227,319	76,244	6,697	395,647
Total natural disasters	93,777	124,848	145,721	85,783	106,595	88,489	108,291	241,840	88,946	23,833	1,108,123
Industrial accidents	1,055	1,942	740	1,770	1,270	1,112	1,444	1,797	2,281	1,801	15,212
Miscellaneous accidents	1,277	747	1,323	1,336	1,725	2,013	1,430	2,115	2,669	1,090	15,725
Transport accidents	5,660	5,898	6,640	8,568	5,854	9,326	7,868	6,417	6,702	7,009	69,942
Total technological disasters	7,992	8,587	8,703	11,674	8,849	12,451	10,742	10,329	11,652	9,900	100,879
Total	101,769	133,435	154,424	97,457	115,444	100,940	119,033	252,169	100,598	33,733	1,209,002

Source: EM-DAT, CRED, University of Louvain, Belgium

[1] Insect infestations and waves/surges.

Note: n.a. signifies "no data available"; ndr signifies "no disaster reported". For more information, see section on caveats in introductory text.

In 2006, reported deaths from natural disasters were at their lowest level of the decade.

Transport accidents and earthquakes each accounted for one fifth of all deaths from disasters in 2006. For transport accidents, this proportion is four times the average for the decade. However, earthquakes have on average claimed one third of all disaster deaths across the decade.

In 2006, deaths associated with extreme temperatures were the second highest of the decade, though much lower than 2003's peak. In both years, deaths were almost entirely attributed to heatwaves in Europe.

The majority of reported deaths caused by droughts and food insecurity during the decade were attributed to the famine in the Democratic People's Republic of Korea.

Table 7 Total number of people reported affected, by type of phenomenon and by year (1997 to 2006) in thousands

	1997	1998	1999	2000	2001	2002	2003	2004	2005	2006	Total[2]
Avalanches/Landslides	34	213	15	215	67	1,021	459	231	10	419	2,684
Droughts/Food insecurity	19,655	35,461	112,591	159,681	166,072	428,279	80,877	34,272	29,631	39,671	1,106,190
Earthquakes/Tsunamis	1,297	3,668	6,856	2,479	9,711	851	4,194	3,147	3,928	3,851	39,982
Extreme temperatures	613	36	725	27	213	104	1,840	2,140	2	63	5,763
Floods	44,955	291,703	149,970	74,093	34,461	167,410	169,166	117,219	75,028	31,134	1,155,139
Forest/scrub fires	53	167	19	39	6	31	184	21	8	3	531
Volcanic eruptions	7	8	34	119	78	278	25	53	332	379	1,313
Windstorms	13,725	27,328	23,768	10,511	30,635	110,464	11,447	21,383	49,114	67,109	365,484
Other natural disasters[1]	29	10	1	17	n.a.	ndr	ndr	n.a.	ndr	ndr	57
Subtotal hydro-meteorological disasters	79,064	354,919	287,089	244,584	231,454	707,310	263,972	175,264	153,793	138,399	2,635,848
Subtotal geophysical disasters	1,304	3,676	6,890	2,598	9,789	1,129	4,219	3,200	4,260	4,230	41,295
Total natural disasters	**80,368**	**358,594**	**293,979**	**247,181**	**241,243**	**708,438**	**268,192**	**178,466**	**158,053**	**142,629**	**2,677,143**
Industrial accidents	113	63	324	17	19	2	646	157	16	137	1,494
Miscellaneous accidents	20	50	12	24	31	61	15	102	77	32	424
Transport accidents	3	4	5	7	3	6	5	48	6	4	91
Total technological disasters	**136**	**117**	**341**	**48**	**53**	**69**	**666**	**307**	**99**	**173**	**2,009**
Total	**80,504**	**358,711**	**294,320**	**247,229**	**241,296**	**708,507**	**268,858**	**178,773**	**158,152**	**142,802**	**2,679,152**

Source: EM-DAT, CRED, University of Louvain, Belgium

[1] Insect infestations and waves/surges.
[2] Since slow-onset disasters can affect the same people for a number of years, it is best to use figures on total numbers affected to calculate annual averages over a decade rather than as absolute totals.
Note: n.a. signifies "no data available"; ndr signifies "no disaster reported". For more information, see section on caveats in introductory text.
Disasters which affected the most people in 2006 were windstorms (67 million affected: 47 per cent of those affected by all disasters), droughts (39.7 million affected: 28 per cent of those affected by all disasters) and floods (31 million affected: 22 per cent of those affected by all disasters).
In 2006, the number of people reported affected by windstorms was the second highest of the decade. For volcanic eruptions, it was the highest of the decade.
Over the decade, hydro-meteorological disasters accounted for 98 per cent of all those affected by disasters, with floods affecting 43 per cent and droughts 41 per cent.
In 2006, industrial accidents accounted for 80 per cent of the number of people affected by technological disasters.

Table 8 Total amount of disaster estimated damage, by type of phenomenon and by year (1997 to 2006) in millions of US dollars (2006 prices)

	1997	1998	1999	2000	2001	2002	2003	2004	2005	2006	Total
Avalanches/Landslides	20	1,136	n.a.	155	80	14	49	11	5	40	1,510
Droughts/Food insecurity	544	887	7,193	4,799	2,620	9,291	931	1,598	2,019	1,043	30,925
Earthquakes/Tsunamis	6,229	3,372	42,441	442	8,209	1,758	9,587	38,767	5,263	3,431	119,499
Extreme temperatures	3,774	5,284	1,211	145	228	n.a.	8,280	n.a.	160	3,910	22,992
Floods	14,526	48,892	17,656	22,258	4,128	29,284	15,712	14,981	17,680	8,048	193,165
Forest/scrub fires	21,368	1,584	594	1,240	n.a.	248	6,676	3	38	889	32,640
Volcanic eruptions	10	n.a.	n.a.	3	17	10	n.a.	n.a.	n.a.	150	190
Windstorms	7,713	24,455	40,807	11,312	15,147	2,147	18,875	64,859	184,364	16,963	386,642
Other natural disasters[1]	4	2	n.a.	141	n.a.	ndr	ndr	n.a.	ndr	ndr	147
Subtotal hydro-meteorological disasters	47,951	82,240	67,461	40,050	22,203	40,985	50,524	81,452	204,267	30,892	668,024
Subtotal geophysical disasters	6,239	3,372	42,441	445	8,226	1,768	9,587	38,767	5,263	3,581	119,689
Total natural disasters	54,188	85,612	109,902	40,495	30,429	42,752	60,110	120,219	209,529	34,474	787,710
Industrial accidents	24	159	4	n.a.	11	11,166	n.a.	961	423	n.a.	12,748
Miscellaneous accidents	32	23	3	505	n.a.	70	n.a.	n.a.	11	1	645
Transport accidents	1	13	n.a.	n.a.	n.a.	n.a.	n.a.	435	n.a.	n.a.	449
Total technological disasters	57	195	7	505	11	11,236	n.a.	1,396	434	1	13,842
Total	54,245	85,807	109,909	41,000	30,440	53,988	60,110	121,615	209,963	34,475	801,552

Source: EM-DAT, CRED, University of Louvain, Belgium

[1] Insect infestations and waves/surges.

Note: n.a. signifies "no data available"; ndr signifies "no disaster reported". For more information, see section on caveats in introductory text. Estimates of disaster damage must be treated with caution, as the financial value attached to infrastructure in developed countries is much higher than in developing countries. While reporting is better for large disasters, the low reporting rates of direct damage make analysis difficult.

The costliest reported disasters of the decade were windstorms (48 per cent), floods (24 per cent) and earthquakes/tsunamis (15 per cent).

In 2006, hydro-meteorological disasters accounted for 90 per cent of total disaster estimated damage, slightly above their average proportion for the decade.

Costs attributed to extreme temperatures in 2006 were 70 per cent above their decade's average, but far below the peak of 2003.

Over the decade, 100 disasters caused damage of US$ 1–10 billion; six disasters caused damage of US$ 10–100 billion (flood in China, 1998; Niigata earthquake in Japan, 2004; forest fires in Indonesia, 1997; Hurricane Rita in US, 2005; Chi-Chi earthquake in Taiwan, 1999; flood in Germany, 2002); and one disaster caused damage of more than US$ 100 billion (Hurricane Katrina in the United States, 2005).

International Federation of Red Cross and Red Crescent Societies

Table 9 Total number of reported disasters, by type of phenomenon, by continent and by level of human development[2] (1997 to 2006)

	Africa	Americas	Asia	Europe	Oceania	HHD	MHD	LHD	Total
Avalanches/Landslides	11	38	115	17	7	25	148	15	188
Droughts/Food insecurity	131	58	79	17	9	38	156	100	294
Earthquakes/Tsunamis	22	44	182	51	8	54	226	27	307
Extreme temperatures	4	38	55	106	1	112	88	4	204
Floods	337	306	547	253	43	425	761	300	1,486
Forest/scrub fires	12	70	23	46	14	101	58	6	165
Volcanic eruptions	7	28	15	1	8	14	42	3	59
Windstorms	72	319	362	121	68	467	429	46	942
Other natural disasters[1]	13	2	6	1	3	2	15	8	25
Subtotal hydro-meteorological disasters	*580*	*831*	*1,187*	*561*	*145*	*1,170*	*1,655*	*479*	*3,304*
Subtotal geophysical disasters	*29*	*72*	*197*	*52*	*16*	*68*	*268*	*30*	*366*
Total natural disasters	**609**	**903**	**1,384**	**613**	**161**	**1,238**	**1,923**	**509**	**3,670**
Industrial accidents	59	37	388	54	0	55	432	51	538
Miscellaneous accidents	104	69	224	75	2	87	321	66	474
Transport accidents	790	287	827	211	9	265	1,358	501	2,124
Total technological disasters	**953**	**393**	**1,439**	**340**	**11**	**407**	**2,111**	**618**	**3,136**
Total	**1,562**	**1,296**	**2,823**	**953**	**172**	**1,645**	**4,034**	**1,127**	**6,806**

Source: EM-DAT, CRED, University of Louvain, Belgium

[1] Insect infestations and waves/surges.
[2] See note on UNDP's Human Development Index country status in the section on disaster definitions in the introduction to this annex.
Note: n.a. signifies "no data available"; ndr signifies "no disaster reported". For more information, see section on caveats in introductory text.
During the decade, Asia accounted for: 41 per cent of all reported disasters, 72 per cent of industrial accidents, 61 per cent of landslides/avalanches, 59 per cent of earthquakes/tsunamis and 47 per cent of miscellaneous accidents.
Africa accounted for: 23 per cent of all reported disasters, 44 per cent of droughts/food insecurity and 37 per cent of transport accidents.
Americas accounted for: 19 per cent of all reported disasters, 47 per cent of volcanic eruptions, 42 per cent of wild fires and 34 per cent of windstorms.
Europe accounted for: 14 per cent of all reported disasters, 52 per cent of extreme temperatures and 28 per cent of wild fires.
Oceania accounted for: 2.5 per cent of all reported disasters, 14 per cent of volcanic eruptions, 8 per cent of wild fires and 7 per cent of windstorms.

ANNEX

Table 10 Total number of people reported killed, by type of phenomenon, by continent and by level of human development[2] (1997 to 2006)

	Africa	Americas	Asia	Europe	Oceania	HHD	MHD	LHD	Total
Avalanches/Landslides	241	1,478	6,230	469	95	440	7,604	469	8,513
Droughts/Food insecurity	1,169	53	458,163	2	60	n.a.	458,453	994	459,447
Earthquakes/Tsunamis	3,321	2,813	370,647	18,584	19	2,707	383,996	8,681	395,384
Extreme temperatures	103	1,786	9,909	78,465	0	77,458	12,397	408	90,263
Floods	9,467	38,222	38,939	1,376	38	3,659	72,954	11,429	88,042
Forest/scrub fires	114	93	71	122	29	217	208	4	429
Volcanic eruptions	201	59	3	n.a.	n.a.	52	11	200	263
Windstorms	1,496	28,311	32,493	652	244	6,200	53,179	3,817	63,196
Other natural disasters[1]	n.a.	3	401	n.a.	2,182	n.a.	2,586	n.a.	2,586
Subtotal hydro-meteorological disasters	12,590	69,946	546,206	81,086	2,648	87,974	607,381	17,121	712,476
Subtotal geophysical disasters	3,522	2,872	370,650	18,584	19	2,759	384,007	8,881	395,647
Total natural disasters	**16,112**	**72,818**	**916,856**	**99,670**	**2,667**	**90,733**	**991,388**	**26,002**	**1,108,123**
Industrial accidents	3,439	381	10,479	913	ndr	482	11,378	3,352	15,212
Miscellaneous accidents	2,889	2,729	8,537	1,534	36	2,018	11,352	2,355	15,725
Transport accidents	24,855	8,008	30,925	5,680	474	7,744	44,681	17,517	69,942
Total technological disasters	**31,183**	**11,118**	**49,941**	**8,127**	**510**	**10,244**	**67,411**	**23,224**	**100,879**
Total	**47,295**	**83,936**	**966,797**	**107,797**	**3,177**	**100,977**	**1,058,799**	**49,226**	**1,209,002**

Source: EM-DAT, CRED, University of Louvain, Belgium

[1] Insect infestations and waves/surges.

[2] See note on UNDP's Human Development Index country status in the section on disaster definitions in the introduction to this annex.
Note: n.a. signifies "no data available"; ndr signifies "no disaster reported". For more information, see section on caveats in introductory text.
During the decade, Medium Human Development countries accounted for: 88 per cent of all reported deaths from disasters, almost all deaths from droughts/food insecurity and 97 per cent of deaths from earthquakes/tsunamis.
High Human Development countries accounted for: 8 per cent of all reported deaths, 86 per cent of deaths from extreme temperatures and half of deaths from wild fires.
Low Human Development countries accounted for: 4 per cent of all reported deaths, 76 per cent of deaths from volcanic eruptions, 25 per cent of deaths from transport accidents and 22 per cent of deaths from industrial accidents.

International Federation
of Red Cross and Red Crescent Societies

Table 11 Total number of people reported affected, by type of phenomenon, by continent and by level of human development[2] (1997 to 2006) in thousands

	Africa	Americas	Asia	Europe	Oceania	HHD	MHD	LHD	Total[3]
Avalanches/Landslides	5	197	2,453	18	11	19	2,359	306	2,684
Droughts/Food insecurity	266,962	25,728	811,061	1,063	1,377	1,021	863,765	241,405	1,106,191
Earthquakes/Tsunami	363	3,662	31,933	3,999	26	836	38,680	468	39,983
Extreme temperatures	n.a.	4,035	896	833	n.a.	45	5,519	200	5,764
Floods	24,616	10,729	1,114,697	4,996	101	6,642	1,129,128	19,370	1,155,139
Forest/scrub fires	9	188	52	259	22	326	201	3	530
Volcanic eruptions	397	599	266	n.a.	50	64	1,138	110	1,312
Windstorms	3,894	29,449	324,918	7,015	207	29,106	335,672	705	365,483
Other natural disasters[1]	n.a.	1	46	n.a.	10	n.a.	57	n.a.	57
Subtotal hydro-meteorological disasters	295,487	70,327	2,254,123	14,183	1,728	37,159	2,336,702	261,988	2,635,848
Subtotal geophysical disasters	761	4,261	32,198	3,999	76	900	39,817	578	41,295
Total natural disasters	**296,246**	**74,588**	**2,286,322**	**18,183**	**1,804**	**38,059**	**2,376,519**	**262,567**	**2,677,143**
Industrial accidents	105	575	744	70	ndr	428	969	98	1,494
Miscellaneous accidents	201	13	196	14	n.a.	20	311	94	424
Transport accidents	14	9	63	4	n.a.	11	72	8	90
Total technological disasters	**320**	**597**	**1,003**	**88**	**n.a.**	**459**	**1,352**	**200**	**2,008**
Total	**296,566**	**75,185**	**2,287,325**	**18,271**	**1,804**	**38,518**	**2,377,871**	**262,767**	**2,679,151**

Source: EM-DAT, CRED, University of Louvain, Belgium

[1] Insect infestations and waves/surges.
[2] See note on UNDP's Human Development Index country status in the section on disaster definitions in the introduction to this annex.
[3] Since slow-onset disasters can affect the same people for a number of years, it is best to use figures on total numbers affected to calculate annual averages over a decade rather than as absolute totals.
Note: n.a. signifies "no data available"; ndr signifies "no disaster reported". For more information, see section on caveats in introductory text.
During the decade, Medium Human Development countries accounted for: 89 per cent of all people reported affected by disasters, 98 per cent of those affected by floods, 97 per cent of those affected by earthquakes/tsunamis and 96 per cent of those affected by extreme temperatures.
Low Human Development countries accounted for: 10 per cent of all people reported affected by disasters, 22 per cent of those affected by droughts/food insecurity and 22 per cent of those affected by miscellaneous accidents.
High Human Development countries accounted for: 1.4 per cent of all people reported affected by disasters, 61 per cent of those affected by wild fires, 28 per cent of those affected by industrial accidents, 11 per cent of those affected by transport accidents and 8 per cent of those affected by windstorms.

ANNEX

Table 12 Total amount of disaster estimated damage, by type of phenomenon, by continent and by level of human development[2] (1997 to 2006) in millions of US dollars (2006 prices)

	Africa	Americas	Asia	Europe	Oceania	HHD	MHD	LHD	Total
Avalanches/Landslides	n.a.	100	1,355	56	n.a.	56	1,455	n.a.	1,511
Droughts/Food insecurity	1,290	9,155	11,219	7,019	2,242	16,528	14,378	19	30,925
Earthquakes/Tsunamis	6,030	8,082	74,796	30,592	n.a.	64,831	52,597	2,072	119,500
Extreme temperatures	1	6,512	7,117	9,135	228	14,742	8,251	n.a.	22,993
Floods	1,983	24,994	115,506	49,284	1,398	78,512	113,720	933	193,165
Forest/scrub fires	12	6,688	21,649	3,693	599	10,749	21,892	n.a.	32,641
Volcanic eruptions	10	173	3	4	n.a.	14	166	10	190
Windstorms	584	281,542	81,875	19,314	3,327	325,452	61,069	121	386,642
Other natural disasters[1]	6	n.a.	n.a.	n.a.	141	141	7	n.a.	147
Subtotal hydro-meteorological disasters	3,877	328,991	238,720	88,502	7,934	446,180	220,770	1,074	668,024
Subtotal geophysical disasters	6,040	8,255	74,799	30,595	n.a.	64,844	52,763	2,082	119,689
Total natural disasters	**9,916**	**337,246**	**313,520**	**119,097**	**7,935**	**511,025**	**273,535**	**3,155**	**787,714**
Industrial accidents	865	n.a.	462	11,421	ndr	11,421	1,327	n.a.	12,748
Miscellaneous accidents	24	85	36	498	n.a.	527	111	5	643
Transport accidents	1	9	440	n.a.	n.a.	n.a.	448	1	450
Total technological disasters	**890**	**94**	**938**	**11,919**	**n.a.**	**11,948**	**1,886**	**6**	**13,841**
Total	**10,806**	**337,340**	**314,458**	**131,016**	**7,935**	**522,973**	**275,421**	**3,161**	**801,555**

Source: EM-DAT, CRED, University of Louvain, Belgium

[1] Insect infestations and waves/surges.
[2] See note on UNDP's Human Development Index country status in the section on disaster definitions in the introduction to this annex.
Note: n.a. signifies "no data available"; ndr signifies "no disaster reported". For more information, see section on caveats in introductory text.
Estimates of disaster damage must be treated with caution, as the financial value attached to infrastructure in developed countries is much higher than in developing countries. While reporting is better for large disasters, the low reporting rates of direct damage make analysis difficult.
During the decade, Americas accounted for: 42 per cent of the cost of all reported damage, 90 per cent of damage from volcanic eruptions and 72 per cent of damage from windstorms.
Asia accounted for: 39 per cent of the cost of all reported damage, 97 per cent of damage from transport accidents, 89 per cent of damage from land-slides/avalanches, 66 per cent of damage from wild fires, 62 per cent of damage from earthquakes/tsunamis and 59 per cent of damage from floods.
Europe accounted for: 16 per cent of the cost of all reported damage, 89 per cent of damage from industrial accidents, 77 per cent of damage from miscellaneous accidents, 25 per cent of damage from earthquakes, 25 per cent of damage from floods and 23 per cent of damage from droughts.

International Federation of Red Cross and Red Crescent Societies

	Total number of people reported killed (1987–1996)	Total number of people reported affected (1987–1996)	Total number of people reported killed (1997–2006)	Total number of people reported affected (1997–2006)	Total number of people reported killed (2006)	Total number of people reported affected (2006)
Africa	**24,654**	**195,023,996**	**47,295**	**296,567,854**	**5,768**	**21,965,254**
Algeria	498	73,956	3,929	367,692	37	60,331
Angola	848	7,700,197	893	724,099	18	237
Benin	34	389,727	288	529,598	54	20
Botswana	28	1,154,807	3	143,736	ndr	ndr
Burkina Faso	38	3,051,004	166	60,304	71	25,674
Burundi	112	3,600	412	6,336,360	82	2,166,310
Cameroon	444	375,004	634	6,398	182	12
Cape Verde	n.a.	6,306	18	40,000	ndr	ndr
Central African Republic	7	21,499	246	95,781	11	20
Chad	95	429,398	225	1,506,334	52	0
Comoros	223	50,200	124	284,343	41	43
Congo, Rep. of	663	16,500	125	176,668	6	5,000
Congo, DR of the	1,371	28,509	2,365	356,620	230	88,243
Djibouti	155	421,075	184	500,399	132	150,049
Egypt	2,422	258,916	3,122	7,056	1,278	696
Equatorial Guinea	15	313	82	5,050	0	750
Eritrea[1]	133	1,615,725	56	11,507,043	ndr	ndr
Ethiopia[1]	1,005	46,711,878	2,056	32,460,679	968	3,034,182
Gabon	102	10,000	50	11	ndr	ndr
Gambia	100	4,000	83	47,406	ndr	ndr
Ghana	331	707,309	672	471,071	162	71
Guinea	473	6,066	352	222,187	43	1,250
Guinea Bissau	15	10,050	218	134,908	0	32,400
Côte d'Ivoire	166	7,187	396	95,193	8	95,000
Kenya	1,456	7,800,294	1,932	106,495,649	353	4,283,444
Lesotho	40	1,094,750	1	1,002,001	ndr	ndr
Liberia	n.a.	1,002,000	70	5,000	ndr	ndr
Libyan AJ	360	121	130	79	ndr	ndr
Madagascar	573	5,695,402	1,067	5,606,323	4	20,516
Malawi	507	33,959,977	796	14,496,361	8	5,160,500
Mali	97	326,667	262	2,077,792	73	1,031,146
Mauritania	107	447,414	167	3,136,423	26	10,643
Mauritius	165	14,307	3	2,050	ndr	ndr
Morocco	1,073	98,203	1,629	867,935	153	2,266
Mozambique	751	9,364,211	1,413	9,963,757	20	1,430,476
Namibia	20	826,400	26	784,309	5	2,300

	Total number of people reported killed (1987–1996)	Total number of people reported affected (1987–1996)	Total number of people reported killed (1997–2006)	Total number of people reported affected (1997–2006)	Total number of people reported killed (2006)	Total number of people reported affected (2006)
Niger	250	4,401,992	159	13,332,696	24	3,046,739
Nigeria	2,151	887,533	10,193	615,516	940	13,137
Reunion (FR)	79	10,261	2	3,700	ndr	ndr
Rwanda	355	163,678	292	1,939,990	24	2,000
Saint Helena (UK)	ndr	ndr	n.a.	300	ndr	ndr
Sao Tome and Principe	ndr	ndr	ndr	ndr	ndr	ndr
Senegal	131	32,925	1,727	918,506	126	25
Seychelles	n.a.	n.a.	8	12,867	ndr	ndr
Sierra Leone	504	200,000	588	15,051	11	26
Somalia	994	642,000	3,356	4,820,019	114	491,510
South Africa	2,187	1,731,691	1,631	15,207,400	128	7,245
Sudan	824	24,038,209	1,169	12,554,959	47	167,000
Swaziland	n.a.	1,500,000	53	4,159,744	1	6,535
Tanzania, UR of	1,398	5,253,815	1,503	16,115,404	185	21,584
Togo	3	586,500	n.a.	97,405	n.a.	2,000
Tunisia	86	152,216	400	27,134	17	n.a.
Uganda	487	1,266,617	1,219	4,519,248	83	605,811
Zambia	545	5,473,432	322	3,341,401	ndr	ndr
Zimbabwe	233	25,000,155	478	18,369,899	51	63
Americas	**32,349**	**30,029,249**	**83,936**	**75,185,000**	**1,555**	**1,447,154**
Anguilla (GB)	ndr	ndr	n.a.	150	ndr	ndr
Antigua and Barbuda	4	76,732	3	24,559	ndr	ndr
Argentina	387	4,961,019	611	861,403	12	4,540
Aruba (NL)	ndr	ndr	ndr	ndr	ndr	ndr
Bahamas	4	1,700	5	12,000	ndr	ndr
Barbados	n.a.	230	1	2,880	ndr	ndr
Belize	n.a.	2,600	69	142,570	ndr	ndr
Bermuda	28	40	22	n.a.	ndr	ndr
Bolivia	246	558,886	932	986,073	91	126,622
Brazil	3,568	5,943,259	2,031	22,618,553	227	116,000
Canada	242	61,935	402	69,059	1	3,900
Cayman Islands (GB)	ndr	ndr	2	300	ndr	ndr
Chile	624	406,605	246	735,019	38	95,867
Colombia	2,588	694,753	2,800	3,138,964	150	238,465
Costa Rica	181	1,136,708	94	133,863	ndr	ndr
Cuba	903	1,431,307	286	10,366,565	2	1,768
Dominica	1	3,711	14	990	ndr	ndr
Dominican Republic	623	1,240,020	1,390	1,081,711	ndr	ndr
Ecuador	5,975	514,306	779	741,457	67	357,939

	Total number of people reported killed (1987–1996)	Total number of people reported affected (1987–1996)	Total number of people reported killed (1997–2006)	Total number of people reported affected (1997–2006)	Total number of people reported killed (2006)	Total number of people reported affected (2006)
El Salvador	207	48,560	1,965	2,170,977	1	9,000
Falkland Islands (GB)	ndr	ndr	ndr	ndr	ndr	ndr
French Guiana (FR)	n.a.	70,000	ndr	ndr	ndr	ndr
Greenland (DK)	ndr	ndr	ndr	ndr	ndr	ndr
Grenada	n.a.	1,000	40	61,860	ndr	ndr
Guadeloupe (FR)	5	11,084	25	153	ndr	ndr
Guatemala	436	196,418	2,639	817,767	81	49
Guyana	n.a.	38,481	44	1,524,174	n.a.	35,000
Haiti	3,430	3,506,645	6,575	724,830	16	39,700
Honduras	811	262,106	14,964	3,814,420	4	1,500
Jamaica	71	1,392,512	37	392,222	1	5,000
Martinique (FR)	10	4,510	n.a.	600	ndr	ndr
Mexico	2,619	862,864	3,551	5,427,435	199	270,720
Montserrat (GB)	11	21,040	32	4,400	n.a.	200
Netherlands Antilles (NL)	2	40,000	15	4	ndr	ndr
Nicaragua	430	718,009	3,492	1,543,404	44	800
Panama	172	48,939	78	81,153	29	7,884
Paraguay	23	400,577	480	303,642	ndr	ndr
Peru	2,715	3,917,321	3,618	6,312,602	177	18,544
Puerto Rico (US)	118	108,553	114	15,499	ndr	ndr
Saint Kitts and Nevis	1	3,100	5	11,180	ndr	ndr
Saint Lucia	49	925	n.a.	200	ndr	ndr
Saint Pierre et Miquelon (FR)	ndr	ndr	ndr	ndr	ndr	ndr
Saint Vincent and the Grenadines	3	1,408	n.a.	1,634	ndr	ndr
Suriname	169	13	13	25,000	3	25,000
Trinidad and Tobago	11	1,230	3	2,177	ndr	ndr
Turks and Caicos Islands (GB)	n.a.	n.a.	43	200	ndr	ndr
United States	4,886	1,239,377	5,682	10,305,282	412	88,521
Uruguay	20	8,240	116	27,559	ndr	ndr
Venezuela	769	72,523	30,715	700,510	n.a.	135
Virgin Islands (GB)	0	10,003	ndr	ndr	ndr	ndr
Virgin Islands (US)	7	10,000	3	n.a.	ndr	ndr
Asia	**507,585**	**1,979,706,904**	**966,797**	**2,287,323,719**	**20,572**	**119,094,718**
Afghanistan	3,810	434,289	10,703	10,597,572	408	2,233,910
Armenia[2]	91	7,000,798	16	319,156	ndr	ndr

	Total number of people reported killed (1987–1996)	Total number of people reported affected (1987–1996)	Total number of people reported killed (1997–2006)	Total number of people reported affected (1997–2006)	Total number of people reported killed (2006)	Total number of people reported affected (2006)
Azerbaijan[2]	482	1,659,123	196	819,008	ndr	ndr
Bahrain	10	n.a.	212	60	69	60
Bangladesh	156,074	180,027,148	9,088	64,628,661	433	238,662
Bhutan	39	65,600	200	1,000	ndr	ndr
Brunei Darussalam	ndr	ndr	ndr	ndr	ndr	ndr
Cambodia	720	17,239,000	537	9,755,614	5	38,000
China, PR of[3]	35,001	1,066,300,124	29,000	1,194,725,145	3,051	88,744,981
East Timor[4]	–	–	4	12,738	n.a.	8,730
Georgia[2]	333	4,165	128	1,415,446	n.a.	600
Hong Kong (CN)[3]	368	12,709	31	4,812	ndr	ndr
India	43,085	564,525,167	83,252	704,211,356	2,071	7,384,760
Indonesia	7,652	5,966,458	181,977	8,553,331	8,210	3,957,720
Iran, Islamic Rep. of	42,510	1,838,948	34,291	113,498,603	243	171,390
Iraq	894	500	1,429	68,912	106	60,004
Israel	68	343	109	1,857	ndr	ndr
Japan	6,530	945,337	1,072	1,976,737	72	25,250
Jordan	66	18,369	124	330,289	10	15
Kazakhstan[2]	230	30,036	132	675,973	41	3
Korea, DPR of	153,458	25,492,967	458,435	49,311,592	278	91,824
Korea, Rep. of	2,789	824,982	1,832	745,832	61	4,633
Kuwait	ndr	ndr	2	200	ndr	ndr
Kyrgyzstan[2]	232	195,306	207	34,661	4	21,125
Lao, PDR	96	3,570,862	129	1,073,005	ndr	ndr
Lebanon	70	105,575	48	17,555	ndr	ndr
Macau (CN)	n.a.	3,986	ndr	ndr	ndr	ndr
Malaysia	918	96,835	313	306,962	11	136,518
Maldives	n.a.	24,149	143	27,314	ndr	ndr
Mongolia	252	105,061	95	3,931,650	ndr	ndr
Myanmar	1,305	597,991	640	352,053	59	70,106
Nepal	4,100	1,411,352	2,924	1,600,524	278	280,052
Oman	ndr	ndr	104	104	ndr	ndr
Pakistan	7,507	23,536,201	79,873	25,788,814	602	8,277
Palestinian Territory, Occupied[5]	ndr	ndr	14	20	ndr	ndr
Philippines	23,999	40,218,457	8,865	26,970,533	3,081	8,645,460
Qatar	ndr	ndr	ndr	ndr	ndr	ndr
Saudi Arabia	2,028	48	1,594	16,095	442	262
Singapore	3	237	n.a.	1,200	ndr	ndr
Sri Lanka	797	6,894,421	36,018	6,636,666	25	333,002
Syrian Arab Republic	46	n.a.	394	668,705	28	29

	Total number of people reported killed (1987–1996)	Total number of people reported affected (1987–1996)	Total number of people reported killed (1997–2006)	Total number of people reported affected (1997–2006)	Total number of people reported killed (2006)	Total number of people reported affected (2006)
Taiwan (CN)	763	24,125	3,352	779,685	8	1,142
Tajikistan[2]	1,718	326,792	281	6,511,623	43	29,157
Thailand	4,043	17,051,221	9,915	18,011,912	280	3,257,308
Turkmenistan[2]	n.a.	420	51	n.a.	ndr	ndr
United Arab Emirates	n.a.	100	183	41	ndr	ndr
Uzbekistan[2]	10	50,400	183	1,225,488	15	n.a.
Viet Nam	4,730	12,287,453	7,960	31,688,544	598	3,349,410
Yemen[6]	758	819,849	741	26,671	40	2,328
Europe	**43,474**	**53,375,749**	**107,797**	**18,271,104**	**5,814**	**256,027**
Albania	75	9,639,190	29	605,009	ndr	ndr
Austria	38	130	261	71,810	n.a.	516
Azores (PT)	172	60	74	1,155	ndr	ndr
Belarus[2]	n.a.	40,000	97	25,319	5	1,820
Belgium	289	2,350	2,166	3,877	940	n.a.
Bosnia and Herzegovenia[7]	ndr	ndr	64	354,180	ndr	ndr
Bulgaria	68	5,319	67	14,487	18	547
Canary Islands (SP)	ndr	ndr	136	869	ndr	ndr
Croatia[7]	96	2,025	847	2,250	n.a.	n.a.
Cyprus	2	1,865	88	1,240	ndr	ndr
Czech Republic[8]	18	4	89	306,460	14	4,315
Czechoslovakia[8]	41	n.a.	ndr	ndr	ndr	ndr
Denmark	55	100	13	2,072	ndr	ndr
Estonia[2]	912	140	25	130	3	n.a.
Finland	ndr	ndr	35	448	ndr	ndr
France	635	14,202	21,637	3,592,737	1,406	622
Germany[9]	358	136,250	9,745	448,887	61	1,328
Gibraltar (GB)	ndr	ndr	ndr	ndr	ndr	ndr
Greece	1,314	34,841	639	129,998	4	3,690
Hungary	58	279	240	179,655	47	32,300
Iceland	34	363	n.a.	199	ndr	ndr
Ireland	46	3,500	n.a.	1,200	ndr	ndr
Isle of Man (GB)	ndr	ndr	ndr	ndr	ndr	ndr
Italy	619	35,632	21,008	111,460	23	268
Latvia[2]	ndr	ndr	76	n.a.	40	n.a.
Lithuania[2]	6	780,000	62	n.a.	n.a.	n.a.
Luxembourg	ndr	ndr	20	n.a.	ndr	ndr
Macedonia, FYR of[7]	198	11,515	43	109,909	n.a.	1,500
Malta	295	n.a.	70	6	28	n.a.
Moldova[2]	17	40,715	25	2,610,957	13	n.a.

	Total number of people reported killed (1987–1996)	Total number of people reported affected (1987–1996)	Total number of people reported killed (1997–2006)	Total number of people reported affected (1997–2006)	Total number of people reported killed (2006)	Total number of people reported affected (2006)
Netherlands	201	262,070	2,016	5,296	1,000	n.a.
Norway	418	4,000	108	2,142	ndr	ndr
Poland	318	294	1,215	245,423	184	670
Portugal	128	5,422	2,884	150,964	41	240
Romania	464	37,356	631	343,509	158	20,963
Russian Federation[2]	4,490	1,044,761	4,192	2,823,618	548	19,929
Serbia and Montenegro[7]	23	6,011	169	120,274	49	36,434
Slovakia[8]	11	200	78	58,493	1	100
Slovenia[7]	n.a.	n.a.	290	1,305	ndr	ndr
Soviet Union[2]	27,573	2,039,558	ndr	ndr	ndr	ndr
Spain	514	36,023,065	15,659	52,331	73	39
Sweden	36	122	71	162	ndr	ndr
Switzerland	53	7,205	1,167	7,305	1	3,000
Turkey	2,642	870,904	20,003	5,148,685	172	63,085
Ukraine[2]	174	2,109,129	1,565	452,673	985	64,661
United Kingdom	674	217,032	193	284,610	ndr	ndr
Yugoslavia[7]	409	140	ndr	ndr	ndr	ndr
Oceania	**1,036**	**23,650,895**	**3,177**	**1,804,895**	**24**	**37,862**
American Samoa (US)	n.a.	n.a.	6	23,063	ndr	ndr
Australia	374	22,623,724	286	59,874	4	10,271
Cook Islands (NZ)	6	2,000	19	2,252	ndr	ndr
Fiji	33	171,372	96	304,719	4	392
French Polynesia (FR)	10	n.a.	13	511	ndr	ndr
Guam (US)	1	6,115	233	22,064	ndr	ndr
Kiribati	ndr	ndr	n.a.	84,000	ndr	ndr
Marshall Islands	n.a.	6,000	ndr	ndr	ndr	ndr
Micronesia Fed. States of	5	203	48	37,431	ndr	ndr
Nauru	ndr	ndr	ndr	ndr	ndr	ndr
New Caledonia (FR)	2	n.a.	2	1,100	ndr	ndr
New Zealand	19	12,442	27	8,240	n.a.	1,200
Niue (NZ)	n.a.	200	1	702	ndr	ndr
Palau	1	12,004	ndr	ndr	ndr	ndr
Papua New Guinea	465	368,139	2,370	1,151,125	16	25,999
Samoa	21	283,000	10	n.a.	ndr	ndr
Solomon Islands	38	89,024	n.a.	1,905	ndr	ndr
Tokelau (NZ)	n.a.	1,832	n.a.	26	ndr	ndr
Tonga	1	3,103	n.a.	23,071	ndr	ndr

International Federation of Red Cross and Red Crescent Societies

	Total number of people reported killed (1987–1996)	Total number of people reported affected (1987–1996)	Total number of people reported killed (1997–2006)	Total number of people reported affected (1997–2006)	Total number of people reported killed (2006)	Total number of people reported affected (2006)
Tuvalu	n.a.	850	18	n.a.	ndr	ndr
Vanuatu	55	70,867	48	84,812	n.a.	n.a.
Wallis and Futuna (FR)	5	20	ndr	ndr	ndr	ndr
Total	**609,098**	**2,281,786,793**	**1,209,002**	**2,679,152,572**	**33,733**	**142,801,015**

Source: EM-DAT, CRED, University of Louvain, Belgium

Note: n.a. signifies "no data available"; ndr signifies "no disaster reported". For more information, see section on caveats in introductory text.

* Since slow-onset disasters can affect the same people for a number of years, it is best to use figures on total numbers affected to calculate annual averages over a decade rather than as absolute totals.

1 Prior to 1993, Ethiopia was considered one country, after this date separate countries: Eritrea and Ethiopia.

2 Prior to 1991, the Soviet Union was considered one country, after this date separate countries. The former western republics of the USSR (Belarus, Estonia, Latvia, Lithuania, Moldova, Russian Federation, Ukraine) are included in Europe; the former southern republics (Armenia, Azerbaijan, Georgia, Kazakhstan, Kyrgyzstan, Tajikistan, Turkmenistan, Uzbekistan) are included in Asia.

3 Since July 1997, Hong Kong has been included in China.

4 Since May 2002, East Timor has been an independent country.

5 Since September 1993 and the Israel-PLO Declaration of Principles, the Gaza Strip and the West Bank have a Palestinian government. Direct negotiations to determine the permanent status of these territories began in September 1999 but are far from a permanent agreement.

6 Prior to May 1990, Yemen was divided into Arab and People's Democratic Republics; after this date it is considered one country.

7 Prior to 1992, Yugoslavia was considered one country, after this date separate countries: Bosnia and Herzegovina, Croatia, Serbia and Montenegro, Slovenia, FYR of Macedonia. In June 2006, Serbia and Montenegro both proclaimed their independence.

8 Prior to 1993, Czechoslovakia was considered one country, after this date separate countries: Czech Republic and Slovakia.

9 Prior to October 1990, Germany was divided into Federal and Democratic Republics, after this date it is considered one country.

Over the last decade, the highest numbers of deaths per continent from natural and technological disasters were reported in: Nigeria (Africa), Venezuela (Americas), Democratic People's Republic of Korea (Asia), France (Europe) and Papua New Guinea (Oceania).

Over the last decade, the highest numbers of disaster-affected people per continent were reported in: Kenya (Africa), Brazil (Americas), China (Asia), Turkey (Europe) and Papua New Guinea (Oceania).

Compared with 1987–1996, the past decade has seen reported disaster deaths rise by 98 per cent and the numbers reported affected rise by 17 per cent.

Table 14 Refugees and asylum seekers by country/territory of origin (2000 to 2006)

	2000	2001	2002	2003	2004	2005	2006
Africa	**3,254,300**	**3,007,000**	**2,907,700**	**3,110,100**	**3,209,300**	**3,196,900**	**3,149,900**
Algeria	–	10,000	–	–	–	900	2,400
Angola	400,000	445,000	402,000	312,000	219,700	213,500	195,000
Benin	–	–	–	–	–	100	100
Burkina Faso	–	–	–	–	–	100	100
Burundi	421,000	375,000	395,000	349,000	472,700	438,500	393,700
Cameroon	–	2,000	–	–	2,300	3,900	4,900
Central African Republic	–	22,000	14,000	41,000	29,700	43,700	73,000[1]
Chad	53,000	35,000	–	3,000	53,000	49,900	84,800[2]
Comoros	–	–	–	–	–	500	–
Congo, Rep. of	22,000	30,000	15,000	14,000	22,700	24,300	18,500
Congo, DR of the	342,000	355,000	393,000	422,000	456,100	450,800	413,300
Côte d'Ivoire	–	–	22,000	51,000	44,900	25,300	27,200
Djibouti	1,000	–	–	–	–	100	200
Egypt	–	–	–	–	–	2,200	3,000
Equatorial Guinea	–	–	–	–	–	200	–
Eritrea	356,400	305,000	285,000	277,000	199,700	215,300	255,400
Ethiopia	36,200	13,000	15,500	14,500	46,800	63,900	77,800
Gambia	–	–	–	–	–	700	900
Ghana	10,000	10,000	10,000	10,000	10,000	10,000	7,900
Guinea	–	5,000	–	–	–	2,600	2,700
Guinea-Bissau	1,500	–	–	–	–	100	100
Kenya	–	–	–	–	10,100	11,400	3,500
Liberia	196,000	215,000	255,300	381,800	323,100	219,800	141,100
Madagascar	–	–	–	–	–	100	–
Malawi	–	–	–	–	2,900	3,800	9,100
Mali	–	–	–	–	4,000	3,300	4,100
Mauritania	45,000	50,000	40,000	20,000	28,600	29,300	28,000
Morocco	–	–	–	–	124,000	117,400	116,800
Mozambique	–	–	–	–	–	400	900
Namibia	–	–	–	–	–	1,200	1,100
Niger	–	–	–	–	–	100	300
Nigeria	–	10,000	15,000	17,000	25,700	22,800	11,300
Rwanda	52,000	60,000	36,000	40,000	45,900	102,500	92,100
Sao Tome and Principe	–	–	–	–	–	–	600
Senegal	10,000	10,000	11,000	13,000	11,600	9,600	16,300
Seychelles	–	–	–	–	–	–	1,400
Sierra Leone	419,000	185,000	115,000	61,000	20,800	26,500	25,000
Somalia	370,000	300,000	282,900	263,300	311,600	328,000	410,300[3]
South Africa	–	–	–	–	–	100	100
Sudan	392,200	440,000	471,000	595,000	697,500	670,900	648,000
Swaziland	–	–	–	–	–	–	200

International Federation of Red Cross and Red Crescent Societies

	2000	2001	2002	2003	2004	2005	2006
Tanzania, UR of	–	–	–	–	4,100	5,400	4,300
Togo	2,000	–	–	4,000	4,200	44,100	24,200
Tunisia	–	–	–	–	–	100	100
Uganda	20,000	20,000	25,000	28,000	29,100	35,100	28,500
Western Sahara	105,000	110,000	105,000	191,000	–	–	–⁴
Zambia	–	–	–	–	–	500	600
Zimbabwe	–	–	–	2,500	8,500	17,900	21,000
East Asia and Pacific	**1,056,000**	**1,104,500**	**1,172,100**	**1,236,100**	**1,366,000**	**1,385,900**	**1,329,000**
Cambodia	16,400	16,000	16,000	16,000	15,000	16,400	13,800
China (Tibet)	130,000	151,000	160,900	139,900	155,300	156,300	158,700
East Timor	120,000	80,000	28,000	–	–	–	–
Fiji	–	–	–	–	–	300	200
Indonesia	6,150	5,500	5,100	23,400	23,500	44,300	39,300
Japan	–	–	–	–	–	100	–
Korea, DPR of	50,000	50,000	100,000	101,700	100,000	51,400	32,400
Korea, Republic of	–	–	–	–	–	300	300
Lao PDR	400	–	–	15,000	12,700	15,700	9,300
Malaysia	–	–	–	–	–	200	100
Mongolia	–	–	–	–	–	400	1,800
Myanmar	380,250	450,000	509,100	584,800	688,500	727,100	693,300
Philippines	57,000	57,000	57,000	57,200	65,000	67,700	69,400
Taiwan (CN)	–	–	–	–	–	–	100
Thailand	–	–	–	–	–	200	2,300
Viet Nam	295,800	295,000	296,000	298,100	306,000	305,500	308,000
South and Central Asia	**3,832,700**	**4,852,000**	**3,878,600**	**2,839,500**	**2,461,700**	**2,725,700**	**3,673,600**
Afghanistan	3,520,350	4,500,000	3,532,900	2,533,200	2,070,500	2,192,100	3,260,300⁵
Bangladesh	–	–	–	–	6,800	45,300	47,000
Bhutan	124,000	126,000	127,000	128,700	120,400	122,300	119,100
India	17,000	17,000	18,000	17,000	11,900	11,700	15,300
Kazakhstan	100	–	–	–	–	500	700
Kyrgyzstan	–	–	–	–	–	200	400
Nepal	–	–	–	–	100,000	201,800	102,500⁶
Pakistan	–	10,000	–	6,700	14,700	16,500	16,500
Sri Lanka	110,000	144,000	148,100	106,400	82,600	79,100	108,900
Tajikistan	59,750	55,000	52,600	47,500	54,800	54,200	–⁷
Turkmenistan	–	–	–	–	–	100	100
Uzbekistan	1,500	–	–	–	–	1,900	2,800
Middle East	**5,426,500**	**4,457,000**	**3,244,500**	**3,220,200**	**3,366,600**	**3,898,800**	**4,763,200**
Iran, Isl. Rep. of	30,600	34,000	24,800	21,000	27,000	31,900	29,100
Iraq	409,300	300,000	237,400	268,200	349,400	888,700	1,687,800⁸
Israel	–	–	–	–	–	500	700
Jordan	–	–	–	–	–	500	700
Lebanon	4,400	–	1,200	–	3,900	700	2,100⁹
Libyan AJ	–	–	–	–	300	100	–

	2000	2001	2002	2003	2004	2005	2006
Palestinian Territory, Occupied	4,982,100	4,123,000	2,981,100	2,927,000	2,986,000	2,971,600	3,036,400
Syrian Arab Rep.	100	–	–	4,000	–	4,400	5,900
Yemen	–	–	–	–	–	400	500
Europe	**760,300**	**666,000**	**517,500**	**438,600**	**226,500**	**230,100**	**274,500**
Albania	–	–	–	–	3,300	2,900	2,800
Armenia	–	9,000	–	–	2,500	4,200	7,300
Azerbaijan	–	–	–	–	11,000	13,000	12,500
Belarus	–	–	–	–	–	1,300	2,000
Bosnia and Herzegovina	234,600	210,000	156,100	121,200	30,300	29,700	33,300
Bulgaria	–	–	–	–	–	1,100	1,000
Croatia	314,700	272,000	250,000	208,900	69,800	59,600	57,300
Czech Republic	–	–	–	–	–	100	–
Estonia	–	–	–	–	–	100	100
Georgia	22,400	21,000	11,400	6,600	20,000	23,100	54,600[10]
Hungary	–	–	–	–	–	200	200
Latvia	–	–	–	–	–	100	100
Lithuania	–	–	–	–	–	200	100
Macedonia, FYR of	–	23,000	3,000	–	–	1,400	1,600
Moldova	–	–	–	–	–	1,500	1,800
Poland	–	–	–	–	–	500	400
Portugal	–	–	–	–	–	100	–
Romania	–	–	–	–	–	900	1,400
Russian Federation	22,700	18,000	27,900	25,600	39,400	34,000	35,400
Serbia and Montenegro	148,900	60,000	52,200	52,800	19,300	24,700	26,100[11]
Slovakia	–	–	–	–	–	–	200
Slovenia	4,400	–	–	–	–	100	–
Turkey	12,600	43,000	16,900	17,600	26,600	25,700	28,600
Ukraine	–	10,000	–	5,900	4,300	5,500	7,700
United Kingdom	–	–	–	–	–	100	–
Americas and Caribbean	**366,750**	**421,000**	**454,200**	**319,000**	**339,800**	**324,000**	**515,700**
Argentina	–	–	–	–	–	300	100
Bolivia	–	–	–	–	–	100	300
Brazil	–	–	–	–	–	600	500
Colombia	2,300	23,000	42,900	230,700	261,000	257,900	453,300[12]
Costa Rica	–	–	–	–	–	100	100
Cuba	1,200	3,000	31,500	26,500	25,100	16,700	13,600
Dominican Republic	–	–	–	–	–	–	100
Ecuador	–	–	–	–	–	200	200
El Salvador	235,500	217,000	203,000	4,500	4,500	5,000	4,700
Grenada	–	–	–	–	–	100	100
Guatemala	102,600	129,000	129,000	10,200	12,600	5,900	4,800
Guyana	–	–	–	–	–	500	400
Haiti	20,600	25,000	30,800	23,800	19,900	17,200	18,100

	2000	2001	2002	2003	2004	2005	2006
Honduras	–	–	–	–	–	1,300	1,500
Jamaica	–	–	–	–	–	300	300
Mexico	–	11,000	–	20,700	4,100	4,900	6,800
Nicaragua	3,800	13,000	15,800	2,600	8,200	5,600	3,400
Peru	750	–	1,200	–	–	2,900	2,900
St. Lucia	–	–	–	–	–	200	200
St. Vincent and the Grenadines	–	–	–	–	–	400	500
Trinidad and Tobago	–	–	–	–	–	200	300
United States	–	–	–	–	–	200	400
Venezuela	–	–	–	–	4,400	3,400	3,100
Total	**14,696,550**	**14,507,500**	**12,174,600**	**11,163,500**	**10,969,900**	**11,761,400**	**13,705,900**

Source: US Committee for Refugees and Immigrants

Notes:

– indicates zero or near zero

All data correct as of May 2007

The number of refugees worldwide rose to 13.7 million in 2006 – the highest figure since 2001.

Almost half of the world's refugees in 2006 were Afghans (3.2 million) and Palestinians (3 million).

In 2006, there were also significant populations of refugees from Iraq (1.6 million), Myanmar (693,000), Sudan (648,000) and Colombia (453,000).

Erratum: some continental totals for the years 2000–2003 were slightly misreported in earlier *World Disasters Reports*, affecting global totals for those years. All past errors have been corrected in this table.

Notes on 2006 data:

[1] **Central African Republic:** conflict between government and rebel forces continued to drive refugees into southern Chad.

[2] **Chad:** conflict in Darfur spread over the border into Chad, leading some Chadians to flee into Sudan. Also, USCRI has begun counting as refugees the population of roughly 15,000 Mahamid Arabs from Chad (who fled to Niger during the 1970s), after the government of Niger threatened to expel them in 2006.

[3] **Somalia:** USCRI has increased the number of Somali refugees in Ethiopia by 50,000, based on a conservative estimate of 20,000 new entries just before the end of the year due to renewed conflict in Somalia, plus new research quantifying the number of unregistered Somalis in and around Addis Ababa as at least 30,000.

[4] **Western Sahara:** this territory is now controlled by Morocco. Hence USCRI is listing Morocco as being the source responsible.

[5] **Afghanistan:** the government of Pakistan completed a census of Afghans in its territory and gave more than 2 million permission to stay in the country, an increase of 1 million on the previous year.

[6] **Nepal:** USCRI cut this number back because the Maoists have largely ceased their guerrilla campaign and are joining the government of Nepal, meaning that fewer of the Nepalis in India are fleeing persecution.

[7] **Tajikistan:** as of June 2006, UNHCR declared that the claim of Tajik refugees to *prima facie* refugee status, which arose during that country's civil war, had ceased. Given the current state of Tajikistan, USCRI stopped counting Tajiks who had not received individual refugee status determinations (RSDs).

[8] **Iraq:** continued sectarian violence and persecution of religious and other minorities continued, driving hundreds of thousands of Iraqis to Syria, Jordan, Lebanon, and Egypt.

[9] **Lebanon:** during the Israel-Hezbollah conflict, some Lebanese formally sought asylum in other countries, creating this small increase. At least 180,000 fled to Syria during the fighting, but the vast majority returned once it ended.

[10] **Georgia:** USCRI has increased the estimate of Georgian refugees in the Russian Federation in 2006 from 20,000 to 50,000, based on new information.

[11] **Serbia and Montenegro:** prior to 3 June 2006, Serbia and Montenegro were considered one country. Following a referendum, Montenegro declared itself an independent nation.

[12] **Colombia:** based on the views of the UNHCR office in Ecuador, USCRI revised upwards the number of Colombians counted as refugees in Ecuador to 207,000. USCRI made a similar, but smaller, increase in Venezuela.

Table 15 Refugees and asylum seekers by host country/territory (2000 to 2006)

	2000	2001	2002	2003	2004	2005	2006
Africa	**3,346,000**	**3,002,000**	**3,029,000**	**3,245,500**	**3,293,500**	**3,176,100**	**3,212,900**
Algeria	85,000	85,000	85,000	170,000	102,000	94,500	95,000
Angola	12,000	12,000	12,000	13,000	14,900	14,900	15,600
Benin	4,000	5,000	6,000	5,000	5,900	32,000	12,200[1]
Botswana	3,000	4,000	4,000	4,500	3,800	3,200	3,200
Burkina Faso	–	–	–	–	–	1,300	1,300
Burundi	6,000	28,000	41,000	42,000	60,700	40,600	20,300
Cameroon	45,000	32,000	17,000	25,000	65,000	58,900	71,200
Central African Rep.	54,000	49,000	50,000	51,000	30,600	26,500	14,300
Chad	20,000	15,000	16,000	156,000	260,000	275,500	286,800
Congo, Rep. of	126,000	102,000	118,000	91,000	71,700	69,600	60,000
Congo, DR of the	276,000	305,000	274,000	241,000	200,700	204,500	208,500
Côte d'Ivoire	94,000	103,000	50,000	74,000	74,200	44,100	40,800
Djibouti	22,000	22,000	23,000	36,000	18,000	10,500	9,300
Egypt	57,000	75,000	78,000	69,000	85,800	86,700	172,900[2]
Eritrea	1,000	2,000	3,000	4,000	4,700	6,000	6,600
Ethiopia	194,000	114,000	115,000	112,000	116,000	101,100	147,300[3]
Gabon	15,000	20,000	20,000	19,000	19,100	13,400	12,600
Gambia	15,000	15,000	10,000	10,000	11,000	8,800	14,400
Ghana	13,000	12,000	41,000	48,000	48,100	59,000	50,500
Guinea	390,000	190,000	182,000	223,000	145,200	67,300	35,400[4]
Guinea-Bissau	6,000	7,000	7,000	10,000	7,700	7,800	8,100
Kenya	233,000	243,000	221,000	219,000	269,300	314,600	337,700
Liberia	70,000	60,000	65,000	60,000	38,600	16,100	16,200
Libyan AJ	11,000	33,000	12,000	–	12,400	12,000	10,900
Malawi	–	6,000	13,000	12,000	7,000	9,600	9,200
Mali	7,000	9,000	4,000	7,000	12,300	13,100	12,500
Mauritania	25,000	25,000	25,000	26,500	30,600	30,600	30,400
Morocco	–	–	2,000	–	2,300	2,300	1,900
Mozambique	2,000	5,000	7,000	8,000	5,500	6,000	6,900
Namibia	20,000	31,000	26,000	15,000	16,900	14,300	6,600
Niger	1,000	1,000	–	–	–	300	15,300[5]
Nigeria	10,000	7,000	7,000	10,000	9,500	9,400	9,400
Rwanda	29,000	35,000	32,000	37,000	36,100	49,500	53,100
Senegal	41,000	43,000	45,000	23,000	23,200	23,400	23,200
Sierra Leone	3,000	15,000	60,000	70,000	65,700	60,100	27,600
Somalia	–	–	–	–	3,000	2,900	2,100
South Africa	30,000	22,000	65,000	104,000	142,900	169,800	171,400
Sudan	385,000	307,000	287,000	280,000	225,900	231,700	296,400[6]
Swaziland	–	1,000	1,000	–	–	1,000	1,000
Tanzania	543,000	498,000	516,000	480,000	602,300	549,100	485,700
Togo	11,000	11,000	11,000	12,000	11,700	9,700	6,800
Tunisia	–	–	–	–	–	100	200
Uganda	230,000	174,000	221,000	231,500	252,300	254,400	277,800
Zambia	255,000	270,000	247,000	239,000	174,000	155,900	120,500

International Federation
of Red Cross and Red Crescent Societies

	2000	2001	2002	2003	2004	2005	2006
Zimbabwe	2,000	9,000	10,000	8,000	6,900	14,000	3,800
East Asia and Pacific	**791,700**	**815,700**	**874,700**	**953,400**	**1,013,200**	**1,029,400**	**944,500**
Australia	16,700	21,800	25,000	22,800	14,600	14,800	14,800
Cambodia	50	1,000	300	100	–	200	200
China	350,000	345,000	396,000	396,000	401,500	352,700	335,400
Hong Kong	n.a.	n.a.	–	–	–	–	–[7]
Indonesia	120,800	81,300	28,700	300	–	100	600
Japan	3,800	6,400	6,500	7,900	6,100	2,600	2,900
Korea, Rep. of	350	600	–	1,700	2,200	2,100	2,400
Malaysia	57,400	57,500	59,000	75,700	101,200	152,700	155,700
Nauru	–	800	100	200	–	–	–
New Zealand	3,100	2,700	1,700	1,200	1,800	1,000	800
Papua New Guinea	6,000	5,400	5,200	7,800	7,800	10,000	10,200
Philippines	200	200	200	2,200	2,200	300	100
Thailand	217,300	277,000	336,000	421,500	460,800	477,500	408,400
Viet Nam	16,000	16,000	16,000	16,000	15,000	15,400	13,000
South and Central Asia	**2,655,600**	**2,702,600**	**2,188,600**	**1,872,900**	**1,724,600**	**1,953,600**	**2,914,200**
Bangladesh	121,600	122,000	122,200	119,900	150,000	150,100	178,100
India	290,000	345,800	332,300	316,900	393,300	515,100	435,900[8]
Kazakhstan	20,000	19,500	20,600	15,300	15,800	7,300	4,500
Kyrgyzstan	11,000	9,700	8,300	8,200	4,200	3,100	900[9]
Nepal	129,000	131,000	132,000	134,600	130,600	130,600	129,600
Pakistan	2,019,000	2,018,000	1,518,000	1,219,000	968,800	1,088,100	2,161,500[10]
Sri Lanka	–	–	–	–	–	200	300
Tajikistan	12,400	4,600	3,500	3,200	3,700	2,600	1,200
Turkmenistan	14,200	14,000	13,700	14,100	13,300	12,000	800
Uzbekistan	38,400	38,000	38,000	41,700	44,900	44,500	1,400[11]
Middle East	**6,035,300**	**6,830,200**	**5,290,300**	**4,353,100**	**4,288,100**	**4,855,400**	**5,650,100**
Gaza Strip	824,600	852,600	879,000	923,000	952,300	986,000	1,017,000
Iran, Isl. Rep. of	1,895,000	2,558,000	2,208,500	1,335,000	1,046,100	994,000	1,025,000
Iraq	127,700	128,100	134,700	131,500	96,600	63,400	46,600
Israel	4,700	4,700	2,100	1,000	4,900	1,500	1,700
Jordan	1,580,000	1,643,900	155,000	163,700	168,300	609,500	862,700
Kuwait	52,000	50,000	65,000	65,000	51,800	14,300	13,600
Lebanon	383,200	389,500	409,000	256,000	265,800	296,800	294,200
Qatar	–	–	–	–	–	100	100
Saudi Arabia	128,500	128,500	245,400	240,900	243,700	240,800	241,000
Syrian Arab Rep.	389,000	397,600	482,400	497,000	701,700	866,300	1,329,300
United Arab Emirates	–	–	–	–	–	200	200
West Bank	583,000	607,800	627,500	665,000	682,700	699,800	722,000
Yemen	67,600	69,500	81,700	75,000	74,200	82,700	96,700
Europe	**1,153,300**	**972,550**	**859,900**	**884,500**	**610,500**	**530,200**	**569,200**
Albania	500	400	100	100	–	100	100
Armenia	–	11,000	11,000	11,000	11,200	11,300	11,500
Austria	6,100	10,800	30,900	17,600	19,300	17,300	43,900

	2000	2001	2002	2003	2004	2005	2006
Azerbaijan	3,600	7,000	11,400	10,300	9,800	3,300	2,700
Belarus	3,200	3,100	3,600	3,400	3,400	2,700	700
Belgium	46,400	41,000	30,300	33,000	24,500	14,100	18,100
Bosnia and Herzegovina	38,200	33,200	34,200	22,500	22,700	10,800	10,400
Bulgaria	3,000	2,900	1,200	800	5,200	5,200	5,400
Croatia	22,500	21,900	8,100	4,200	3,700	2,900	2,500
Cyprus	300	1,300	1,800	5,300	10,600	14,300	13,400
Czech Republic	4,800	10,600	6,300	3,900	2,700	1,300	4,800
Denmark	10,300	12,200	5,200	2,800	2,000	2,000	2,700
Finland	2,600	2,100	1,200	2,300	–	2,400	2,000
France	26,200	12,400	27,600	34,900	22,900	25,500	46,400
Georgia	7,600	7,900	4,200	3,900	2,600	2,500	1,400
Germany	180,000	116,000	104,000	90,800	83,300	64,200	21,600[12]
Greece	800	6,500	1,800	5,200	10,200	11,300	5,800
Hungary	4,200	2,900	1,200	1,500	8,000	8,800	1,500[13]
Iceland	50	–	–	–	–	300	–
Ireland	7,700	9,500	6,500	5,800	10,800	2,400	4,000
Italy	13,700	9,600	5,200	5,600	5,800	5,800	5,100
Liechtenstein	–	–	–	–	–	200	100
Lithuania	150	300	200	100	–	600	600
Macedonia, FYR of	9,000	3,600	2,700	2,300	2,200	2,200	3,100
Malta	–	–	–	200	–	2,400	200[14]
Moldova	–	300	300	100	–	200	100
Netherlands	29,600	31,000	17,200	14,600	12,800	14,400	8,700
Norway	8,600	13,200	5,900	11,000	8,900	4,300	5,900
Poland	2,300	1,800	300	1,500	8,700	6,200	2,100
Portugal	1,600	50	–	–	–	400	–
Romania	2,100	200	100	200	2,400	2,300	1,600
Russian Federation	36,200	28,200	17,400	161,300	150,000	149,200	187,400[15]
Serbia and Montenegro	484,200	400,000	353,000	291,100	76,500	78,600	77,900[16]
Slovak Republic	400	3,100	4,500	4,700	3,300	3,100	6,100
Slovenia	12,000	2,700	400	100	–	200	400
Spain	1,100	1,000	200	200	–	1,600	5,500
Sweden	18,500	18,500	24,900	25,600	19,400	19,400	23,900
Switzerland	62,600	57,900	44,200	38,300	31,200	10,500	8,200
Turkey	9,900	12,600	10,000	9,500	7,800	7,300	8,900
Ukraine	5,500	6,000	3,600	3,100	6,400	4,000	3,500
United Kingdom	87,800	69,800	79,200	55,700	22,200	14,600	21,000
Americas and the Caribbean	**562,100**	**597,000**	**756,500**	**543,500**	**535,600**	**475,000**	**648,900**
Argentina	1,000	3,100	2,700	2,300	3,900	3,900	4,000
Bahamas	100	100	–	–	–	–	–
Belize	1,700	–	1,000	900	–	700	500
Bolivia	–	400	400	500	–	500	600
Brazil	2,700	4,050	3,700	3,900	3,800	3,700	3,900

International Federation
of Red Cross and Red Crescent Societies

	2000	2001	2002	2003	2004	2005	2006
Canada	54,400	70,000	78,400	70,200	54,800	39,500	43,500
Chile	300	550	400	500	–	900	1,500
Colombia	250	200	200	200	–	200	200
Costa Rica	7,300	10,600	12,800	13,600	10,600	12,200	11,800
Cuba	1,000	1,000	1,000	800	–	700	700
Dominican Republic	500	500	300	500	–	1,000	2,000
Ecuador	1,600	4,300	9,100	16,500	45,100	47,400	207,500[17]
El Salvador	–	–	–	200	–	–	–
Guatemala	700	700	700	800	–	400	400
Jamaica	50	–	–	–	–	–	–
Mexico	6,500	6,200	4,000	2,900	4,500	3,400	3,500
Nicaragua	300	–	–	300	–	200	200
Panama	1,300	1,500	1,700	2,000	–	2,200	11,200
Paraguay	–	50	–	–	–	–	100
Peru	750	750	900	800	–	1,200	1,400
United States	481,500	492,500	638,000	244,200	232,800	176,700	147,200
Uruguay	50	100	100	100	–	100	200
Venezuela	100	400	1,100	182,300	180,100	180,100	208,500[18]
Total	**14,544,000**	**14,920,050**	**12,999,000**	**11,852,900**	**11,465,500**	**12,019,700**	**13,939,800**

Source: US Committee for Refugees and Immigrants

Notes: – indicates zero or near zero

n.a. indicates not available or reported estimates unreliable

All data correct as of May 2007

In 2006, Pakistan hosted more refugees (over 2.1 million) than any other country in the world.

The Middle East hosted 40 per cent of the world's refugees in 2006, notably in the Gaza Strip and West Bank (1.7 million), Syria (1.3 million), Iran (1 million) and Jordan (862,000).

Other significant populations of refugees were reported in Tanzania (485,000), India (435,000) and Thailand (408,000).

Erratum: some continental totals for the years 2000–2002 were slightly misreported in earlier *World Disasters Reports*, affecting global totals for those years. All past errors have been corrected in this table.

[1] **Benin:** more than 17,000 of the 26,000 Togolese who fled post-election violence in 2005 voluntarily returned in 2006.

[2] **Egypt:** the increase reflects 80,000 Iraqi refugees, mostly new arrivals during 2006.

[3] **Ethiopia:** USCRI has increased the number of Somali refugees in Ethiopia by 50,000, based on a conservative estimate of 20,000 new entries just before the end of the year due to renewed conflict in Somalia, plus new research quantifying the number of unregistered Somalis in and around Addis Ababa as at least 30,000.

[4] **Guinea:** roughly 33,000 Liberians voluntarily repatriated.

[5] **Niger:** USCRI has begun counting as refugees the population of roughly 15,000 Mahamid Arabs from Chad (who fled to Niger during the 1970s), after the government of Niger threatened to expel them in 2006.

[6] **Sudan:** the increase includes 20,000 new arrivals from Chad, nearly 9,000 new arrivals from Eritrea and an improved count of Eritrean refugees by UNHCR.

[7] **Hong Kong:** As of 1997, figures for Hong Kong are included in the total for China.

[8] **India:** the decrease results from a downward adjustment of Nepali refugees, because the Maoists in Nepal have largely ceased their guerrilla campaign and are joining the government, meaning that fewer of the Nepalis in India are fleeing persecution.

[9] **Kyrgyzstan:** the decrease is a result of UNHCR's decision, in June 2006, that the claim of Tajik refugees to *prima facie* refugee status, which arose during that country's civil war, had ceased. Given the current state of Tajikistan, USCRI concurred and stopped counting Tajiks who had not received individual refugee status determinations (RSDs). This applies to Uzbekistan as well.

[10] **Pakistan:** the government completed a census of Afghan refugees in its territory and gave more than 2 million permission to stay in the country, an increase of 1 million on the previous year.

[11] **Uzbekistan:** the decrease results from UNHCR's decision no longer to recognize the claim of Tajik refugees to *prima facie* refugee status. See note above on Kyrgyzstan.

[12] **Germany:** the decrease results from a decline in the number of asylum claims/grants reported by the government.

[13] **Hungary:** the decrease results from a decline in the number of asylum claims/grants reported by the government.

[14] **Malta:** the decrease results from a decline in the number of asylum claims/grants reported by the government.

[15] **Russian Federation:** USCRI has increased the estimate of Georgian refugees in the Russian Federation in 2006 from 20,000 to 50,000, based on new information.

[16] **Serbia and Montenegro:** prior to 3 June 2006, Serbia and Montenegro were considered one country. Following a referendum, Montenegro declared itself an independent nation.

[17] **Ecuador:** USCRI adjusted the number of Colombian refugees upwards, based on the input of UNHCR and local NGOs.

[18] **Venezuela:** USCRI adjusted the number of Colombian refugees upwards, based on the input of UNHCR and local NGOs.

Table 16 Significant populations of internally displaced people (2000 to 2006)

	2000	2001	2002	2003	2004	2005	2006
Africa	**10,527,000**	**10,935,000**	**10,730,000**	**13,099,000**	**12,163,000**	**11,921,300**	**11,026,000**
Algeria	100,000	100,000	100,000	100,000	400,000	400,000	300,000[1]
Angola	2,000,000	2,000,000	2,000,000	1,000,000	60,000	61,700	61,700
Burundi	600,000	600,000	400,000	400,000	145,000	117,000	100,000
Central African Republic	–	5,000	10,000	200,000	200,000	200,000	200,000
Chad	–	–	–	–	–	–	113,000[2]
Congo, Rep. of	30,000	2,000,000	100,000	60,000	48,000	48,000	7,800[3]
Congo, DR of the	1,500,000	50,000	2,000,000	3,200,000	2,330,000	1,664,000	1,100,000[4]
Côte d'Ivoire	2,000	5,000	500,000	500,000	500,000	500,000	750,000
Eritrea	310,000	90,000	75,000	75,000	59,000	50,500	40,000
Ethiopia	250,000	100,000	90,000	90,000	132,000	150,000	100,000
Guinea	60,000	100,000	20,000	20,000	82,000	82,000	19,000[5]
Kenya	100,000	200,000	230,000	230,000	360,000	381,900	431,000[6]
Liberia	20,000	80,000	100,000	500,000	464,000	48,000	13,000[7]
Nigeria	–	50,000	50,000	57,000	200,000	200,000	200,000
Rwanda	150,000	–	–	–	–	–	–
Senegal	5,000	5,000	5,000	17,000	–	–	64,000[8]
Sierra Leone	700,000	600,000	–	–	3,000	–	–
Somalia	300,000	400,000	350,000	350,000	400,000	370,000	400,000
Sudan	4,000,000	4,000,000	4,000,000	4,800,000	5,300,000	5,335,000	5,355,000
Togo	–	–	–	–	–	3,000	1,500
Uganda	400,000	500,000	600,000	1,400,000	1,330,000	1,740,500	1,200,000
Zimbabwe	–	50,000	100,000	100,000	150,000	569,700	570,000
East Asia and Pacific	**1,670,000**	**2,266,000**	**1,349,000**	**1,400,000**	**1,160,000**	**992,000**	**1,000,000**
East Timor	–	–	–	–	–	–	100,000[9]
Indonesia	800,000	1,400,000	600,000	600,000	500,000	342,000	250,000[10]
Korea, DPR of	100,000	100,000	100,000	50,000	50,000	50,000	30,000
Myanmar	600,000	600,000	600,000	600,000	550,000	540,000	500,000
Papua New Guinea	–	1,000	–	–	–	–	–
Philippines	140,000	135,000	45,000	150,000	60,000	60,000	120,000[11]
Solomon Islands	30,000	30,000	4,000	–	–	–	–
Europe	**3,539,000**	**2,785,000**	**2,560,000**	**2,455,800**	**2,226,500**	**2,013,700**	**2,506,300**
Armenia	–	50,000	50,000	50,000	50,000	8,000	8,400
Azerbaijan	575,000	572,000	576,000	571,000	528,000	558,400	579,000
Bosnia and Herzegovina	518,000	439,000	368,000	327,200	309,200	183,400	180,000
Croatia	34,000	23,000	17,000	12,600	12,600	4,900	4,200
Cyprus	265,000	265,000	265,000	265,000	150,000	150,000	140,000
Georgia	272,000	264,000	262,000	260,000	260,000	240,000	222,000
Macedonia, FYR of	–	21,000	9,000	–	2,700	800	700
Russian Federation	800,000	474,000	371,000	368,000	339,000	265,000	190,000[12]
Serbia and Montenegro	475,000	277,000	262,000	252,000	225,000	247,400	228,000
Turkey	600,000	400,000	380,000	350,000	350,000	355,800	954,000[13]

International Federation
of Red Cross and Red Crescent Societies

	2000	2001	2002	2003	2004	2005	2006
Americas and Caribbean	**2,176,000**	**2,465,000**	**2,518,000**	**2,742,000**	**2,912,000**	**2,970,000**	**2,960,000**
Colombia	2,100,000	2,450,000	2,500,000	2,730,000	2,900,000	2,900,000	2,900,000
Haiti	–	–	6,000	–	–	–	–
Mexico	16,000	15,000	12,000	12,000	12,000	10,000	10,000
Peru	60,000	–	–	–	–	60,000	50,000
Middle East*	**1,700,000**	**1,670,000**	**2,646,000**	**2,346,000**	**1,648,000**	**1,792,000**	**2,192,000**
Palestinian Territory, Occupied	–	20,000	26,000	–	–	–	24,500[14]
Iraq	700,000	700,000	1,100,000	800,000	1,000,000	1,300,000	1,700,000[15]
Israel	200,000	200,000	250,000	276,000	10,000	9,000	8,500
Jordan	–	–	800,000	800,000	168,000	160,000	172,000
Lebanon	350,000	250,000	300,000	300,000	300,000	250,000	216,000
Syrian Arab Rep.	450,000	500,000	170,000	170,000	170,000	73,000	71,000
South and Central Asia	**1,542,000**	**2,402,000**	**2,023,000**	**1,511,000**	**1,205,000**	**1,282,800**	**1,484,400**
Afghanistan*	375,000	1,000,000	700,000	200,000	167,000	153,200	132,000
Bangladesh	60,000	100,000	60,000	61,000	65,000	65,000	65,000
India	507,000	500,000	600,000	650,000	500,000	600,000	600,000
Nepal*	–	–	100,000	100,000	100,000	100,000	100,000
Pakistan*	–	2,000	–	–	17,000	20,000	84,000[16]
Sri Lanka	600,000	800,000	563,000	500,000	353,000	341,200	500,000[17]
Uzbekistan	–	–	–	–	3,000	3,400	3,400
Total	**21,154,000**	**22,523,000**	**21,826,000**	**23,553,800**	**21,314,500**	**20,971,800**	**21,168,700**

Source: US Committee for Refugees and Immigrants

Notes: – indicates zero or near zero

All data correct as of May 2007

* Estimates of the size of internally displaced populations are frequently subject to great margins of error and are often imprecise, particularly in these countries and regions.

According to USCRI, estimated numbers of global internally displaced people (IDPs) remained around 21 million in 2006 – below the 23.5 million peak in 2003.

Africa accounted for over half of all IDPs in 2006, with 5.3 million in Sudan, 1.2 million in Uganda and 1.1 million in the Democratic Republic of the Congo.

Other significant populations of IDPs included Colombia (2.9 million), Iraq (1.7 million), Turkey (954,000) and Côte d'Ivoire (750,000).

Erratum: the total number of IDPs in Africa for 2002 was misreported in earlier *World Disasters Reports*, affecting the global total for that year. The error has been corrected in this table.

[1] **Algeria:** decrease of 100,000 due to subsiding insecurity.

[2] **Chad:** increase of 113,000 due to major new fighting.

[3] **Congo, Rep. of:** decrease of 40,200 due to many returns to home areas (total for 2005 may also have been too high).

[4] **Congo, DR of the:** decrease of 564,000 due to many returns to home areas.

[5] **Guinea:** decrease of 63,000 based on evidence from a new study by the UN's Office for the Coordination of Humanitarian Affairs.

[6] **Kenya:** increase of 49,100 due to evictions in the Rift Valley.

[7] **Liberia:** decrease of 35,000 due to many returns to home areas.

[8] **Senegal:** increase of 64,000 due to new fighting in Casamance.

[9] **East Timor, now Timor-Leste:** increase of 100,000 due to new fighting (plus omission of data for 2005).

[10] **Indonesia:** decrease of 92,000 due to many returns to home areas.

[11] **Philippines:** increase of 60,000 due to new displacement on Mindanao and based on evidence from a new study by the UN's World Food Programme.

[12] **Russian Federation:** decrease of 75,000 due to return to home areas of Chechens and others.

[13] **Turkey:** increase of 598,200 based on evidence from a new study by Turkey's Hacettepe University.

[14] **Palestinian Territory, Occupied:** increase of 24,500 due to Israel's security wall and factional fighting.

[15] **Iraq:** increase of 400,000 due to new fighting.

[16] **Pakistan:** increase of 64,000 due to fighting in Baluchistan.

[17] **Sri Lanka:** increase of 158,800 due to new fighting.

Index

INDEX

International Federation
of Red Cross and Red Crescent Societies

INDEX

INDEX

International Federation of Red Cross and Red Crescent Societies

INDEX

INDEX

INDEX

INDEX

UN Office of the High Commissioner for Human Rights (OHCHR) 39

UN Office of the Special Envoy for Tsunami Recovery 148, 167

UN Principles for Older Persons 70

UN Security Council 136

UN Special Rapporteur on Disability 27, 89

UN Standard Rules on the Equalization of Opportunities for Persons with Disabilities 89

United States 18, 37, 47-49, 94, 98, 102, 105, 107, 109, 138, 140, 172, 177-179, 181-183, 188, 192, 199, 207, 211
    see also America
    see also California
    see also Chicago
    see also Hurricane Katrina
    see also Louisiana
    see also Mississippi
    see also Northridge earthquake
    see also New Orleans
    see also New York

Universal Declaration of Human Rights 12, 114

University of the West Indies 14

US Committee for Refugees and Immigrants (USCRI) 177-179, 207, 211, 213

US Department of Justice 123

Valencia-Rodriguez, Luis 38

Vaux, Tony 147, 155

victim(s) 14, 24, 28, 47, 48, 52, 75, 78, 89, 95, 96, 102, 103, 119, 120, 132, 154
    see also affected communities
    see also affected population(s)

village 31, 37, 40, 55, 63, 78, 79, 81, 82, 92, 93, 143, 147, 152, 154, 155, 163
    see also Kashtara
    see also Puthukudierupu

Villupuram 152
    see also district
    see also India
    see also Tamil Nadu

Vintila, Maria 40, 41

violation(s) 17, 28, 44, 58, 91, 113, 115, 117, 118, 120, 121, 124, 125, 132

violent(ce) 26, 44, 88, 95, 96, 97, 123, 130, 151
    see also domestic violence
    see also sexual violence

visibility 102, 153, 155

volcanic 42, 80, 173, 189-196
    see also lahar
    see also volcano
    see also volcanic mudslides

volcanic mudslides 42
    see also lahar
    see also volcano
    see also volcanic

volcano 42
    see also lahar
    see also volcanic
    see also volcanic mudslides

volunteer(s) 11, 40, 52, 53, 54, 73, 77, 82, 101, 104, 113, 130

vulnerable(ility) 9, 11-13, 15, 17, 20, 25, 28, 30, 32, 34, 37, 44, 46, 51, 53, 54, 65, 67-71, 74, 76, 78, 80, 81, 83, 87, 91, 94, 97, 110, 118, 120, 121, 123, 124, 126, 127, 129-132, 144, 145, 151, 153, 156, 157, 162, 163

Vulnerability and Capacity Assessment (VCA) 53, 56, 57

Wajir 45
    see also Kenya

war 4, 11, 22, 24, 27, 65, 72, 75, 76, 95-97, 165, 178, 207, 211

Wario, Ali 45

war-wounded 4, 96

International Federation
of Red Cross and Red Crescent Societies

INDEX